God and the Processes of Reality

Routledge Religious Studies

Advisory Editor: Professor Stewart Sutherland, Principal, King's College, University of London

God and the Processes of Reality
Foundations of a credible theism

David A. Pailin

Routledge
London and New York

First published in 1989
by Routledge
11 New Fetter Lane, London EC4P 4EE
29 West 35th Street, New York, NY 10001

© 1989 David A. Pailin

Printed in Great Britain by T.J. Press (Padstow) Ltd., Padstow,
Cornwall

British Library Cataloging in Publication Data

Pailin, David A. (David Arthur), 1936–
    God and the processes of reality,
    1. Theism
    I. Title
    211'.3

Library of Congress Cataloging in Publication Data

Pailin, David., 1936–
    God and the processes of reality: foundations of a credible theism/
    David A. Pailin.
    p.   cm.
    Includes index.
    ISBN 0–415–02106–5
    1. God.   2. Theism.   3. Process theology.   I. Title.
    BT102.P28 1989
    231—dc19

Ivcvndæ Laetæ Carissimæ

Contents

Preface

The fundamental problem facing theistic belief today is not the challenge of applying its understanding to the issues of human freedom and fulfilment. Important as are the concerns inspiring liberation theologies as they investigate the challenges of Christian thought to sexist, economic, social, and political forms of oppression, the justification of those theologies depends upon the credibility of the underlying theistic understanding. The fundamental problem for theism is that that credibility is currently questioned – and radically so. Often this issue is considered to be that of proving the rational justifiability of assenting to the existence of God. There is, however, a prior question which requires an answer, namely, 'Can a coherent concept of God be identified?' Unless a satisfactory answer to that question is established, the question of the existence of the God of theistic belief may be considered to be as pointless as the question of the existence of a square circle or a married bachelor. Such a concept must be both adequate to the holiness and ultimacy of the divine and significant for human thought and practice.

This study is an attempt to develop such a concept. It does so in the conviction that ideas put forward by so-called 'process thought' – especially in the works of its dual founders, Alfred North Whitehead and Charles Hartshorne – provide important resources for the task. What is presented in the following pages, however, is not a straightforward exposition of those ideas. It uses and modifies them, sometimes radically, in order to suggest a coherent concept of the God of theistic belief and a credible understanding of the relationship of that God to the processes of reality.

Some of the issues which are discussed in the following chapters have been the topic of papers which I have previously published elsewhere. In particular in more or less modified forms (and sometimes the modifications are considerable), I have used material originally discussed in the following papers: 'The incarnation as a continuing reality' in *Religious Studies* (1970); 'Process theology – why and what?' in *Faith and Thought* (1972); 'Neville's critique of Hartshorne' in *Process Studies* (1974); 'The humanity of the theologian and the personal nature of God' in *Religious Studies* (1976); 'God and creation – a process view' in *Epworth Review* (1982); 'God as creator in a Whiteheadian understanding' in *Whitehead und der Prozessbegriff,* edited by Harald Holz and Ernest Wolf-Gazo (Freiburg/München: Verlag Karl Alber, 1984); 'The genuinely active God' in *The Modern Churchman* (1985); 'The utterly absolute and the totally related: change in God' in *New Blackfriars* (1987); 'History, humanity and the activity of God' in *Religious Studies*; 'The poet of salvation' in *Freedom and Grace,* edited by I. Jones and K. Wilson (London: Epworth Press, 1988); 'Process-theology and evolution' published in *Evolution and Creation,* edited by A. R. Peacocke and Svend Andersen (Aarhus University Press, 1987). I am grateful for permission to use these materials.

David A. Pailin
31 December 1987

1 The problem of God today

In some famously — some might say infamously — provocative
letters from prison in June and July 1944 Dietrich Bonhoeffer
reflects on the human situation and belief in God. He suggests
that in the modern age people have learnt to cope with 'all
questions of importance without recourse to the "working hypothesis" called "God"'. As a result 'in human affairs generally,
"God" is being pushed more and more out of life, losing more
and more ground' (Bonhoeffer 1971: 325f).

This may not cause concern when it happens in the sciences
and the arts, or even in politics and ethics. Many believers,
however, find it worrying that it has also 'become increasingly
true of religious questions'. In response some of them try to find
ways of evoking in people a sense of 'existential despair' in order
to find a role for God. Bonhoeffer condemns such apologetic
activity, which he describes as 'secularized methodism',[1] as
pointless (because it tries to foist problems on to people), ignoble
(because it attempts to exploit their weaknesses for alien purposes), and unchristian (because it identifies the will of Christ
with a stage in human development that has now been super-
seded). Fortunately, it is also massively ineffectual. While a few
'intellectuals' and 'degenerates' (whom, somewhat disturbingly,
Bonhoeffer apparently equates!) may be brought to worry about
themselves, most people have 'neither the time nor the inclination' to be bothered about 'existential despair'. Their share of
happiness may be modest but they do not see it 'as a trial, a
trouble, or a calamity' (ibid.: 326f.).

There is little point in regretting this situation. Once we have
grown up there is no creditable way back to the world of
childhood, whatever its attractions once we have left it. Bonhoeffer, however, does not merely accept that this is the current
human situation. He positively affirms human autonomy as an
actualization of the divine will for humankind. He writes, for
example, that:

> we cannot be honest unless we recognize that we have to
> live in the world *etsi deus non daretur* [as if there were no

---

[1] This is a not inappropriate comment on the traditional Methodist approach,
following that of John Wesley's sermons, of preaching the law in order to
bring about a sense of sin as a prelude to conversion.

God] . . . God himself compels us to recognize [this] . . . God would have us know that we must live as men who manage our lives without him. The God who is with us is the God who forsakes us (Mark 15: 34). The God who lets us live in the world without the working hypothesis of God is the God before whom we stand continually. Before God and with God we live without God . . . Christ helps us, not by virtue of his omnipotence, but by virtue of his weakness and suffering.

(ibid.: 360)

This view of God is held to distinguish Christianity from other religions. For authentic Christian faith, God is not an almighty power who may be expected to determine the course of events by acts of overwhelming force. The God who truly helps humanity is the divine that is known in powerlessness and suffering (ibid.: 361).

Bonhoeffer's comments suggest a way in which theists may reconcile their faith in the reality of God with what is widely regarded as the current experience of humanity. The absence of credible instances of divine intervention in the course of nature and history may thus not be regarded as evidence against the reality of God. Instead, the lack of such events may be held to indicate how the divine is properly to be understood. God is not to be expected to rescue people from tyranny, to dampen fleeces, or to light sacrifices (cf. Exodus 2ff; Judges 6: 36ff; I Kings 18: 36ff). Indeed, when some claim that God has committed arson on a cathedral to manifest the divine (dis)pleasure or has miraculously healed someone, many sensitive believers are justifiably embarrassed. Not only is it notoriously hard to find convincing reasons for holding that an event, however unusual or surprisingly opportune, is due to divine agency. Such claims also raise in an acute way the problem of evil and the worshipfulness of God. If, for example, the divine purposes are compatible with certain powerful interventions in natural, historical, or personal situations, it is hard to envisage why God does not intervene more frequently to prevent suffering. To try to find an answer to the problem posed by the apparent paucity (or absence) of divine interventions by arguing that we are not in a position to judge the merits of God's behaviour seems suspiciously like trying to find excuses for dereliction of duty. It is less objectionable and more realistic to maintain that God is not the protecting and intervening saviour to whom believers have typically looked for practical help.

This latter view of God may be judged to make a virtue of necessity as it establishes an empirical fit between theistic belief and human experience. It also provides the basis for a kind of theodicy in that it challenges fundamental notions about the nature of divine activity which are presupposed in the standard way of formulating the problem of evil. These benefits, though, are obtained at a high price. Sceptics may well retort that if belief in the reality of God and the evidence of experience have to be so interpreted in order to make them compatible with each other, the interpretation takes away the point of theistic belief. If God is not to be praised — or blamed — for what happens, what is the significance of such belief? Would it not be simpler to abandon belief in God altogether and to adopt a secularistic view of things?

In order to meet these challenges theists need to show that they have convincing warrants for maintaining that theistic understanding provides a credible way of making sense of the ultimate ground, nature, and purpose of reality. Pretensions to such insight, though, are liable to be regarded as incredible by 'down to earth' positivists. According to many of these critics Kant is correct when he holds that human reason 'stretches its wings in vain' when it attempts 'to soar above the world of sense' and to find, by its own speculative powers, answers to ultimate questions (Kant 1933: 500). In the face of such scepticism — or 'realism' — many are doubtful whether theism can be rationally justified.

In any case, so some critics of theism further argue, the intellectual case is unimportant. In practice we do not need God. Theistic belief is a relic of humanity's childhood. Its stories — or, rather, delusions — are no longer required to underwrite our morals and to boost our morale in coping with life. It is a point classically made by Sigmund Freud. He popularized (rather than originated) the view that religion is unnecessary and, in many ways, unhelpful to human fulfilment. With a confidence in science which is more typical of the nineteenth century than of today, he closes his classic study of religion, significantly entitled *The Future of an Illusion,* by stating that it would be 'an illusion' to consider 'that what science cannot give us we can get elsewhere' (Freud 1962: 52). The limitation does not disturb Freud. He is convinced that through the sciences people will find genuine solutions to their real problems. Equally, though, he is convinced that religion is not one of the sciences.

Experience of the effects of scientific discoveries and technological advances in the past half-century has undermined the kind of confidence which underlies Freud's expectations about future scientific achievements. We have become aware of the limits of science and technology to solve problems and of their ability to create terrible new ones (cf. Küng 1977: 38ff). This realization has not, however, been accompanied by a noticeable growth in rationally credible belief in God. On the contrary, while pockets of theistic faith continue and while there are occasional and, in some places, extensive outbursts of forms of theistic faith which radically renounce the canon of sound reason, for some time the prevailing trend in educated and affluent western society — it is debatable whether education or affluence is the more potent influence — has been one of increasing dominance by a secular view of reality. In both thought and behaviour, furthermore, this secularization takes the form of an appreciation of human autonomy which is largely secularist in its presuppositions (cf. Ogden 1967: 7ff, for the distinction between secularization and secularism).

Although Bonhoeffer (1971: 325, 359) suggests that the roots of the movement towards secularization may be traced back to the thirteenth century, its strength so far as theistic belief is concerned has been particularly obvious from the eighteenth century onwards. During that diffuse movement in thought called the Enlightenment, fundamental questions were raised about the truth and significance of belief in God. They are questions which continue to require from theists convincing answers if their fundamental faith is to be deemed rationally responsible. For an increasing number of people, though, they are also questions to which satisfying answers have yet to be found.

The result of the failure to identify such answers is that theistic faith has become more a chronic invalid than the ground of vibrant life in contemporary western society. One symptom of its sickness is the widespread view that theism is a distinct and optional aspect of human being in the world. Such a view implies that, whatever in principle may be theism's claim to provide the basic orientation for thought and activity, in practice it has become peripheral. To the extent that people consider that they may choose whether or not to entertain theistic belief, they show that they do not consider it to be fundamentally determinative for private and social existence. And this is how it is currently regarded by many people in the secular world of the west, whether in the massively non-church-going communities of Britain or in the strongly 'religious' areas of the Bible-belt and 'the moral majority' of the United States.

4

Such people do not regard differences over theistic faith and practice as a major source of fundamental disagreement about human being. Religious disputes are not like divisions over whether it is right to own slaves or permissible to torture infants. They are perceived to be more like differences of opinion between neighbours over which is the best make of car to buy — with some aggravating 'greens' stirring the debate by questioning whether any car needs to be purchased! It is consequently considered to be a sorry state of affairs if such disagreements lead to serious disruptions in relationships. In any case, they do not affect the shared consensus over what are regarded as 'serious matters' — for example, the need for security, sewage systems, and honest police.

Where, then, religion in general and theistic faith in particular are identifiable as a separable mode of understanding and practice which has marginal significance, it is clear that they do not constitute the faith which is the fundamental and pervading ground of human existence. That faith is to be found, if anywhere, in the principles and presuppositions which determine the choice made about the 'religious' option.

Popular responses made to the religious debates of the past quarter of a century provide another symptom of the fact that theistic faith as traditionally understood has lost its fundamental significance in the predominantly secularist culture found, for example, in contemporary Britain. On the one hand, although the so-called 'Death of God' theologies[2] stirred a certain amount of interest in the United States, they created hardly a ripple in Britain. On the whole this was not because British people in the 1960s were too sophisticated to be attracted by the latest intellectual ephemera from across the Atlantic. It was because the news of this 'demise' was too stale to arouse interest. Like the proverbial use of the report 'Queen Anne's dead', people were more surprised that it was newsworthy than troubled to understand what it might imply for their lives.

On the other hand, populist politicians and other media-seeking pundits have in recent years been quick to attack attempts by certain theologians (for example, Maurice Wiles, David Jenkins, and John Hick) to discern intellectually credible understandings of the Christian faith. Attempts by Church leaders (for example, Bishops Stockwood, Montefiore, Shepherd,

---

[2] The 'movement' is preferably described as one of 'theologies' for the phrase 'the death of God' was used to cover a wide range of positions (cf. Pailin 1967, 1969).

Jenkins, and Warlock) and by 'liberation' theologians to clarify the social demands of the Christian faith have aroused similar hostility. The critics make out that their concern is to maintain the integrity of the true faith. In some cases that is probably what they honestly consider that they are doing. Consideration of their comments according to a hermeneutics of suspicion, however, raises the question of whether a deep, perhaps unconscious, motive for many of the reactions may not be that of preventing the Christian faith from becoming a real threat to comfortable (perhaps complacent) forms of thought and practice. An effective way to neutralize the authentic demands of faith in God would be to confine its self-understanding to traditional forms which can be pontificated over by the ignorant, dismissed as incredible by the sensible, and treasured as curious museum pieces (while locked away for reverent preservation in hermetically sealed glass cases) by the nostalgic.

While the widespread separation of 'religion' from life as a whole and recent reactions to revisionary expressions of theistic faith are symptoms of the current secularist situation, there has been a variety of responses in western culture during and since the Enlightenment to doubts about theistic faith. Some of these responses cast light on the significance of the question of the reality of God; some suggest the need for changes in traditional conceptions of that reality; and some indicate major difficulties attending any attempt to establish the truth and significance of theistic faith. In the remainder of this chapter, therefore, the nature and implications of five of these responses will be considered. They indicate the importance of attempting to establish a significant relationship between God and the processes of reality, and some of the problems which need to be overcome if any such attempt is to be successful. This discussion thus sets the context for the study of theistic understanding to be developed in the following chapters.

For some authors the idea that we exist in a godless universe (which they hold to be a true insight) is something which should properly evoke terror. At the end of the eighteenth century, for example, Jean Paul Friedrich Richter saw the affirmation of atheism as one which splinters the world into an utterly lonely multiverse of 'innumerable . . . individual personalities, running hither and thither at random, coalescing and parting asunder without unity, coherence, or consistency' (Richter 1877: 260). Those who appreciate the ultimate horror of godlessness perceive that the question of God's existence cannot be discussed as 'chillheartedly as though it were a question of the existence of the kraken or the unicorn'. To hold that there is no God is to shatter life into nothingness, to replace the sense of purposed belonging with one of unrelievable abandonment (ibid.: 261; cf. 261-5).

In the twentieth century Franz Kafka's stories portray a horrifyingly empty, meaningless, incoherent, lonely world. Its total godlessness is characterized by the absence of even an awareness of the question of God's reality. The 'gruesomeness of the living present', furthermore, makes people 'eager . . . to obliterate' it (Kafka 1961: 79). Samuel Beckett's descriptions of the pointless chaos that is human being are sometimes, but not always, relieved with humour. Trapped in the cylinder of existence 'the lost ones' decline through imperceptibly growing languor until they arrive unwittingly at 'their last state'. Then light will be 'extinguished as purposeless' and 'every body will be still' (Beckett 1972: 15). The second law of thermodynamics determines the character of the eschaton. In *Waiting for Godot* Pozzo's response to the temporal structure of life, 'They give birth astride of a grave, the light gleams an instant, then it's night once more', is echoed by Vladimir's 'Astride of a grave and a difficult birth. Down in the hole, lingeringly, the grave-digger puts on the forceps. We have time to grow old. The air is full of our cries. But habit is a great deadener.' Even though Vladimir goes on to remark that he is noticed by 'someone', it apparently has no significance (Beckett 1965: 89ff). Godless reality is a succession of pointless events. Through them 'hollow men' meaninglessly grope in the shadow towards 'the way the world ends, / Not with a bang but a whimper' (Eliot 1961: 80).

These responses to the godlessness of reality show neither the truth nor the necessity of belief in the reality of God. So far as theistic understanding is concerned, believing that something is so does not make it so. Although such believing may obscure the nature of things, it cannot change (let alone determine) their intrinsic actuality. To hold otherwise is to convert belief into delusion. Nor is it intellectually legitimate to defend the validity of theistic belief on the grounds that it is convenient or comforting. Bertrand Russell is justified in finding 'indifference to truth . . . extremely dangerous' and in feeling 'profound moral reprobation for those who say that religion ought to be believed because it is useful, and that to ask whether it is true is a waste of time' (Russell 1975: 156f). Attempts to defend theism by ignoring the question of truth (and the virtue of intellectual integrity which decides 'vexed questions in accordance with the evidence' (ibid.: 154)) are fundamentally atheistic. They worship human wishes rather than the ultimate reality.

On the other hand, so far as these responses are correct in holding that a godless world is horrific in its ultimate incoherence and pointlessness, they do indicate the importance of the question of theism. It is not a remote intellectual puzzle for investigation by those who have finished the crossword and can find nothing better to do. Its answer is critical for the determination of whether being in general and human lives in particular are to be understood as having fundamental meaning and value. In this respect, the question of God is inescapably the question of everything. It is the question of wholeness or nothingness. It is the question which haunts self-conscious existence. Those who tackle it may be presumptuous but they should not be embarrassed. They are tackling the question whose solution determines the meaning of being itself.

Other authors, though, are not traumatized, at least not to a significant extent, by their judgement that we are part of a godless reality. They see it as 'one of those things' which, like gravity, the price of books, and ageing, just has to be accepted. There is no point in agonizing over it. This is how the world is. 'God' neither explains what happens nor provides security against what the future may bring (cf. Shideler 1966: 112). In their view what is important is to accept that reality is godless and to get on with living — and with living in as whole and as satisfying a manner as is then possible.

This is the kind of attitude to life put forward, for example, by Jacques Monod. Whether or not his view of the ultimate bleakness of human being is warranted by his researches into genetic biology, he apparently regards it with equanimity. The innate demand for complete explanation and the search for the meaning of existence traditionally met by 'mythical or philosophical ontogenies' are to be seen as an inheritance from earlier forms of humankind. Then such drives had survival value (cf. Monod 1972: 155ff). Now it is time to recognize the character of reality:

> man must at last wake out of his millenary dream and
> discover his total solitude, his fundamental isolation. He
> must realize that, like a gypsy, he lives on the boundary of
> an alien world; a world that is deaf to his music, and as
> indifferent to his hopes as it is to his suffering or his crimes.

> (ibid.: 160)

In particular, people must recognize that values originate in human decisions and are subject to human choice.

The prospect does not daunt Monod. Rather he sees it as an invigorating challenge which humanity is capable of meeting. Having emerged 'only by chance' out of 'the unfeeling immensity of the universe', 'man' must grasp that 'neither his destiny nor his duty have been written down. The kingdom above or the darkness below: it is for him to choose' (ibid.: 167). For Monod, then, scientific realism reaches the same conclusion as atheistic existentialism: existence precedes essence. Human beings determine the meaning and values by which the significance of their lives is to be judged.

From a religious perspective Robert Adolfs finds a similarly positive acceptance of the godlessness of reality expressed in the 'quiet indifference' to questions of theistic belief 'which develops in people who discover that they can be complete human beings without religious faith'. Such people display 'a deliberate acceptance of the temporal' which emerges from their realization that 'work, knowledge, art, politics are worthwhile in themselves.' The outcome of such cases is a kind of 'positive indifference which undermines' faith in God (Adolfs 1967: 83).

This attitude towards life is illustrated in modern classics by Ernest Hemingway and Albert Camus. In *For Whom the Bell Tolls*, Hemingway's Anselmo, 'having been brought up in religion', confesses that he misses God but, convinced by his experiences in the Spanish Civil War that there cannot be a God, he now holds that 'a man must be responsible to himself' (Hemingway 1955: 43). He thus gets on with doing what has to be done, unpleasant at times as it may be. It is an attitude also portrayed by heroic characters in Camus's *The Plague*. Recognizing that 'on this earth there are pestilences and there are victims', they grope their 'way through the darkness . . . and try to do what good' lies in their power. In this way they show 'that there are more things to admire in men than to despise' in 'the never-ending fight against terror and its relentless onslaughts' (Camus 1987: 204, 186, 248).

Nicolas Berdyaev describes this godlessness as 'calm, even full of goodwill'. It 'arises from compassion, from love for what is good and just'. It may be seen in those who, like the godless Marxists, protest in the name of human fulfilment against the perverted forms of theism used to crush the human spirit (and which, regrettably, are often the only forms of theism of which these critics are aware). Thankful that there is no God, such people feel that they are 'free to settle down on the earth', quietly to make the best of living there (Berdyaev 1953: 93; cf. 93ff).

The question for theism posed by this response to the godless-ness of reality is whether theistic belief can justifiably be held to make a significant contribution to human living. Are its beliefs, practices, stories, and values important — or are they only interesting entertainments for antiquarian musings? Wrapped up in this question of 'importance' is a bundle of subordinate questions. Is it correct to maintain that people can get along reasonably happily without reference to God? If they can, why should they be expected to take the question of God seriously? If they cannot find happiness in godlessness, why should discernment of the reality of God be expected to make any difference — and what real difference does it make? Attempts to discern the significance of God in relation to the processes of reality at least need to indicate how such questions may be answered even if they do not address all of them directly.

A third response to theism found in modern western thought takes the form of an excited announcement that there is no God. The recognition of this is held to be a necessary condition for the full expression of authentic human being. Those who promote this understanding are not only confident about humanity's ability to cope without God: they present the godlessness of reality as something to be celebrated. Church bells should peel, bonfires be lit, and parties be organized because the threatening stories of a transcendent tyrant are now seen to be self-induced nightmares. The abolition of theistic faith is the fundamental act of human liberation.

Berdyaev classes Friedrich Nietzsche among those who find suffering and tragedy in the affirmation of the 'death' of God (cf. Berdyaev 1953: 93, 103). But this is only one facet of Nietzsche's response to this state of affairs. He does see the godlessness of reality as indicating that human being is 'straying as through an infinite nothing' of chill 'empty space' (Nietzsche 1954: 95). More typical, however, is his strident summons to rejoice over the freedom that the 'death' of God — the recognition, that is, of the unreality of God and of the fictitious character of theism — brings to human being. Identified as 'the One and the Plenum and the Unmoved and the Sated and the Permanent', the deity is 'evil' and 'misanthropic'. A being so characterized destroys the possibility of any significance in human creativity (ibid.: 198; cf. 198f). Since, therefore, Nietzsche regards the only being properly conceivable as God as 'the declaration of war against life, against nature, against the will to live' (ibid.: 585), he finds 'the great liberation' in the announcement of God's death. Now we can see that 'there is nothing

10

which could judge, measure, compare, or sentence our being'. By denying God 'we redeem the world' (ibid.: 500f). The news that 'God has ceased to be believable' is a matter of 'happiness, relief, exhilaration, encouragement, dawn' for now 'at last the horizon appears free again' (ibid.: 448). The threat that human being is absolutely nothing because God is absolutely all is an illusion; humanity should rejoice because it is now clear that it is free to be its own creator and valuer.

Another illustration of this reaction to theistic belief is found in Don Cupitt's claim that the proper development of human being is only possible by 'taking leave of God'. He rejects 'theological realism' (his phrase for belief in the existence of 'a god who is conceived of as an infinite, almighty and commanding being quite distinct from the believer, who requires absolute obedience' (Cupitt 1980: xii)) on the grounds that it produces 'a heteronomous consciousness'. Consequently it prevents human autonomy, the internalization of values, and spiritual growth. It is, therefore, a position which 'no normal person ought now to have' (ibid.: 12).

Cupitt offers three arguments to support his rejection of theism. One is that people have justifiably 'lost confidence' in the 'proofs' which have traditionally been supposed to support belief in God (cf. ibid.: 21ff). A second is that if God is held to be unchangeable, human activities can have no ultimate significance since they can make no impression upon the divine (cf. ibid.: 104). The third is that if God is regarded as a personal ruler, human autonomy is threatened by morally corrupting capriciousness and flexibility: 'however good the despot, life under personal rule is inevitably bad for everybody's morals' (ibid.: 104). Hence theism is to be rejected in favour of the notion of 'God' as 'a unifying symbol' or '*focus imaginarius*', a personified representation of 'everything that spirituality requires of us' (ibid.: 9f). So far, then, as authentic religion is concerned, Cupitt maintains that the reality of God is to be replaced with an idea of divinity which is a product of human thought and consistent with human flourishing.

The criticisms of theism illustrated by these references to Nietzsche and Cupitt are arguably based upon serious misconceptions of the proper attributes of the God of theistic faith. Nevertheless, it would be a mistake to ignore the charges. They provide vivid reminders of ways in which doctrines about God traditionally assumed to be part of theistic thought apparently undermine affirmations of the freedom, fulfilment, and significance of human being.

It is, though, a position which some theists have appreciated and sought to counter. In *The Reality of God*, for example, Schubert Ogden agrees that those who maintain that God is in every respect *actus purus* and hence 'a statically complete perfection incapable in any respect of further self-realization' are thereby committed to holding that God 'can be as little affected by our best actions as by our worst'. Such a being 'must be in the strictest sense wholly indifferent' to both human actions and human suffering (Ogden 1967: 17f). Likewise, to hold that God determines all events, foreknows the future, has a monopoly of power, is totally impassible, or is incapable of any change is to accept a view of the deity which radically contradicts the conviction that human being has 'its proper autonomy and significance' (ibid.: 20; cf. Page 1985: 139f for a Maori story recognizing this point). The only way in which theistic belief can be compatible with, let alone positively ground and promote, the affirmation of the worth of human being is therefore through overcoming 'the inadequacies of this traditional theism' (Ogden 1967: 19). The discussion in later chapters will indicate what this means. It involves a thorough reconstruction of some of the basic conceptions of the attributes of God.

A fourth response to theism found in the contemporary world considers the question of God to be pointless. According to this position, whatever deity might credibly be held to exist must be too remote from human affairs to have any significance for human being. A proper appreciation of the essential ultimacy and intrinsic otherness of God is thus judged to involve a recognition of the irrelevance of theism for actual living. Whatever may ultimately be the case in reality, in practice it does not matter whether the universe is godless or not.

Whether consciously recognized or not, this understanding probably lies behind — and explains — the findings of some empirical studies of religious belief. When asked about such matters, many people reportedly reply that they believe that there is a God. Other questions and observations, though, fail to detect any way in which that profession influences their lives. Such people are probably not giving false answers: they just do not see how theistic belief could have any practical significance. This understanding of theism also underlies the widespread suspicion that those who apparently find little difficulty in describing the nature, will, and activity of God are more likely to be projecting their own fantasies than perceiving the reality of the divine.

Three factors — religious, theological, and cultural — help to form this view of theism. From the religious point of view there is a perceived need for theistic understanding to avoid anthropomorphic conceptions which make sense of God at the price of destroying an essential awareness of the otherness of the divine. The more sophisticated and ostensibly appropriate conceptions of God become, however, the more they are liable to approximate towards vacuity. In the pursuit of adequacy for the divine, some theologians even go so far as to assert that God is 'ineffable' — although nearly all those who do affirm this proceed to show that they do not consider that this alleged 'un-utterability' prevents them from saying a great deal about the divine! Those who do maintain that God is 'wholly other' should take seriously Ludwig Wittgenstein's remarks at the end of the *Tractatus*. Having affirmed that 'there are, indeed, things that cannot be put into words' — things which he calls 'mystical' — he concludes that 'what we cannot speak about we must pass over in silence' (Wittgenstein 1961: 151). It is a truism which is often ignored in the passage from the principles to the practice of theistic discourse.

While few believers and theologians (for the latter it would be professional suicide!) may be prepared to 'retreat into silence' on the grounds that the things of God belong 'to the class of things that just cannot be said' (McPherson 1955: 133), many of their defining remarks about God leave readers wondering whether they convey anything materially significant. Nicholas of Cusa, for example, addresses God as 'Very Absolute Infinity':

> Thou art without beginning and end; Thou art beginning without beginning and end without end; Thou art beginning without end and end without beginning; Thou art equally beginning as end and end as beginning, yet neither beginning nor end, but above beginning and end, absolute infinity itself, blessed for ever!
>
> (Nicholas of Cusa 1960: 60, 65)

It may seem to be the right kind of thing to say about God — and to God — but what does it mean? Somewhat similarly, in a recent philosophical study of spiritual development, Robert Neville asserts that 'the ontological cause' of all things 'is neither finite nor infinite, existent or non-existent, one or many, or any other categorial thing'. Accordingly in religious traditions awareness of this 'absolute ground which itself can be no thing can be described as atheism as well as theism'. It is awareness

13

of what 'can be called Absolutely Empty as well as Pure Act, Nothingness as well as Fullness, Brahman without Qualities as well as Brahman with Qualities' (Neville 1978: 64f).

Puzzling remarks like these are not only put forward as religiously appropriate ways of referring to the divine; they are also used to express what some theologians and philosophers consider to be required theologically by rational reflection on the nature of God. Neville, for example, states that it is a mistake to conceive of God as 'a lover, or a loving creator' because such metaphors 'refer to definite created things' whereas God is 'the absolute foundation of things . . . or the abyss whence arises the world as it is' (ibid.: 91f). God is not determinate but the transcendent ground of all determinations (cf. ibid.: 105). Similarly, according to Paul Tillich, God is 'being-itself or the absolute'. As such the being of God 'cannot be understood as the existence of a being alongside others or above others'. Nor can the attributes of God be expressed by means of superlatives: 'when applied to God, superlatives become diminutives' because 'they place him on the level of other beings while elevating him above all of them'. Instead God must be recognized to be 'the ground of the ontological structure of being without being subject to this structure himself' (Tillich 1953: 261, 265). More recently Robert Scharlemann has wrestled with the problem of the proper significance of God-talk and reached the conclusion that the word

> 'God' designates one who can never be the predicate in a judgment and whose name, grammatically, can never be an adjective. God can never be predicated of another, and of God the only predication to be made is that God is God: *God* is God, and God is *God*.

> (Scharlemann 1981: 161)

It may be argued with some justification that theological conclusions such as these are required by a proper appreciation of the deity of God. Nevertheless, the way in which they draw attention to the mysterious otherness of the divine leads some to conclude that what is so ultimate and general can have no particular significance for the life of individual persons and societies — or even for the being of humanity as such.

This theological conclusion is reinforced for many people by cultural reflection on what modern investigations into cosmology indicate about the extent of the universe and the character of its processes. Underlying the resulting appraisal of theism is the assumption that if there is a God, then God must be in some significant way the creator of all. The significance of theism becomes problematic, though, when attempts are then made to envisage the nature of divine creativity in a way that is compatible with what is known about the cosmos.

In *God and the New Physics*, for example, Paul Davies suggests that 'the most surprising evidence for a grand design' of the cosmos lies in its dependence upon the 'fundamental constants' having certain values. Since 'only in those universes where the numbers come out just right would life and observers form', it is possible to argue for cosmic design (and divine designer) from 'the delicate fine-tuning in the values of the constants' required for the present structure of the universe to exist (Davies 1984: 187ff). An article in the *Guardian* newspaper of 6 April 1987 reports Davies as suggesting that God possibly provides the simplest logical explanation of why the physical laws are such that they provide the basis for a self-conscious universe: a transcendent God 'creates the laws of physics, which then go on to create the universe, which then creates us'. Along the way the complexifying interactivity of fundamental forces not only leads to particles, atoms, and molecules but also to complex chains of DNA and RNA molecules with possibilities of mutation as well as of massively consistent replication. It is an interesting story to which we will return in Chapters 7 and 8; it may well be the best one which we have at present; and it may be more or less correct. It is, however, a story which leaves many with the impression that the creative providence of the deity is extremely remote from the particular states and events of contingent existence.

Religious concern to respect the divinity of God, theological attempts to recognize the ultimacy of the deity, and cultural awareness of the nature of things thus reinforce one another in suggesting to many people that any divine reality that there may be is too remote from the day-to-day concerns of personal living for theistic belief to be important for it. Theism may be an interesting idea for those who enjoy mystical musing and metaphysical speculation. They do not see it, however, as able to provide both a credible and an adequate basis for a living faith which gives significance to human being.

This appraisal of theism indicates a further set of problems which confronts any attempt to establish the credibility and significance of belief in God. The religious, theological, and cultural sources of doubt about the importance of theism, granted the reality of the divine, are not to be ignored. A theism which

15

does not do justice to these considerations shows thereby that it is not properly concerned with *God*. On the other hand, if theism is to be the ground of a living faith, it must also show that the divine which is so perceived is also to be understood as the ground of the significance of human being. It may not be easy to reconcile these requirements but their satisfaction is a condition of a credible theistic faith. Accordingly the consideration of God and the processes of reality in the following chapters must seek to satisfy them both.

The final response to theism to be mentioned is one which draws attention to intrinsic difficulties, and especially to apparent contradictions, in the concept of God. It is suggested by some that these problems do not merely raise doubts about the content of that concept. They radically threaten the possibility of any coherent thought about the reality of God. Some of these problems are obvious — as, for example, when it is held that God is both providentially caring and totally impassible, or is both unchanging and responsively active. Others are only teased out by reflection on the implications of what is being stated. Such may be the case with conjoint claims that the divine is both intentionally creative *and*, being perfect, is without potentiality, or that all events are eternally co-present to the divine awareness *and* that God has a gracious personal relationship with human beings.

When these problems are recognized, they are judged by some to show that theistic faith cannot (logically cannot) be a real option for responsible assent. Nothing can exist the essential attributes of which are incompatible with being real; and nothing can exist (nor can the concept of it make sense) the essential attributes of which are mutually contradictory. Reflection on the basic notion of deity thus leads some to conclude that the concept of God is no more to be entertained as a serious basis for understanding than talk about square triangles, pregnant fathers, or invigorating influenza.

Internal difficulties in the concept of God have long been recognized to exist. In the *Proslogion*, for example, Anselm is aware of problems in affirming that God is both omnipotent and yet not capable of all things, both compassionate and yet affected by no sympathy for the wretched, and both supremely just and yet merciful to the wicked (cf. Anselm 1962: 13ff). Using his logical acuity, however, he suggests ways by which these notions may be so defined that each pair of apparently conflicting attributes can coherently be affirmed of the divine. Whether or not his solutions are wholly satisfactory (in the case

16

of the divine compassion, for instance, it comes to holding that God is felt by us to act 'compassionately' although there is no correlative sense of compassion in God), they are typical of many attempts in traditional theology to overcome the puzzles and paradoxes apparently intrinsic to descriptions of the divine.

Other thinkers have not been as sanguine about finding solutions to these problems. David Hume, for instance, suggests that it is meaningless playing with words to hold that there can be a 'mind' which not only thinks, reasons, wills, and loves but is also 'wholly simple and totally immutable' (Hume 1935: 197). If the divine has to be so conceived, then atheism is the only reasonable option. Ludwig Feuerbach similarly argues that an atheistic position is warranted by a wide range of contradictions which are present in descriptions of the divine. God is said, for example, to be both universal and personal, both the abstract idea of being and an individual existence, both existing independently of all others and one for whom humanity is an essential predicate, both personal and not personal, and both conscious and not conscious. In such cases 'one half of the definition [of God] is always in contradiction with the other half' and hence 'the fundamental idea' is self-annihilating. While theologians attempt to conceal this by 'sophistry', Feuerbach sees his analyses as uncovering the inescapable implications of theologically approved language about God and thereby as radically destroying theism (Feuerbach 1957: 213; cf. 185ff).

In recent decades similar views have been put forward by philosophers influenced by language philosophy. J. N. Findlay, for example, once argued that the notion of God (as 'that of a Being in whom Essence and Existence lose their separateness') is not merely 'barely intelligible'. The demands of religious worship require that God be conceived as possessing certain qualities necessarily, including that of necessary existence. According to post-Kantian understanding, however, such conceptions are 'self-evidently absurd'. Hence, Findlay concludes, no such state of being as that ascribed to the divine could possibly be the case (Findlay 1955: 52ff, 73). Although Findlay (1964: 515ff) has since accepted that some sense can be made of the notion of necessary existence and so no longer endorses this argument, it is a reminder of the danger that theistically adequate descriptions may show the impossibility of the reality which they purport to identify.

Ronald Hepburn suggests that when theists consider themselves compelled to develop a notion of God which excludes all limitations and unworthiness, they may 'elevate God not only out of imperfection, but also and equally out of personal existence of any kind'. When, furthermore, they say that God is 'beyond being', there seems no way of distinguishing between their position and that of atheists (Hepburn 1958: 196). Another, less sympathetic, example of this response to theism is found in the work of Antony Flew. For him the question of the fundamental consistency of theistic language seems particularly to arise when we compare what theologians affirm (or should properly affirm) about God as 'the infinitely powerful Creator' with what they consider equally strongly to be true about human being, namely that 'his creatures can, and regularly do, disobey' the divine will (Flew 1966: 143). In Flew's view of the notions involved, these claims are incompatible. Accordingly he states that 'if creation is in' (with the implication that God is the 'controller of every thought'), then human 'autonomy is out' (ibid.: 47).

As will be indicated in later chapters (especially Chapters 4, 5, and 6), convincing replies can be made to such attempts to rule out theistic belief in principle on the grounds that it is essentially incoherent. It is arguable (and will be argued) that these attempts either rely upon faulty analyses of the content of the concepts used to describe the attributes of God or they presuppose (in order to destroy) a notion of God that is theistically inappropriate. On the other hand, while these critical responses to the language of theism may be countered by more exact and rigorous analyses of the concepts involved (cf. Hartshorne 1964: vii, 6ff; 1953: 110), they should not be ignored. Negatively they are useful in that they draw attention to deeply unsatisfactory elements in traditional ways of thinking and talking about God. Positively they are valuable in that they force theists to reconsider the proper content of the concepts used to describe the divine and to find more adequate modes of expression.

The five responses which have been discussed do not, as some of their presenters claim, show that theism must be either ignored or rejected on the grounds that it is unnecessary, insignificant, inimical to human being, or a jumble of mutually contradictory ideas. They do, however, set some of the agenda for the development of a proper understanding of the notion of God. Although the following chapters do not take up directly all of the arguments that have been used to illustrate these responses, the discussion in general is formed by the intention to reply to them by showing how theism can justifiably claim to be a coherent, significant, and credible faith for people today. Furthermore, underlying the discussion is the conviction that proper theistic understanding (and, as will be seen in the next chapter, what is implied by 'proper' here is a matter of considerable controversy) is not only the most adequate apprehension of the ground and goal of being but also is the true perception of that ground and goal so far as they are currently apprehensible by human beings. The problem of God today sets a demanding agenda. It is time, though, to move from outlining the problem to considering in more detail what is meant by the concept of 'God' and why its use in theological understanding raises doubts about its coherence.

2   The concept of God: demands and difficulties

Isaiah expresses a strongly held religious conviction when he has God state that 'my thoughts are not your thoughts, and your ways are not my ways', (Isaiah 55: 8). Towards the end of *The Cloud of Unknowing* the author affirms that neither 'outer knowledge gained through the senses' nor deep understanding 'of all spiritual things ever created' can lead to a knowledge of 'an uncreated spiritual thing . . . which is none else than God!' Appeals to Scripture and learned authorities provide excuses for 'parading one's ingenuity and erudition' rather than developing understanding of the divine. Between the human and the divine there is 'a cloud of unknowing'. The highest understanding is found by entering this cloud and knowing that one is in it. God is thus properly known in the recognition that it is God that limits human understanding. The author cites Pseudo-Dionysius with approval: 'the most godlike knowledge of God is that which is known by unknowing' (*The Cloud of Unknowing*, 1961: 136f; cf. 58ff).

Remarks such as these warn philosophers and theologians that they are straying into dangerous territory when they try to understand the nature and activity of the divine. The difference between the divine and the human, the creator and the created, the ultimate and all else, is such that attempts by the latter to make sense of the former are liable to result in hilarious pretentiousness. Voltaire has a point when he teases about a mole and a June bug arguing as to whether it was a powerful mole or a talented bug that built the toilet at the end of his garden (Voltaire 1962: 240). Are human beings on stronger ground when they assume that their modes of understanding are significant for understanding the divine?

In the face of such doubts it is tempting to give up the task of theistic understanding. Agnostics and sceptics hold that whatever may be humanity's success in achieving metaphysical insight into the ultimate and universal character of reality, attempts to perceive the relationship between God and the processes of reality go beyond what can be credibly ascertained. On the other hand, the question of the nature and purposes of the divine is the question of the significance of being as such and of human being in particular. Hence whatever may be the difficulties of determining the divine character, the question of God is one that self-conscious human self-understanding cannot eschew if it is to seek intellectual satisfaction.

If, then, theistic understanding is not to be abandoned as a quest for an unattainable sangrael, the primary theological importance of warnings such as those cited from Isaiah, Pseudo-Dionysius, and *The Cloud of Unknowing* is to remind those engaged in seeking such understanding that they must, so far as they are able, direct their thought towards a notion of God which is appropriate to being 'God'. Acknowledgement of the inescapable limitations of human apprehension of the divine does not justify content with what is recognizably less than adequate. In this respect thought about God must fulfil three defining characteristics: religious, rational, and theological. Conceptions of the divine which do not satisfy all these criteria are thereby revealed to be deficient as ways of grasping that which is the ground, goal, and object of theistic understanding.

From the religious point of view the notion of God is the notion of that which is the proper object of worship. This, though, is by no means a simple quality. On the one hand it points to what Rudolf Otto (1950) classically described in terms of the sense of the 'holy'. The divine is that which evokes a sense of profound mystery, shuddering awe, profane creatureliness, and overpowering attraction. The sacred is not to be trifled with; the story of Uzzah (II Samuel 6: 6f) is a biblical reminder of the widespread conviction that in the case of the intrinsically taboo thoughtlessness can be fatal. At the same time the terrifying Other is irresistibly fascinating. It is good to be in the presence of God. According to one strong tradition in theistic understanding the vision of God is the fulfilment of human being. Nothing greater can be desired. In this respect it is possible that the practice of speaking of God as 'Thou' when such language had become unfashionable in common use was a valuable reminder of the sacred quality of the deity. God is the holy one.

On the other hand, to define 'God' as 'the One Who is Worshipped' (Hartshorne 1967: 3) is also to direct thought to the unsurpassable character of the divine. God is the one who is unhesitatingly adored. No one and nothing does or possibly ever could surpass the divine — for otherwise God would not justify the unreserved commitment that is authentic worship. It is this aspect of the divine being to which Hartshorne typically turns when considering questions about the definitive nature of 'God'. In *Anselm's Discovery*, for example, he shows that he is

21

persuaded of the correctness of Anselm's definition of God as 'that than which nothing greater can be conceived'. Although, as we shall see, he has some important criticisms of the way in which Anselm and most other theologians elucidate what is meant by 'greater' in this regard (cf. Hartshorne 1965: 26ff; 1964: 6ff; 1962), he endorses without reservation the conviction that 'by "God" is meant the universal object of worship' (Hartshorne 1965: 26). From this two further points follow. First, because worship is most adequately understood as 'a consciously unitary response to life' (Hartshorne 1967: 5) in which the individual finds wholeness, God is to be identified as 'the all-inclusive reality' which 'cherishes all creatures' and desires for them good 'not yet attained'. Secondly, since 'only supreme love can be supremely lovable', God must be understood as all-embracingly loving — 'a cosmic love' (or, perhaps better, a cosmic lover). Only so is the divine worthy of the total devotion — 'love with the whole of one's being' — that is true worship (ibid.: 12ff; cf. 4; 1964: 3).

From the point of view of rational reflection, the definitive characteristics of the notion of 'God' are those of primacy and ultimacy. These defining qualities, though, have various aspects. God is that which — or the one who — is ultimate in being, value, and understanding. Ontologically, that is, God is the one on whom all being depends but who is dependent on nothing. Although the so-called ontological and cosmological arguments do not convincingly demonstrate the existence of the divine, they do make clear the unique quality of the divine mode of being. As Hartshorne frequently points out, the divine existence is properly to be described as 'necessary existence'. While, *pace* Hartshorne's understanding of the modal form of the ontological argument, it does not follow from the attribution of this mode of being to the divine that it must be true that God exists (cf. Pailin 1968; 1969a; 1986: 176ff), it does follow that God is to be conceived as one whose being is not derived from and whose continuation is not dependent upon any other. In this respect God is primary and omnitolerant. If it is coherent to think of a beginning to there being something rather than nothing (a notion which will be examined in Chapter 7), God must be thought of as the origin of that beginning. Furthermore, whether or not there was a beginning to being, the being of whatever is is finally grounded in the divine. The little girl in the cartoon who prayed 'and please God look after yourself for if you go we're all done for' had grasped one aspect of the ontological status of the divine! But she had not grasped all that it entails. God is not only the ground of all being: God is also unable not to be. Nothing other than the divine could threaten the divine existence and it does not seem coherent to think of God as ever threatening God's own being. A being, however terrifying, that could even contemplate the real possibility of self-destruction would neither be worshipful nor the ultimate in being.

The definitive ultimacy of the divine presupposed by rational reflection is not, however, merely a matter of ontological primacy. The notion of God also essentially refers to that which is ultimate in value. This may be seen as another rational correlate of the intrinsic worshipfulness of the divine. The conundrum 'Is it good because God wills it, or does God will it because it is good?' is fundamentally mistaken. The nature of goodness — i.e. the positive standard of value — is not something dependent upon divine choice. This would render it arbitrary. There could be no reasons for such choice if the choice itself determines the values which decide what are sound reasons! Neither is it satisfactory to regard divine judgement about what is good as dependent upon a standard of value external to the divine. This would deny the ultimacy of God since it would imply that God is to be reckoned perfect only contingently — so far, that is, as the divine actions are in total accord with this standard. Instead, the essential ultimacy of the divine means that God must, by definition, be held to be necessarily perfect and hence to instantiate the good. From this it follows that God is that by which (or the one by whom) the goodness of all else is finally to be judged but is not subject to judgement. Similarly, in terms of understanding, the ultimacy of God means that God is to be seen as the one whose nature and purposes determine what it is finally to understand. Whether or not we can ever in practice apprehend the divine reality, in principle God is the answer of which no further question may coherently be asked. The intellect here finds that which is intrinsically satisfying. The divine nature essentially makes final sense without reference to what is other than the divine.

Finally, an adequate understanding of the divine must meet certain theological criteria. These arise from the definitive role of God in theistic faith as the basis of confidence in the meaningfulness and worth of being. An essential characteristic of the notion of God, that is, is its status as the key to understanding all that is. The divine being is not only the intrinsically ultimate in rationality as the reality whose being answers any coherent question that can be asked about it: God is also the one whose nature and purposes are the final ground for understanding all that is and all that might possibly be the case.

In this respect theology may justifiably be described as 'the queen of the sciences'. This does not mean that earlier interpretations of the title were correct in considering that theology enjoys privileged access to truths which allow it to 'queen' it over all other ways to knowledge. Whatever claims to revelatory insight may permit, they do not give theistic understanding the authority to overrule the findings of other disciplines. What talk about the 'queenship' of theology — and so of theistic understanding — properly draws attention to is the role of theology in making sense of the universe as a *uni*verse, that is, as a unity whose constituent processes combine in a coherent story which gives both the parts and the whole a completely satisfying purpose. If, that is, theism is correct, what happens in nature and in history is not in the final analysis to be seen as the random product of blind chance and pointless necessity. It has a point, a meaning, a value — and that point, meaning, and value have their ground in the divine as purposively agential. From this it follows that a concept of God cannot be considered adequate unless it refers to a divine which is commensurate with the task of making sense of reality. And this means, among other things, being capable of taking account of what all forms of human enquiry have discovered about the nature of reality.

But while this theological requirement for an adequate concept of God may appear obvious in principle, its satisfaction in practice raises major difficulties for the credibility of theism. For example, as will be considered in later chapters, it is not easy to meet the demand that theism show that its concept of God is capable of making sense of what modern science discloses to be the physical and evolutionary processes of the cosmos in terms of an overall divine purpose which gives meaning to the parts and to the resultant whole. Furthermore, theistic understanding not only claims that things 'make sense' intellectually. It also maintains that being in general and human being in particular have worth and that this worth is grounded in God. Accordingly a concept of the divine is not fully adequate unless it shows the divine as establishing that every actuality has value as well as point. This is an issue which will be considered further in the final chapter.

The religious, rational, and theological criteria which have been outlined suggest that a theistically satisfactory concept of the divine must conceive of the divine as being intrinsically holy, ultimate, personal, and agential. Only such a reality can be the proper object of worship, the final ground of understanding, and the justification of faith's confidence in the meaningfulness and worth of being. It is, however, one thing to hold that any adequate form of theistic understanding must satisfy such demands. It is another to show that such a concept is possible. On reviewing the criteria, it may well be suspected that theism makes impossible demands. Is the suspicion justified? Can the concept of God no more be developed in a coherent, adequate, and credible way than can discussions of the joys of debating with the hobbits in the cherry orchard, of non-temporally ordered activity, and of colours at infra-red wavelengths? Or is it possible to overcome the known objections to the coherence of the concept of God? If theistic understanding of God and the processes of reality is not to be ruled out *ab initio*, it is important to show that the demands of the concept of God do not render theism impossible.

One common argument against the possibility of theistic understanding maintains that it is ruled out by the inadequacies of language. As has been mentioned in Chapter 1, some critics allege that it is impossible to say anything about the divine which both has content and is appropriate to its reference. They argue that when theistic understanding attempts to identify the character of its ground, namely God, it is caught on the horns of a dilemma. On the one hand it seems able to describe the nature of the divine only by using notions dependent upon human experience and reflection. In that case, so it is claimed, it gives content to its remarks about the divine by falling into the error of using anthropomorphic descriptions. The result of this, the critics further allege, is that the essential otherness of the divine is lost and we are presented only with projections of human qualities. The supposedly divine is the human magnified. On the other hand, if the nature of the divine as the transcendent, ultimate, and holy other is properly appreciated, it is argued that the divine will be seen to be strictly ineffable — and what cannot be spoken about *cannot* be spoken about. Theists are thus held to face the choice between saying something qualitatively inappropriate and saying nothing at all about the divine. If they say anything, it is wrong; if they say nothing, theistic understanding dissolves like the Cheshire cat, leaving only a bemused smile.

Such criticisms of the possibility of expressing and so of apprehending authentic theistic understanding depend, however, upon posing unwarrantably extreme options. It is not self-evident that all language used of God must be either empty or utterly inappropriate. For one thing, not all anthropomorphic descriptions are equally bad. It is possible to grade such usage from the crude (as when God is described as being without an umbilicus) to the sophisticated (as when God is held to have a direct awareness of a person's state of mind). There is, it must be admitted, a danger that as the qualities attributed to the divine become more sophisticated, they also become more elusive. Nevertheless, it is arguable that the line of development from the crude to the sophisticated at least gives pointers towards the nature of the divine even if no humanly based experiences can ever be regarded as thoroughly adequate to provide direct descriptions of that nature.

Secondly, for all the fun that may be made of anthropomorphisms, the only material qualities that we can envisage are those that we have experienced as human beings. Even if in some cases the non-human surpasses the human (e.g. eagles have better sight, dogs have a better sense of smell, and hamsters breed faster than human beings!), we are only aware of such qualities through our own experiences of them. Furthermore, the highest form of being that we appear to be able to envisage is the personal one which we have as self-conscious, environmentally aware, responsive, purposive, and agential beings. To ascribe such a mode of being to God is, therefore, not necessarily to demean the divine. It is to treat the divine as having (at least) what is for us the highest imaginable mode of being. In addition, while the actualization of material qualities in the divine may surpass their highest human forms in unknowable ways, it does not follow that the latter cannot provide any inklings of the divine reality. At this point, though, it has to be recognized that the search for theistic understanding, like all other realms of thought, finally depends upon the faith that human rationality provides a significant way of grasping the truth about reality. Since, however, this act of faith necessarily underlies all attempts at understanding, its rejection would not only destroy theism. It would undermine all forms of understanding.

Finally, in reply to those who challenge the possibility of adequate statements about the divine, it ought not to be forgotten that such statements normally include both formal terms which are not subject to the charge of anthropomorphism and 'qualifiers', as I. T. Ramsey (1957: 49ff) names them, which indicate that the material terms used of the divine are not to be taken in a simplistically literal manner. In the case of the former, terms such as infinite, ultimate, and eternal mark off the divine from all else. These descriptions properly apply only to God. Even if our grasp of their contents is primarily or wholly negative (the divine as not limited, as neither derivative from nor surpassable by others, as without beginning or end, for example), they directly express something of the character of the divine being.

In the case of the latter, the role of adverbs such as purely, perfectly, and absolutely, of the prefix 'omni-', and of references to symbolic and analogical usage is to draw attention to the peculiar status of material qualities justifiably attributable to the divine. When applied to an adjective connoting such a quality, they indicate that what is being communicated thereby is thought directed towards a limit rather than a literal characterization of the divine nature. Although, for instance, it may not be possible to comprehend what it is to be 'perfectly' loving, such a description suggests that in this respect God is to be considered as the ideal terminus of the range from hating to loving and from the less to the more loving. Such a quality may in itself be beyond our grasp but the language indicates what direction thinking about the divine ought to take if it is to be more rather than less appropriate.

To argue, however, that it is possible to find terms which may be used significantly of the divine nature is to counter only one basic objection to the possibility of theistic understanding. Another, potentially even more devastating challenge maintains that theism is in principle impossible because its basic concept of God is self-contradictory. Whatever arguments might be put forward to justify the possibility of predicating qualities of the divine being are pointless because there is no coherent subject to which they may be applied. Talk about God is as nonsensical as talk about faithful adulterers, square circles, and desirable toothache. Pretences at theistic understanding are thus necessarily ridiculous.

Hartshorne's major achievement in theistic understanding — and the core of the theological development of process thought — is to have perceived why it has often been considered that theism is bound to make apparently contradictory statements about the divine and, even more importantly, how it is possible to talk coherently of God. The remainder of this chapter, therefore, will discuss the nature of the problem and various responses that have been made to it. Three questions will be taken up: first, why is it arguable that the basic structure of the concept of God found in much western theology is fundamentally unsatisfactory? second, why have theologians traditionally considered that the concept of God must be so understood? and third, how have theologians previously responded to the problems that arise with this concept of God? The treatment of these three issues in this chapter will indicate the problem to which Whitehead, Hartshorne, and other thinkers have responded by developing the so-called 'process' or 'neo-classical' concept of God to replace the one traditionally put forward in theological understanding. The following two chapters will then discuss the metaphysical basis and fundamental form of this concept while the subsequent chapters will attempt to put flesh on to the bones of the logical structure of the concept of God there delineated.

The basic reason why some modern theologians, especially those who share the insights of 'process' thought, criticize the theistic understanding traditionally found in western theology is that they consider that it responds to the twofold structure of that theology by putting forward incoherent remarks about God. What is this structure and what are the allegedly incoherent things that are said as a result of observing it?

On the one hand, theology is the attempt to express a religious faith. For western theology this means faith as found in the Judaeo-Christian-Muslim theistic tradition. In this respect theology sees itself as descriptive, subject to judgement by reference to the faith which it purports to express. On the other hand, because it attempts to give a rationally coherent expression of that faith, it is also potentially, if not actually, revisionary. It seeks to 'revise' or 'modify' or 'clarify' or 'correct' the initial, crude, and often implicit self-understanding of that faith in order to make it conform to what it regards as the standards of rationality. Serious problems arise in theology when it appears that these two approaches seriously conflict — for example, when it appears that the concept of God, in order to be a rationally acceptable concept of the divine, must include notions which contradict what religious faith in God presupposes. It is because they consider that western theology is generally characterized by insoluble tensions of this sort that Hartshorne and other process theologians have put forward a significantly different concept of God.

The fundamental difficulty is that the convictions of faith and the demands of reason are understood to make incompatible demands. Particularly when they have been conscious of philosophical considerations, theologians have regularly talked about God as being, among other things, absolute, necessary, unchanging, unchangeable, infinite, eternal (generally understood in the sense of being 'beyond' or 'outside time'), *actus purus* (pure actuality, without any potentiality whatsoever), *ens realissimum* (having all perfections), and impassible. These notions, however, if taken seriously, apparently contradict any talk about God as creating, loving, pitying, deciding, and acting in relation to the world. There thus arises a fundamental conflict between some of the notions which theologians have considered to be essential parts of a rationally adequate description of God and believers' faith in God as a personal being who acts purposively, responsively, and caringly and so is a proper object of their trust. In addition, since not all values are compossible, it is questionable whether such notions as those of an *ens realissimum* and an *actus purus* — in the way that they are generally interpreted — can be used coherently to describe any actual being.

This description of the 'fundamental problem' may be suspected of being a tendentious caricature. In order, therefore, to indicate that the difficulty is not a pseudo-problem invented by philosophical theologians wanting to be different, remarks made by three theologians, two of whom at any rate are of seminal importance in the development of western theology, will be cited to illustrate it. Their statements show how the demands of rationality may be considered to require views of God which are incompatible with an understanding of theistic faith as the believers' perception of God as one who personally calls, loves, and forgives them.

In the *Proslogion*, for instance, Anselm expounds the nature of God according to the principle that God, as that 'than whom nothing greater can be conceived', must be 'whatever it is better to be than not to be'. On this basis he concludes that God is 'just, truthful, blessed' because 'it is better to be just than not just; better to be blessed than not blessed' (Anselm 1962: 10f). So far his argument seems to develop by a priori reasoning a proper understanding of God's nature. On the basis of the same principle, though, he goes on to hold that among the qualities of the divine, God must be thought of as both 'compassionate' and 'passionless'. The divine must be thought of as 'compassionate' because a non-compassionate being is to be judged, presumably intuitively, inferior. In Anselm's judgement, however, God's blessedness and impassibility would be respectively impaired and contradicted if God were affected by sympathy for those who suffer and thereby are candidates for divine 'compassion'. He therefore seeks to escape the dilemma by holding that God is 'compassionate in terms of our experience, and not compassionate in terms of [God's] being'. He asserts, that is, that God is 'both compassionate' in being one who saves 'the wretched' and 'not compassionate' because the divine is 'affected by no sympathy for wretchedness' (Anselm 1962: 13f).

God and the processes of reality

This attempt to harmonize an affirmation of compassion with impassibility in the divine nature by describing God's actions as expressions of compassion while denying that there is anything in God which can correspond to our experiences of compassion seems to be intrinsically unsatisfactory as well as contrary to the Christian faith which Anselm shares. It is intrinsically unsatisfactory because it involves the denial of an essential element in the notion of compassion when the notion is applied to God. Talk of 'compassionate' acts which do not express some feeling of 'sympathy for the wretched' is talk which contradicts itself. It is also contrary to the Christian believer's faith in God as one who is significantly to be described as grieving over the fate of a people, caring for them with parental love, pitying those who suffer, and longing for the restoration of those who are lost — the God, that is, who is described by the stories of the burning bush, Hosea, the parables of the lost sheep, the lost coin, and the prodigal son, and whose nature and will are held to be supremely revealed in the suffering of Jesus. Anselm's attempt to explicate God's nature thus leads him into fundamental difficulties because he accepts, apparently without question, that God as perfect must be regarded as impassible, as unaffectable by others.

Aquinas's considerable — and in some ways unfortunate — contribution to Christian theology was to attempt to express it in Aristotelian terms. His acceptance of this structure of thought with its underlying principles led him, in a way similar to Anselm, to conclusions about the nature of God which contradict how Christian believers implicitly understand their relationship to God. In his *Summa Theologiae*, for example, he comes to the conclusion that 'it clearly follows that God cannot change in any way' because God, as 'first existent', must be 'sheerly actual and unalloyed with potentiality, since actuality, simply speaking, precedes potentiality' (i.e. God must be *actus purus*) (Aquinas 1964: 2, 127ff). Accordingly he holds that there are no reciprocal relationships between God and created beings by which the latter can in any way affect the former. According to his understanding of the situation,

> since God is altogether outside the order of creatures, since they are ordered to him but not he to them, it is clear that being related to God is a reality in creatures, but being related to creatures is not a reality in God, we say it about him because of the real relation in creatures.

(Aquinas 1964: 3, 75)

Attributes of God which apparently imply God's 'relation to creatures' are not to be interpreted as indicating 'any change' in God but only 'a change in the creatures'. To clarify the point he picks up an illustration offered by Aristotle: in the case of my relation to a pillar 'we can say that the pillar has changed from being on my left to being on my right, not through any alteration in the pillar but simply because I have turned round' (ibid.: 3, 73ff; cf. 2, 87; 4, 55f; 6, 25ff, 39).

To conceive of the divine nature in this way means that references to God's activity can only make sense in terms of the attraction of a final causality. It is incompatible with descriptions of God as deciding and acting. It implies that God cannot in any serious way be described as living: the divine existence is understandable only as unchanging self-contemplation. It is difficult, though, to imagine how this picture of a narcissistic being could ever represent a convincing object of worship, let alone be reconciled with stories of God being revealed in Jesus as one 'who for our salvation came down from heaven'.

A third example is provided by William Beveridge's commentary on the Thirty-nine Articles in which he seeks to prove that they are 'consonant to Scripture, Reason, and Fathers'. In the course of his argument he states that these three authorities agree that God is 'not subject to, nor capable of love, hatred, joy, grief, anger, and the like, as they daily arise in us imperfect creatures; but he is always the same unmovable, unchangeable, impassible God' (Beveridge 1846: 26). Consequently 'it is impossible for God, who is a most pure act, to be subject' to 'suffering' (ibid.: 30). Furthermore, it is argued, since the divine is essentially and wholly perfect, God can neither ever have been nor ever become imperfect. Therefore God cannot change for change must be either from or to an inferior state. Beveridge offers biblical and patristic texts as well as some rational reflections in order to justify his position. Nevertheless, what he presents is a view of God which is irreconcilable with faith in God as one who knows, cherishes, cares for, responds to, and aids people in their contingency and freedom.

These brief references illustrate a view of God which has been widely adopted, more or less uncritically, by most western theologians. Their works put forward a concept of God which seems at first to be intellectually satisfactory, even rationally necessary, since any theistically adequate notion of God apparently needs, implicitly or explicitly, to conceive of the divine as being absolute, necessary, eternal, and wholly perfect. A being who is not absolute or not necessary or not eternal or not perfect would not be 'God'. Unfortunately, as the above references illustrate, when theologians have drawn out the implications of such a concept of God they have generally produced the concept of something that is more like an ideal value than like the living God in whom the believer enjoys the personal relationship of theistic faith.

Why have theologians traditionally considered that the concept of God must be understood in this way? It seems that they have reached their conclusions because, on the one hand, they have accepted — as they must if their views are to be rationally coherent — the principle of non-contradiction and, on the other hand, have been persuaded, again correctly, that certain descriptions are required by any rationally adequate understanding of God. These descriptions include the qualities of being absolute, necessary, unchanging, infinite, and eternal. A being to which these qualities could not be attributed in some significant sense would not satisfy the defining criteria for the divine. Each of these qualities, though, has a contrary: necessary — contingent; absolute — relative; unchanging — changing; infinite — finite; and eternal — temporal. On the basis of the principle of non-contradiction, it is therefore assumed that if one of these pairs of qualities is properly used to describe God, the other must be denied any applicability to the divine. Thus if God is held to be necessary, then it is entailed that God is not contingent; if absolute, then not relative; if unchanging, then not changing; if infinite, then not finite; and if eternal, then not temporal.

The attribution of these qualities to God and the corresponding denial of their contraries create fundamental problems for theistic faith. They make it impossible to predicate coherently of the divine many things that such faith also holds to be the case. The divine relationship to human being, for example, is widely maintained to be one of love. It is impossible, however, to affirm coherently that a 'God' who is in every respect absolute and unchanging 'loves' anything which is in some essential respects a changing, autonomous agent — i.e. anything like the morally responsible, self-determining beings which we consider ourselves to be. What is absolute and unchanging cannot, that is, enter into the kind of changing relationship with such an object which is presupposed by significant talk about 'loving' it. In certain respects 'love' cannot in practice be a totally unchanging state: its actualization requires responses to its object which differ according to the differing states of that object. To take a humdrum example, a father's love for his 3-year-old son will involve different expressions according to whether the son is trying to draw a car, suffering from chicken-pox, expressing infantile rebellion, or splashing on a beach. To say that God is *in all respects* unchanging is to deny that the divine 'love' has the varying responsiveness which is part of the relationship of love. It implies that the divine 'love' is a kind of universal smile which, unaware and unfeeling, radiates throughout the cosmos, quite unconscious of the contingent states of what it falls upon.

Similar arguments can be presented for holding that a necessary, absolute, unchanging, infinite, and eternal being, such as God is frequently understood to be in every respect (on the grounds that the contrary qualities cannot be ascribed to the divine without contradiction), cannot coherently be said to have intentions, act creatively, know a contingent and changing world, and share the experiences of its constituents. If taken seriously these conclusions imply that the divine is a static, self-centred, only self-knowing absolute. Such a reality might satisfy some of the defining characteristics of the divine but it is far from the living, personal agent that is the object of theistic faith and understanding.

How have theologians responded to the problems that thus arise with the concept of God? There have been four major forms of response, each of which enjoys a certain degree of plausibility.

Some theologians choose to let the demands of reason, as they understand them, control their understanding of God. They may, for example, follow Aristotle's view of what reason requires and find the determining norms of their concept in such notions as those of 'the Unmoved Mover' and *'actus purus'*. The result of adopting this position is that talk about God as loving, caring, feeling sympathy, intervening, and so forth are treated as pious and comforting but basically misleading anthropomorphisms.

The 'God' of this theological stance shares the absolute, necessary, and unchanging qualities of an ideal value and a multiplication table. Here theology has in effect abandoned theistic faith and become a kind of religious metaphysics. Its object may be described as the vision of God or as the vision of the Good. For some people, especially for those who find peace in contemplation of the ideals of beauty, truth, and goodness, the faith expressed by such a theology is completely satisfying. For others, though, it is only partially attractive. It fails to meet intellectual questions about the meaning and purpose of reality; it offers no justification for human hope, let alone confidence, in the final worth of human being; and it gives no support to the conviction that ultimately reality is structured by a conscious concern for the flourishing of humane values.

An alternative response to problems concerning the compatibility of faith and reason challenges the authority of the demands of reason in order to allow religious faith, as it is understood, to determine the contents of talk about God. The Bampton Lectures by H. L. Mansel illustrate one form of this type of solution. Influenced by the ideas of Sir William Hamilton, he argus that 'the fundamental conceptions of Rational Theology' are 'self-destructive'. Contradictions, for example, result from attributing to 'one and the same Being' any two of the three conceptions of 'the Cause, the Absolute, and the Infinite' (Mansel 1858: 50, 47). These contradictions, however, do not belong to the nature of God. They are the product and reveal the limits of human understanding. According to Mansel, the correct theological solution to this problem is to recognize that human reason is incompetent to judge matters concerning the divine nature and, accordingly, to base theistic understanding wholly upon God's self-revelation to humanity.

Initially this may appear to be an attractive way out of the difficulty since it places on God the responsibility for correct theistic understanding. Who are human beings to challenge what God declares about the divine? Unfortunately it is a spurious solution. Some control by rational reflection seems inescapable — even if not explicitly acknowledged — in identifying supposed revelatory insights and in determining their authenticity and meaning. The recognition and explication of alleged revelations consequently are not and cannot be wholly free from presuppositions about the nature of God. They reflect those prejudgements even though they may also modify them. A notable example of this is provided by Karl Barth's exposition of the biblical revelation, especially in his earlier writings. Whereas the Bible seems to many commentators to speak of a God who is constantly present with people and who reveals Godself in personal terms, Barth finds the Bible witnessing primarily to what Søren Kierkegaard describes as 'the infinite qualitative distinction between time and eternity' (Barth 1933: 10). In spite of Barth's insistence that his theology should be determined by and should expound the biblical witness, what he finds in the Bible seems to be conditioned by his prior conviction about the Kierkegaardian understanding of the relationship between the divine and the human. It is a pattern which is liable to repeat itself wherever theologians seek to avoid responsibility for their ideas by appealing to the dictates of authority.

A third response to the problem posed by the incompatibility of what are considered to be rationally required views on the nature of God with believers' faith in God is to refuse to take the offending terms too seriously. This response is found in theologians who use the problematic concepts but are not prepared to accept all their implications. Charles Gore, for instance, wants to assert that God is 'absolute' while rejecting certain unwelcome implications of this description. He states that 'the revealed religion undoubtedly postulates a God who is the absolute' but immediately qualifies this by adding 'not, of course, that the universe is identical with God its Creator' and by interpreting the notion in terms of God as 'the one and only ultimate source' of all that 'exists in the universe'. According to Gore, that is, God is to be described as 'the absolute' although there is something over against Godself, albeit something that is also ultimately dependent upon Godself. Furthermore, while Gore says in this sentence that God 'contains ... all that is', he goes on to say in the next one that 'this absoluteness of God must ... be qualified so as to admit of the existence, by the creative will of God ... of free spirits' whose dependence upon God does not prevent them having 'the power of disordering ... the world as God would have had it be' (Gore 1926: 147). What we have here is an attempt to describe God on the one hand as 'the absolute' and, on the other, as not the totality of reality but as limited in certain respects by partially autonomous realities (even if realities which the divine has created) distinct from Godself. This is to use the term 'absolute' while rejecting part of its meaning in a way that leaves it uncertain whether or not God is properly to be described as 'absolute' and, if so, what the description signifies.

A fourth — and more sophisticated — response to the problem of apparent conflicts between the demands of reason and the supposed perceptions of theistic faith affirms that both must be correct even though it acknowledges that there is no obvious way to reconcile them. This position is often justified by reference to the supposed limits of the human intellect. Gilbert Burnet, for example, in his *Exposition of the Thirty-nine Articles of the Church of England* (1705), is clearly unhappy with the kind of interpretation of the divine attributes that Beveridge presents. He takes up the problem of how God can be held to know all distinct created things not by 'successive Thoughts' but 'by one single Thought', and to act freely but yet 'by a necessity of Nature'. Since it seems that theistic understanding requires the affirmation of such conflicting claims, his solution is to appeal to human ignorance:'the Divine Essence being so infinitely above us, it is no wonder if we can frame no distinct Act concerning its Knowledge or Will.' In view of the difficulties in the way of understanding, therefore, 'the wisest and safest course' for us is 'to adore what is above our Apprehensions, rather than to enquire too curiously, or determine too boldly in it'. In effect Burnet recognizes the intellectual problem only to ignore it. He concludes his discussion thus:

> It is certain that God acts both freely and perfectly: Nor is he a Being subject to change, or to new acts; but *he is what he is*, both Infinite and Incomprehensible: We can neither apprehend how he made, nor how he executes his Decrees. So we must leave this Difficulty, without pretending that we can explain it, or answer the Objections that arise against all the several ways by which Divines have endeavoured to resolve it.

> (Burnet 1705: 26f)

Some advocates of this 'solution' stress, even glory in, the absurdity of the contents of faith. What else should be expected when we try to apprehend the divine?

A variant of the latter two responses attempts to overcome problems with the coherence of the concept of God by baptizing the difficulties as 'paradoxes'. By this means it tries to make apparent contradictions in theism's traditional self-understanding acceptable. It may be asserted, for example, that it is not self-contradictory nonsense but theistically appropriate paradox to hold that God is both unchanging and acting, or both impassible and loving. A rather different version of this defence maintains that each of the apparently incompatible concepts must only be understood in a way that is compatible with its associated (and apparently self-contradictory) one. Thus the 'impassibility' of God is, paradoxically, to be understood in a way that is compatible with the divine 'love'.

This response to problems about the coherence of faith's traditional view of God is basically to trust that that view is correct although it is not possible to perceive how it makes sense. It thus leaves the impression that theologians are 'trying to have their cake and eat it'. They are attempting to assert, for example, that God is absolute and unchanging (on the grounds that a 'God' who does not have these qualities cannot be believed in as God) while refusing to admit that these descriptions, when taken seriously, have implications which rule out other claims which they wish to make about God — such as that God is aware of people's contingent states and responds to them. The basic weakness of such a view of claims about God is that it is unclear what is being affirmed in such cases. Since, as Newman points out in *The Grammar of Assent* (1870), what cannot be apprehended cannot be held to be believed, it is questionable whether this position can be regarded as a genuine solution to the problem of the coherence of claims about the divine.

What, then, is the theologian to do? None of the above responses to fundamental problems with the concept of God is satisfactory. Reason and faith seem to require that we talk of God in some respects as absolute, necessary, unchanging, infinite, and eternal and in other respects as relative, contingent, changing, finite, and temporal. Can it be done without falling foul of the principle of non-contradiction? Can, that is, the theist find a way of using both sets of descriptions in a coherent manner or must theism be given up as an inescapably self-contradictory and so meaningless form of understanding? In the following chapters it will be argued that process thought offers a way of understanding the nature of God which overcomes this fundamental problem in a way that meets the demands of both religion and reason and which opens up a fruitful way of understanding the relationship between God and processes of reality. But before we examine Hartshorne's 'dipolar' solution to the concept of God, it is important to take note of the metaphysical foundations of process thought.

3   God, metaphysics, and process thought

So far as theism is concerned, two currently widespread (and mutually opposed) views are that references to 'God' are not to a reality and that understanding the reality of God does not involve metaphysics. Both these attempts to avoid problems in thought about the God of theistic faith and understanding are fundamentally mistaken. The first of them seeks to overcome difficulties with the definitive notion of God by converting it into something else; the second ignores the inescapable conditions of all thought about God. One corollary, though, of perceiving the radical unsatisfactoriness of these suggested solutions is the recognition that any attempt to achieve an adequately self-aware understanding of God and the processes of reality must involve the conscious adoption of a metaphysical understanding of the necessary structure of any possible world as well as an appreciation of the fundamental nature of the actual world in which we find ourselves and of which God is God. Consequently, after the first two points have been considered, the discussion in this chapter will take up the issues raised by this corollary. It will be suggested that the general perception of the character of reality presented by what is known as 'process thought' may, with some modifications of its classical form, provide the proper ground for theistic understanding.

The view that references to God do not denote a reality is sometimes put forward by people who consider that the notion of God has a significant use and yet are convinced that attempts to identify and to justify claims about the divine as a reality are irretrievably defective. In order, therefore, to preserve some form of religion and of talk about God, they maintain in one way or another that statements about God have a non-cognitive role. Such statements may report commitment to a style of living, or announce the ultimate status of various values (those used to describe the attributes of 'God'), or express a certain way of looking at reality, or present a particular attitude to life. In each case, though, it is crucial to recognize that, whatever the surface grammar of statements about God may appear to indicate, they are misunderstood when they are apprehended as providing descriptions of a particular entity, even though a notably peculiar

entity. The function of 'God' is correctly analysed according
to these interpretations when it is perceived that it is used
descriptively, as an adjective rather than as a noun. It does not
denote a subject but connotes a predicate ascribed to a subject.

D. Z. Phillips, for example, suggests that talk about the attributes of God is 'radically misconstrued' when it is taken to
describe a subject which exists independently of the believer.
Instead, the divine 'attributes' are to be understood to inculcate
qualities by whose instantiation the believer not only participates
in but also, apparently, constitutes the reality of God (Phillips
1970: 55). Less subtly Don Cupitt similarly holds that statements
about 'God's creation of the world', for example, are to be
apprehended as mythical and inspiring assertions about human
creativity: 'The creation-myth in effect says, "You can do it;
here's how"; and the god functions as a guiding standard or
norm' (Cupitt 1985: 181; cf. 212).

Another example of non-cognitive understanding of the role
of 'God' underlies Harold Schulweis's notion of 'a predicate
theology'. According to his analysis of religious language what
appear to be the subject and the predicate in statements about
God are correctly apprehended when they are reversed — a view
which strongly echoes a claim made by Feuerbach (cf. 1957: 60).
On the basis of this hermeneutical understanding of God-talk
Schulweis finds a solution to the problem of evil. God is not a
subject, an agent, whose attributes entail disturbing questions
about divine responsibility for evil in the world. Statements
about the nature and will of God must be interpreted so that
'the predicates are ... the proper subject of theology' while the
term 'God' or 'godliness' (which is the grammatical subject of
statements containing those predicates) refers to the status,
organization, and interrelatedness of the qualities described in
those apparent predicates (Schulweis 1984: 122, 131). What,
then, appears to be talk about God affirms that certain qualities
are 'godly' and hence to be adored and emulated (cf. ibid.: 124).

While such analyses clarify the use — and hence the
meaning — of some statements (or part of the content of some
statements) which refer to God, they are crucially inadequate as
ways of identifying what may be called the characteristically
'theistic' use of that reference. As Joseph Runzo puts it in
criticizing Phillips's position, 'from the standpoint of traditional
monotheism' — which is what I mean by 'theism' — 'non-
cognitivist views of religion are basically a-theistic ... for
traditionally monotheists have quite clearly *intended* to be
making truth-claims about the nature and acts of God' (Runzo

1986: 182). Theistic talk about God, furthermore, is not talk about just another entity among those contingent beings which constitute the world. Theism, at least the theism which is the subject of this study, is fundamentally a matter of understanding the ultimate ground, nature, and purpose of reality. Accordingly references to God definitively concern that reality which intrinsically constitutes the totally satisfying explanation of the ground and goal, the meaning and purpose, of all things. However limited may be the human apprehension of the divine, in principle God is ontologically, valuatively, and rationally the final and proper answer to the questions of why there is something rather than nothing and of what that something — which is everything — is 'for' or 'about'. Existentially theism finds in God that which answers the ultimate questions about life which haunt self-reflective human being.

If, though, references to God concern that which properly satisfies this fundamental and definitive human quest for understanding, statements about God must be recognized necessarily to have cognitive functions. This does not imply that any non-cognitive functions which are also to be detected in them must be regarded as derivative. What it does imply is that a cognitive element is primary and essential. The reason for this is that what is real can only be adequately understood by reference to that which is itself in some appropriate way real. Authentic explanations of what was, is, and is to be are not free-floating ideas which appear 'out of the blue yonder' and simply hang in the air. They can finally satisfy our intellect only if they make sense of things by reference to what is also the case.

Alfred North Whitehead makes this point in terms of what he calls 'the ontological principle'. It asserts that 'actual entities are the only *reasons*; so that to search for a *reason* is to search for one or more actual entities' (Whitehead 1978: 24). More pithily he summarizes the principle as 'no actual entity, then no reason' (ibid.: 19). In order, therefore, to answer the human quest for understanding theism identifies as holy the reality of that which necessarily exists, is ultimate in rationality and value, and, as purposive, is the ground of and determines the goal of all else. Theism, that is, seeks to satisfy the intellect by discerning that sacred reality which is the brute non-contingent fact where all questions must stop since at that point there is nothing more to say besides, 'But that is what is ultimately the case.' When, therefore, Whitehead affirms the basic conviction of theism — namely, that it is 'in the nature of God' that 'reasons of the highest absoluteness' are found (ibid.: 19) — it is important to remember that, in order to provide those reasons which are the ground of all understanding, God must be a definite actual entity.

The other widespread error which was mentioned at the start of this chapter is that theistic understanding does not involve metaphysics. It is a claim popularly asserted by those who profess to have, or who wish to be provided with, a 'simple faith'. Such people often complain that theologians and philosophers — indeed, all who seek to think clearly about the nature and will of God — only manage to muddle what is straightforward and to obscure what is easy to grasp.

It is not because, as one who teaches philosophy of religion, I have my profession to defend that I judge this wish to eschew metaphysics to be mistaken! While critics justifiably point out that in practice some thinkers befog rather than clarify what they attempt to understand, this is an indictment of the competence of those thinkers rather than a repudiation of the validity of their task. Even for the most powerful minds thought about God, since it is thought about that which is holy, ultimate, necessary, and universal, is to be expected to be at the limits of and beyond what can be apprehended. Its object is not only unique. As that which instantiates the ground and goal of being it is also that in terms of which all else is finally to be understood rather than being itself understandable in the same way as other objects. Whereas, for example, the existence of each contingent thing is partly to be understood in terms of the 'causes' which produced it (including its own powers of self-determination), the divine, as that which is ontologically ultimate, necessarily exists as that on which all else is dependent but which is not dependent on (and hence is not to be understood by reference to) anything ontologically prior. Similarly the non-divine is to be praised to the extent that it emulates the qualities of the divine; but God, as that by which all else is to be judged, is the standard of judgement and so not open to being praised. For reasons such as these it needs to be recognized that a 'simple' theistic faith is a contradiction in terms. God is not that kind of an object.

It may be claimed, though, that while thought about the reality of God is essentially puzzling, it can do without the complications of metaphysics. Theologians should concentrate on God and leave metaphysical issues to others. To introduce metaphysical considerations is to aggravate needlessly an already difficult problem. Such claims, however, collapse once it is perceived that some form of metaphysical understanding underlies all cognitive thought, whether its metaphysical basis be consciously recognized or not. The way to clear and justifiable understanding of reality is not by avoiding metaphysical considerations but by determining the appropriate metaphysical foundations for such thought. Since, therefore, theism is a cognitive matter of making sense of reality, thought about God cannot avoid involving metaphysics. As contributing to 'the complete circle of knowledge', the immediate experience of religion and of its theological insights must both influence and be influenced by 'some metaphysical way of conceiving the most penetrating description of the universe' (Whitehead 1927: 66). Accordingly theologians should not aim to do without metaphysics. Instead they should seek to become aware of the metaphysics which they use as well as to subject it to critical scrutiny in order to determine whether, out of those available, it provides the most adequate basis for understanding reality.

What is meant by metaphysics in the above comments? If it is foundationally important for thought about God, it will be as well to be clear about what it is before we consider the value of process thought in providing the metaphysical basis for theistic understanding.

In considering this issue in *Creative Synthesis and Philosophic Method* (1970), Hartshorne proposes twelve views of metaphysics which he considers to differ only 'in emphasis and focus of explanation'. They define it, for example, as 'the unrestricted or completely general theory of concreteness', 'the clarification of strictly universal conceptions', 'the search for unconditionally necessary or eternal truths about existence', and 'the attempt to make non-exclusive or purely positive statements' (Hartshorne 1970: 24, 33). What these formulas make clear is that metaphysics is not just a matter of determining the presuppositions underlying an intellectual system in order to examine them for internal coherence and external applicability. While such critical identification of the principles which determine domains of thought is important because of the light which it throws on the proper appreciation and development of those domains, metaphysical understanding goes beyond the realm of ideas alone. Its goal is the perception of concepts which identify the character of any possible as well as of all actual reality. When, therefore, Whitehead states that 'metaphysics is nothing but the description of the generalities which apply to all the details of practice' (Whitehead 1978: 13; cf. 1927: 72n), it is important to interpret his remark as referring to whatever could possibly be as well as to what has been and is the case.

For much of the twentieth century in Britain metaphysical understanding has been suspected of being a speculative attempt to achieve what is impossible, essentially confused, or simply erroneous. Three factors have supported such an adverse attitude. In the first place it is maintained that no previous attempt to achieve metaphysical knowledge has managed to gain widespread consensus, at least not for any length of time. Whereas scientific understanding grows as later theories take up points discerned in earlier ones and modify them to incorporate further discoveries and insights, the history of metaphysical understanding is held to indicate that it is incapable of such productive development. This apparent failure after so much effort by so many brilliant minds thus leaves some with the impression that the task is impossible and ought to be abandoned. Second, the various forms of linguistic philosophy which have dominated British philosophy for much of this century have been in certain respects a justified reaction against the speculative excesses of some metaphysics, especially as found in neo-Hegelianism. Such conclusions as that the only reality is the Absolute and that temporal distinctions are unreal have been judged to be not brilliant insights into the paradoxical character of reality but the confused products of a misunderstanding of language. Third, there has been a growing recognition of the subjectivity of thought. From Hamann and Kant in the eighteenth century through Coleridge and Kierkegaard in the nineteenth to Wittgenstein, Bohr, and the advocates of the anthropic principle in the twentieth, it has been pointed out that we cannot stand 'outside' reality and view it objectively. We are part of the reality which we want to understand; what we observe as real is affected by our observation of it; and how we understand it is to some extent determined by the prior structures of understanding with which we try to make sense of it.

While these considerations indicate some of the difficulties inherent in seeking metaphysical understanding and warn against overconfident claims for the products of such a quest, they are not sufficient grounds for ruling out all attempts to achieve it. In the first place, past failures do not show that all attempts must be erroneous — and inspection may reveal that some past attempts have more to be said for them than recent prejudice has been willing to allow. Second, it is clearly important not to be misled by language and, in particular, not to fall into the trap of regarding abstractions as names of actual realities — what Whitehead calls 'the fallacy of misplaced concreteness' (Whitehead 1927a: 64ff). This, though, warns of the dangers inherent in using our conceptual tools rather than imposes a ban on metaphysical thought as such. Finally, the subjectivity which affects all observing and thinking does not entail that understanding must be dismissed as simply the product of the thinker's mind. What it does indicate is that all thinking must seek, as far as possible, to be self-critically aware of its relativity and, hence, open to revision.

In any case the demand to make sense of reality seems to be basic to human rationality and, as was indicated earlier, every attempt to meet that demand inescapably presupposes some form of metaphysical understanding, whether or not it is explicitly recognized to be such. Consequently, rather than waste time agonizing further over the difficulties — or impossibilities — of the task, it will be more profitable to risk the dangers of dialectical illusion and to consider the metaphysical understanding which arguably provides the most adequate basis for theistic understanding. Furthermore, it must not be forgotten that even an 'empiricist' or 'secularist' denial of metaphysics is itself a metaphysical position.

The importance of this task is highlighted once it is recognized how problems may arise in a theistic understanding which is tied to an unsatisfactory metaphysical position. As was noticed in Chapter 2, classical perceptions of Christian theism, such as are found in Thomist thought, are moulded to their detriment by some of the ideas of perfection put forward in Greek (particularly in the case of Thomism, Aristotelian) philosophy. Recent examples of the same kind of problem are found in works by Richard Braithwaite and Paul van Buren. When, for instance, Braithwaite presented *An Empiricist's View of the Nature of Religious Belief* (1966), the presupposed 'empiricism' forced him to interpret statements about God as statements about believers' behaviour-policies and their supportive stories. That is all that seems to be 'empirically' testable in such matters. Van Buren was similarly constrained in his deliberately 'secular' interpretation of 'the Gospel' by what in effect amounts to a secularist metaphysics. This holds as a basic principle that there is no 'transcendent realm' (Buren 1963: 1). Accepting the validity of this metaphysical position, van Buren's discernment of the Gospel is accordingly governed by the basic principle that 'our inherited language of the supernatural' can no longer be regarded as referring to a reality (ibid.: 4). The significance of the Gospel is thus put in terms of the 'expression of a historical perspective'. As van Buren admits, however, this 'empirical' approach is likely to seem to others to provide an 'inadequate' grounding for the language of the Christian faith (ibid.: 193). It is certainly not possible to make sense of theistic understanding on the basis of such metaphysics.

One response to problems which arise from the use of an unsatisfactory metaphysics in theistic understanding maintains that the proper procedure for finding the appropriate metaphysical insights for such understanding is to adopt a 'critical' approach. According to this position, just as the general principles governing all thought and the particular principles governing different realms of thought are to be discovered by analysing thought in practice in order to discern what is necessary to it, so the metaphysical basis of theistic understanding is to be found by extrapolating its presupposed principles. This, for example, is an approach suggested by Karl Barth.

On the grounds that 'theology is *ministerium verbi divini*' (Barth 1933: x), Barth asserts that a theologian's ontology should be subject 'to criticism and control by his theology, and not conversely' (Barth 1967: 91). What this may entail is illustrated by Barth's discussion of angelology (Barth 1960: 369ff). Applying the supposed 'Anselmian' principle of 'credo ut intelligam' (I believe in order that I may understand), Barth holds that in dogmatics 'an *intelligere* worthy of the name' may only be attained by giving to the *credere* of the biblical witness 'full and exclusive attention' (ibid.: 403; cf. 372). Since, therefore, 'the witness of Scripture' introduces angels 'in connexion with the revelation and work of God', a Christian dogmatics must concern itself with them although there is no independent 'philosophical' reason to affirm their reality (ibid.: 372f). Indeed, Barth warns that if we attempt to find angels elsewhere than in the biblical witness 'our philosophy will spoil our theology, and our theology our philosophy' (ibid.: 404).

In principle such an approach accepts as normative rather than critically reviews a particular received understanding of theism. Furthermore, by seeking the proper metaphysical basis for theistic understanding in that authoritative expression, it endorses not only its understanding of God and reality but also the metaphysical conceptions which form it. In consequence it may well help to perpetuate a mode of theistic understanding which lacks credibility either because it requires general assent to a view of reality which is no longer regarded as tenable or because it produces a split between reality as faith envisages it and reality as currently experienced in secular life. Once, though, it is appreciated that all expressions of theistic understanding, including the witness of faith contained in the Bible, are moulded

45

by the metaphysical presuppositions of their authors, and that however authoritative those expressions may be, their metaphysical basis is not necessarily the most appropriate for theistic understanding, even those who are committed to the authoritative status of some such expressions may recognize that their metaphysical basis is not an authoritative given. From this it follows that the answer to the question of the proper metaphysical ground for theistic understanding is not to be found necessarily by examining existing forms of that understanding, whatever their classical status. If, though, the metaphysical ground for theistic understanding is not laid down by past forms of that understanding, how is it to be established? It is by the reflection which is appropriate for discerning the necessary structure of all that is and all that could ever possibly be.

But before we consider how it may be possible to determine 'the metaphysical first principles' which 'can never fail of exemplification' (Whitehead 1978: 4), it is important to note that the apprehension of these principles is limited. Their essential universality means that no verbal expression can ever formulate them in a completely adequate way. This is because language, like observation, normally proceeds 'by the method of difference'. We notice, name, and conceive a particular object because of the ways in which it is distinct from other objects. 'Sometimes we see an elephant, and sometimes we do not. The result is that an elephant, when present, is noticed' (ibid.: 4). It can accordingly be described — as can any other contingent entity. When, in contrast, we seek to characterize that which is necessarily true of all possible as well as of all actual realities, empiricism's method of 'detailed discrimination' is no longer appropriate. Imagination is needed to perceive those principles, and metaphorical language, in which 'words and phrases' are 'stretched towards a generality foreign to their ordinary usage' (ibid.: 4), is required to express them. Consequently when metaphysical claims about reality are made, it must be remembered that what is being provided is not a direct description but, in intention, the most adequate way of expressing these insights in terms of human thought and human experience.

But how is a perception of the metaphysical truths which are necessarily the case for all reality, both actual and possible, to be achieved? Charles Hartshorne advocates a systematic, a priori, method of argument. In one recent paper he sums up the 'technical basis' of his metaphysics in the following two rules: 'exhaust the conceptual options, judge each option by rational rules of conceptual coherence' (Hartshorne 1985: 119; cf. 1973:

102 (E4)). What this means in practice may be seen, for example, in the chapters 'Ideas of God: an exhaustive division' and 'Six theistic proofs' in *Creative Synthesis and Philosophic Method* (1970). In the former chapter he lists the nine possible ways of conceiving divine existence in terms of the metaphysical contraries of necessity and contingency (in both their transcendent and their non-eminent forms), and then considers which of those combinations is able to meet 'nine reasonable requirements' of the character of divine existence. His argument is that since the requirements 'are fully met' by only one of 'the categorial possibilities for conceiving deity', all but that one ought to be eliminated as deficient (Hartshorne 1970: 266, 274; cf. 263ff). In the latter chapter he offers six arguments for divine existence which depend upon the requirements of the very general and abstract concepts that are involved in them (cf. ibid.: 294). In one of them, for instance, he offers a revised form of the argument from design according to which there are only four possibilities for us to choose between:

There is no cosmic order.
There is cosmic order but no cosmic ordering power.
There is cosmic order and ordering power, but the power is not divine.
There is cosmic order and divine power.

(ibid.: 281)

The first is ruled out on the grounds that 'a merely chaotic world must be unknowable'; the second because 'any order is infinitely threatened' if there is 'no supremely influential' agent among the free agents; the third because 'the cosmic ordering power' must be conceived as 'the supreme or eminent form of awareness'. If, then, the first three possibilities are ruled out and there can be only four coherent possibilities in relation to cosmic design, the fourth one must be true.

What is of interest here is not the cogency of Hartshorne's arguments but their method. In its strongest form, the argument lists all the conceptual possibilities in a particular respect and then demonstrates by careful analysis that all but one of these possibilities is 'not only unacceptable as true but absurd, not genuinely conceivable' (ibid.: 281). A weaker form of the argument has to be content with showing that all but one of the possible options are, more or less, not credible. The remaining possibility must therefore be held to be true because none of the alternatives to it is acceptable. In each case the reasoning is not 'empirical in the sharp sense defined by Popper, that its premises could conceivably conflict with observation' (ibid.: 278). It depends upon discerning the coherence or incoherence of the concepts involved.

In spite of his confidence (and delight) in such a priori arguments and of the rigour of his analyses, Hartshorne himself recognizes that no argument for theism 'is so evidently cogent that there can be no reasonable ground for rejecting it'. What he does maintain is that while there is 'room for intelligent disagreement in this matter', the arguments which have been formulated, when 'taken together, convince me and . . . I think are free from obvious fallacy' (Hartshorne 1982: 18). It is arguable, however, that although Hartshorne's individual arguments are conceptually and logically cogent, the basic method is not convincing as a way to determine the ultimate and necessary character of reality. In Hume's *Dialogues concerning Natural Religion* Philo points out that non-metaphysicians are often suspicious of a priori arguments even if they cannot explain their dissatisfaction (Hume 1935: 236). Justifying this commonsense response are reasonable worries about the adequacy of the concepts employed, the exhaustiveness of the perceived options, and the validity of the arguments used. Whitehead, for instance, warns that 'weakness of insight and deficiencies of language' prevent philosophers from ever being able to achieve a final formulation of the metaphysical first principles (Whitehead 1978: 4). So far as he is correct in this, a priori arguments about these matters may require a precision in their conceptual data which is unattainable.

Above all, though, there is worry about the relation between our concepts and reality. This last concern is classically expressed in Kant's warnings against the danger of dialectical illusion and his criticism of attempts, as in the ontological argument, to argue from concepts to reality. A priori consideration of concepts shows how the basic nature of our thinking requires us to understand things. By itself, though, it cannot show that reality necessarily is as our structures of thought compel us to think about it. In order to be reassured about that relationship it is necessary to move from purely a priori reflections to considering what may be called, in Ian Ramsey's phrase, the 'empirical fit' (cf. Ramsey 1964: 17, 38ff; 1965: 82, 85) between the thought by which we try to understand things and things as they are experienced — bearing in mind throughout this exercise that what we 'perceive' to be 'there' is always to some extent moulded by the ways in which we can 'conceive' it.

In order, then, to identify the metaphysical first principles which determine the fundamental nature of all reality, Hartshorne's preference for an a priori rationalist approach needs to be augmented, though not necessarily replaced, by a procedure which is critically aware both of the relativity of all understanding and of the need to test understanding against reality as experienced. While it is a need of which Hartshorne is aware, in this respect Whitehead's view of the way to achieve philosophical discovery has much to commend it. Whitehead stresses the need for 'the play of a free imagination, controlled by the requirements of coherence and logic' in the attempt to identify the metaphysical first principles. Using a metaphor which is more appropriate to the relatively low-flying, open-cockpitted aeroplanes of the 1920s than to the isolation of today's encanned flights, he describes the appropriate method thus:

> The true method of discovery is like the flight of an aeroplane. It starts from the ground of particular observation; it makes a flight in the thin air of imaginative generalization; and it again lands for renewed observation rendered acute by rational interpretation.

> (Whitehead 1978: 5; cf. 1927: 76, 110)

Here imagination, rational reflection, and observation all play a part.

Since 'we can never catch the actual world taking a holiday' from the 'sway' of the metaphysical first principles, it is difficult, if not impossible, to identify them by the method of difference. Imaginative thought is thus important: in spite of deficiencies in its penetrative power (cf. Whitehead 1978: 4), it alone is likely to be able to apprehend 'factors which are constantly present' in all reality by supplying 'the differences which the direct observation lacks' (ibid.: 55). Rational reflection is also important in order to ensure that the metaphysical first principles, as the products of 'imaginative construction', satisfy the necessary conditions of 'coherence and logical perfection'. These principles must both be adequate to what is found to be the case and show the solidarity of a connected system (ibid.: 6; cf. 6f). Observation, finally, is important because it both provides starting-points for imaginative generalization and tests the applicability of the resulting 'synoptic vision' of 'notions which apply to all facts' (ibid.: 5; cf. 1927: 110).

As later discussions will indicate, Whitehead and Hartshorne do not only differ in their approach to the metaphysical question.

They also differ somewhat in their answers. Indeed while Hartshorne describes himself as 'a "process philosopher" or "neoclassical" metaphysician' and while he recognizes that he has learnt much from Whitehead, 'the most recent of the great speculative philosophers', he states that he does not consider himself 'a Whiteheadian' (Hartshorne 1983: ixf, xiiif). Nevertheless, whatever the differences between them, Whitehead and Hartshorne basically share a common insight into the processive quality of the fundamental character of reality. It is also a metaphysical position which, with some modifications, provides the most adequate ground for a theistic understanding of God and the processes of reality. The remainder of this chapter will outline its main points.

The view that reality is processive is not new. Heraclitus affirmed the unending flux of things in the fifth century BC. On the whole, however, the dominant view throughout the history of western thought has been that the ultimate reality — and so, as the 'complete' reality, the perfect — must be unchanging. This view has been justified by the argument that change entails movement either towards or away from the state of ultimacy (and perfection): consequently it cannot be coherently attributed to that which is intrinsically ultimate (and perfect). Philosophers have thus considered that only unchanging qualities may be ascribed to the ultimate reality.

Plato, for example, responding to the Heraclitan position epistemologically by finding unchanging objects for knowledge in his theory of the Forms, maintains that 'true philosophers' seek to identify the 'eternal and immutable truth' of 'Reality itself' (Plato 1955: 238, 244). In Aristotle's view the ultimate and perfect is to be conceived as the Unmoved Mover. Such notions of an essential link between the perfect and the unchanging harmonize, furthermore, with human awareness of the loss of the past, of the impermanence of the things we cherish, and of the frightening unknowability of the future. The result has been a deeply embedded prejudice against change in western metaphysics as it inherits ideas from Greek thought.

Traditionally, therefore, philosophers have sought to understand the metaphysical structure of reality on the basis of reflection on the state of apparently static objects such as tables and chairs. In the past two centuries, however, this prejudice for the unchanging has been challenged. To live is to change. At the level of human existence it has been recognized that the values of creativity and of personal relationships, the avoidance of boredom and the enjoyment of fulfilment are only possible in terms of a changing mode of reality. More broadly it has been argued that reality as we experience it is deprived of intrinsic significance if it is at best a striving towards the unchangeably perfect (to which it can therefore contribute nothing) and at worst an illusion.

As a consequence, where metaphysical understanding is sought, notions of historical development and of biological evolution have been generalized, whether warrantably or not. Combined with a sense of the worth of human being, the result has been an atmosphere more amenable to the recognition that the structure of reality, even at the ultimate level, needs to be approached in dynamic terms if it is both understandable and to be adequately understood. Such an approach was offered by different strands of Hegelian thought in the nineteenth century and has been most notably — and variously — pursued in this century by Bergson, Smuts, Lloyd Morgan, Samuel Alexander and Teilhard de Chardin. Most significant — and most influential — of all, however, has been the development by Whitehead and Hartshorne of what the former called 'the philosophy of organism' and what is now most widely known as process philosophy.

As its name indicates, the defining principle of process thought is that to be actual and hence to be a concrete reality is to be in process. Not only organic or living beings change: all actual entities, as actual, are momentary constituents of the process of reality. Enduring objects are sequences of these momentary actualities, each of which massively inherits the qualities of its predecessor. They are subject to change both internally and externally. Whether I consider my own being, the chair on which I am sitting, or reality as a whole, the continuing object of my attention is constantly altering in its internal constitution as well as in its relationships with all other actualities. Positively this means in terms of the process of becoming that for anything to be actual is for it to be at the point where the indeterminate becomes determinate — to be where, that is, a previously yet-to-be-determined range of possibilities at that moment ends in the realization of one particular state of being now that actual entity. Or, to make the same point in terms of the movement from past to future, in no case is a concrete reality without a predecessor from which it has just emerged into being what it is and without a successor to whose form its present state will immediately (and massively) contribute as a datum. Negatively this means that only what is dead, past, abstract, or purely formal is unaffected by the processes of change. Unchangingness, for example, is applicable to the internal relationships of abstractions from the real (such as descriptions of a state at a particular instant) and to formal notions (such as are found in pure mathematics).

In terms of Whitehead's view of philosophical method, process thought may in certain respects be seen as an imaginative generalization from what physicists and evolutionary biologists on the one hand, and, more importantly, self-awareness on the other tell us about what it is to 'be'. According to the discoveries of modern physics, for example, even an object like a bar of gold or a marble bust whose rate of visually observable change is minimal is in fact composed of an enormous number of elementary 'particles' or, perhaps, foci of forces whose configuration changes from moment to moment. Such an object appears to be unchanging because we do not perceive the actual entities which compose it but only the successive resultants of the interactions of a huge number of them. In reality its constituent actual entities are continually changing in response to each other and to the influences of other forces acting upon them as that object. What is the case with inorganic objects is even more dramatically the case with living organisms. They are what they are because of their evolutionary inheritance of an enormous sequence of changes and because of their present response to their environment.

If, furthermore, we reflect upon the nature of that mode of existence whose reality it is impossible for us to deny, namely our own, we similarly find that to 'be' is to be involved in change. My existing as this self is not a static, unchanging persistence. It is a continuity through change which is not only continuity through a changing environment but also continuity as a changing subject. When, for example, I write the next paragraph, I will not be exactly the same person as I am writing this one. Experiences will have happened to 'me' and responses will have been made by 'me' that ensure that 'I' will have changed to some extent — even if so slightly that the changes are utterly trivial. Over longer periods (such as between my writing the first and last chapters or between my being a schoolboy and a pensioner), though, the aggregate of what may be individually minute changes may produce significant changes in who 'I' am. In contrast to the Platonic notion of the soul, my 'I' is not some unchanging substance which continues unaffected by what 'I' experience and what 'I' do: my 'I' is the self that experiences and responds and in so doing changes.

This understanding of what it is to be a self may cause puzzles for those who are troubled about the identity of the present 'I' with itself in former or in later states but they are the same kind of puzzles which arise when thought tries to impose upon reality generally structures which are alien to it. They are also puzzles whose roots lie to some extent in the nature of language. Apart from alleged exceptions like the language of the Hopi ('alleged' because I am not in a position to judge reports about their language), the basic structure of language is of nouns and verbs. The nouns refer to things; the verbs refer to what the things do or suffer. Underlying this linguistic structure, though, is the presupposition that the nouns refer to things that stay the same. It is a presupposition which becomes a law of thought with the principle of identity. Process thought, however, has difficulty with this presupposition since, as has been noted, it considers that an enduring object is a series of bundles of actual relationships which change from moment to moment even if, as in the case of what we call this stone or that table, the changes in the internal relationships of the actual constituents of such objects from one moment to the next are undetectable by us.

In the case of Whitehead's understanding of actuality, the structure of language seems to have combined with his mathematical understanding of points and calculus and his appreciation of recent developments in quantum theory in physics to produce a corpuscular model of reality. The basic constituents of reality are held to be actual occasions. Each of these is an individual drop of reality (or 'experience') which momentarily comes to concrescence and then perishes, to be succeeded by another actual occasion which massively inherits its characteristics but has some limited possibilities for change. Continuity is a matter of a nexus of successive actual occasions. The objects which we observe and talk about are bundles of such nexus. The process of reality is thus treated as a series of discrete instances. It jerks along rather than flows.

The corpuscular model provides a way of recognizing both continuity and creativity in the processive character of reality. The continuity comes from the way in which each actual occasion in coming to be ('concrescing' is the Whiteheadian term) grasps ('prehends') its immediate predecessor so that it massively incorporates it. Creativity comes from the decision (which Whitehead stresses does not entail conscious selection but only a 'cutting off' (1978: 43)) by which, out of the possibilities open to it, each concrescing occasion determines the particular novel synthesis that its own being actualizes. It is arguable, furthermore, that it

53

is preferable to think of the process of reality as a matter of drops of being changing by minute jerks rather than as a continuous flow since this allows for each successive step in the process to be precisely defined. According to this way of understanding, then, an actual occasion at the indivisible moment t_1 is a particular state and its immediate successor at the next moment t_2 is another (minutely distinct) state.

As a way of understanding how an actual occasion 'affords knowledge of the past and the future' (and so makes sense of both memory and induction) (Whitehead 1927a: 55) in a definite form, the corpuscular model may be regarded as fruitful. It has, however, two major difficulties. In the first place its definiteness is achieved at the cost of breaking up into individual droplets what may be more appropriately understood as a continuum of forces within which there are foci or centres of concentration. What Whitehead identifies as the 'fallacy of simple location' in time and space — which is a form of the fallacy of misplaced concreteness that affirms the individual independence of actual occasions (cf. 1927a: 61ff; 1978: 137) — suggests that while the corpuscular model provides notional perceptions of precise states in a continuum rather like points in mathematics, what are so identified are best understood as theoretical abstractions from a continuous flow of responses to changes in the determinate in the light of the indeterminate and to changes in the indeterminate in the light of the determinate. Whatever the insights given by quantum theory in sub-atomic physics, the feedback procedure of reality means that actuality at any moment is not as precisely graspable as our language and conceptual understanding imply. This does not imply that what is actual is only vaguely so. What is actual is what it is — exactly this and not anything else. Nevertheless, while being actual is a passing state of being at a point where the indeterminate finally becomes completely determinate, the reality of a determinate actuality essentially spreads from that point with increasing degrees of vagueness into what has been and what may be. So far as understanding is concerned, precision is a characteristic of the past: it is found by abstracting from actuality.

A second difficulty with the corpuscular model derives from what seems to be a corollary, namely, that the determinateness of each actual occasion (whether this be a precise droplet or a point marking the momentary end of a proceeding continuum) involves internal relations. The way this is presented seems to require a panpsychic view of reality but, on reflection, it is doubtful whether such a view makes sense. Even though the degree of 'mentality' involved may be held to be enormously attenuated, there are even more enormous difficulties in seeing what can be meant by ascribing mental modes of activity to the actual occasions that combine in physical objects. While it is plausible to speak of the dominant occasion that is my 'I' as prehending the data provided by the past and the possibilities of the future and then deciding upon a particular creative synthesis of them, it is not at all clear that such language makes sense when applied to the actual occasion of an electron.

In this respect, though, it must be emphasized that Whitehead himself states that when he speaks of a concrescent occasion becoming actual by a ' "decision" whereby what is "given" is separated off from what for that occasion is "not given" ' the word 'decision' does not necessarily imply 'conscious judgement'. As has already been mentioned, it is used 'in its root sense of a "cutting off" ' to express 'some activity procuring limitation' (Whitehead 1978: 42f). An actual occasion, that is, becomes what it is by an act of determination whereby its being at this point is fixed in what was a range of possibilities open to it. The difficulty is that it seems impossible to give content to this notion of self-determination in a way that is appropriate to internal, as opposed to external, relations determining its being, without implicitly carrying with it some sense of conscious awareness and selection. Further discussion of this problem must wait until Chapter 8 when the relation of God as creator to the processes of nature is discussed.

In spite of these difficulties, what emerges from this understanding of reality as being in process is not simply insight into the basic nature of the contingent objects which we are as selves and which constitute the world which we experience. The principles of process thought are metaphysical truths which apply to any possible as well as to every actual reality, including God. Although, as Robert Neville (1980) points out, questions may be asked as to whether Whitehead is wholly consistent in working out his claim that God is the 'chief exemplification' of 'all metaphysical principles' (Whitehead 1978: 343), the following principles characterize all reality.

First, as we have considered at some length, what is actual is a point in a process of movement where, on the one hand, the possibilities of the indeterminate end in the fixing of the determinate and, on the other, the determinate is faced by the possibilities of the not-yet-determined. From this it follows, second, that to be actual is to be in some temporal order constituted basically by the distinction between the determinate and the indeterminate. To be allegedly 'outside time' is not to be. Whatever is actual has a past and a future. From the past it inherits data to which it responds in determining its being as a creative synthesis; to its future it presents that creative synthesis as a datum to which succeeding actualities will respond. Third, what is real is essentially related. A concrescing occasion massively prehends not only its immediate predecessor but, with a graded scale of importance down to the utterly trivial, the determinate being of all else. Each actual entity, that is, affects all concrescing entities. This is another reason why the notion of simple location must be abandoned as a way of describing 'the primary way in which things are involved in space-time' for, as Whitehead puts it, 'every spatio-temporal standpoint mirrors the world' and itself affects 'every other location' (1927a: 114). Hartshorne (1953) similarly describes reality as 'a social process'. Fourth, so far as the creative synthesis which determines the form of each actual occasion can be understood to be a matter of autonomous internal relations, ultimate power lies in the attractiveness of that which lures concrescing occasions into co-operation with its purposes. It will do this by presenting to them visions of love, beauty, and rational harmony in which they will find satisfaction (cf. Whitehead 1978: 346). Fifth, reality is ultimately a unity. Not only do all concrescing occasions take account of all actual ones according to the social structure of reality. All that is, furthermore, is contained within a universe whose ground, being, and goal are given, embraced, and directed by God. At this point, then, it is time to turn from metaphysics to the question of the nature of the divine according to process thought.

4 The dipolar structure of the concept of God

In *Religion in the Making* Whitehead defines religion, with reference to doctrine, as 'a system of general truths which have the effect of transforming character when they are sincerely held and vividly apprehended' (1927: 5). Authentic religion thus involves both the perception of fundamental truths about reality and their appropriate expression in the way that people live. In the latter respect its goal is a personal one, concerned with cleansing and developing character. Collective activities and external authorities are merely 'its passing forms'. Its proper end is 'individual worth of character', produced in the 'solitariness' in which an individual moves 'from God the void to God the enemy, and from God the enemy to God the companion' (ibid.: 6f). Although religion may take demonic forms, it has the potential to be and in a few cases actually has been 'the main instrument' of human progress (ibid.: 26). Religion, however, also has an intellectual goal. At least so far as it instantiates that 'rational religion' which Whitehead regards as its highest form, it is 'the wider conscious reaction of men to the universe in which they find themselves' (ibid.: 31). As such it is a matter of the perception and entertainment of universally valid truths which are properly to be used for the 'ordering of all experience' (ibid.: 21). An adequate description of religion takes account of both these aspects.

The universality and ultimacy of metaphysical truth provide the critical norm as well as the goal for religious understanding. 'A purified religion' in which the goodness of God is studied in order to be imitated is said, for instance, to be one which is 'rationalized under the influence of a world-concept' (Whitehead 1927: 30). Since, then, rational religion seeks to be 'that metaphysics which can be derived from the supernormal experience of mankind in its moments of finest insight' (ibid.: 21), Whitehead makes it clear that rational reflection is needed to criticize the meanings and verify the truth of the beliefs arising from such experiences. They are to be tested by what he considers to be the criteria for metaphysical descriptions of reality, namely, 'logical coherence, adequacy, and exemplification' (ibid.: 76). In particular it is the manifest universality of the religious understanding of reality which shows that it is not 'a passing fancy' (ibid.: 123). By applying the principle that 'generality is the salt of religion' (ibid.: 32), reason thus safeguards religious understanding of reality by securing for it 'the general coherence denied to hysteria' and to particularism (ibid.: 53; cf. 71). In the case of the Christian Gospel this means that 'the conversion of the Gentiles is both the effect of truth and the test of truth' (ibid.: 123).

Whitehead's recognition of the metaphysical character of religious belief and his view that Christianity is 'a religion seeking a metaphysic' (Whitehead 1927: 39) do not result in a simple system of beliefs, remote and utterly abstract notions of God, and an arid faith. While he emphasizes the metaphysical goal of theistic understanding, he is suspicious of claims to completeness for any metaphysic. 'A neat little system of thought' may well have been achieved at the cost of over-simplification (ibid.: 40). It is a defect which readers of Whitehead's own attempts at metaphysical insight, particularly in *Process and Reality* (1978), will not be likely to accuse him of sharing! So far as religion is concerned, he states that any attempt to reduce its dogma to 'a few simple notions' is wrecked, if nowhere else, on 'the rock of the problem of evil' (Whitehead 1927: 64f). An important contribution from rational religion to modern culture is hence claimed to be its insistence that 'we know more than can be formulated in one finite systematized scheme of abstractions', however valuable such a system of ideas may be in certain respects (ibid.: 128). Although dogmatic statements are possible and necessary ways of safeguarding the truth perceived by religion, it must not be forgotten that the goal of religion includes a personal 'intuitive response' to reality which goes beyond dogma's 'partial expression' of it in 'abstract concepts' (ibid.: 129). By such remarks Whitehead indicates that he insists on the metaphysical aspect of religious faith in order to expand understanding of it creatively rather than to inhibit it to narrowly established forms.

The foundation of Whitehead's religious — and so metaphysical — understanding involves a concept of God which is in important respects in marked contrast to widespread notions of the divine as unrelated, unchanging, and impassible deity. Rejecting a number of the assumptions about divine perfection which produces some of the problems for the doctrine of God considered in Chapter 2, Whitehead suggests a view of God which comes closer to the belief embodied in actual theistic (and particularly Christian) faith. The term 'suggests' is important, though, for he does not develop his theistic position at length. Nevertheless, its main points are clear.

Although Whitehead criticizes the simplifying tendency in liberal theologians, various remarks in *Religion in the Making* indicate that he shares their preference for the Gospel of love supposedly presented by the Evangelists, especially John, in contrast to that of fear expressed in the Pauline letters (1927: 63f). In comments reminiscent of Hatch and Harnack, for example, he says that while Paul adapted Jesus's doctrine for 'popular survival', in the changes 'something was added and something was lost' (ibid.: 19). Fortunately, though, the Gospels have survived. While, therefore, he accepts that it is only a superficial rendering of the situation, he affirms that the modern world, which 'has lost God and is seeking him', will find God 'only through love and not through fear, with the help of John and not of Paul' (ibid.: 64).

It is in the final part of *Process and Reality*, however, that Whitehead's understanding of the divine nature is most evocatively expressed. His comments show that whatever the abstruse complexity of his metaphysical system, in some — though not in all — respects his perception of the nature of God can be put in attractively concrete images. He contrasts, for example, images of God as 'an imperial ruler', 'a personification of moral energy', and 'an ultimate philosophical principle' with the image of the divine suggested 'in the Galilean origin of Christianity'. The latter does not 'emphasize the ruling Caesar, or the ruthless moralist, or the unmoved mover' but

> dwells upon the tender elements in the world, which slowly and in quietness operate by love; and it finds purpose in the present immediacy of a kingdom not of this world. Love neither rules, nor is it unmoved; also it is a little oblivious as to morals. It does not look to the future; for it finds its own reward in the immediate present.

> (Whitehead 1978: 343)

A little later the divine judgment on the world is portrayed as that of 'a tenderness which loses nothing that can be saved' and of 'a wisdom which uses what in the temporal world is mere wreckage'. God is described as 'the poet of the world, with tender patience leading it by his vision of truth, beauty, and goodness' (ibid.: 346) and 'the great companion — the fellow sufferer who understands' (ibid.: 351).

God and the processes of reality

These images are not rhetorical flourishes which lie uneasily beside Whitehead's metaphysical ideas. Nor are references to God an extraneous element forced to be included in the work because it originated as Gifford Lectures (in days when electors and elected respected the wishes of the benefactor). Although, as Lewis Ford's studies (1978a, 1984) make clear, Whitehead's ideas about the role of God developed as he worked on *Process and Reality* and although, as perceptive critics like Donald Sherburne (1971, 1971a, 1986) and Robert Neville (1980, 1981) point out, the place of God in his metaphysical understanding has problems, the powerful pictures of the divine with which he concludes this work can be seen as a religious development of a coherent, fundamental, and necessary part of that understanding. It is a position, furthermore, in which the divine is held not to be 'an exception to all metaphysical principles, invoked to save their collapse' but 'their chief exemplification' (Whitehead 1978: 343).

What, then, is the nature and role of God in Whitehead's metaphysics? According to his understanding the divine has two main aspects which are called the 'primordial nature' and 'the consequent nature' of God. Whitehead's use of the term 'nature' in this respect, though, does not imply that these phrases refer to independent entities or to some kind of division in the divine reality. They describe two facets of God's being as it relates to the world.

The primordial nature of the divine refers to God's role as the ground of possibility in the processes of reality. Each actual occasion, in creating the synthesis which is its final concrescent form, not only 'physically' prehends its immediate predecessor and, with graded degrees of importance, all other previous occasions. It also 'conceptually' prehends the possibilities for that synthesis. In accordance with the ontological principle that 'actual entities are the only reasons' (Whitehead 1978: 24), these possibilities — the 'pure potentials' which Whitehead speaks of as the 'eternal objects' — do not subsist of themselves. They are only prehensible as opportunities for novelty in concrescing occasions so far as they have a locus in actuality as being envisaged by God. God's primordial nature, then, is the divine awareness of all genuine possibilities — 'the unlimited conceptual realization of the absolute wealth of potentiality' (ibid.: 343) — which is the condition of all creation and which 'at once exemplifies and establishes the categoreal conditions' of all that may come to be (ibid.: 344).

When, though, Whitehead states that 'the primordial created fact is the unconditioned conceptual valuation of the entire multiplicity of eternal objects' (ibid.: 31), he does not only mean that God's primordial nature is coextensive with possibility as such. He is further asserting that each possible state of affairs is primordially envisaged in its particular definiteness by God. This implies that each possibility, however minute its differentiation from another possibility, has always been conceptually grasped by the divine. For example, not only has God up to now everlastingly envisaged my present actual state as a possibility, the primordial nature of the divine has also for ever included a full and precise grasp of all the other possible states that could now have been the case for me — for example, my being with a single hair more on my scalp or a speck of dust less on my spectacles.

In claiming that God eternally envisages each particular possibility in its precise specificity, this interpretation of the primordial nature of the divine presents a doctrine of the divine awareness which not only seems to be fantastic and incredible but, more importantly, is philosophically and theistically questionable. Philosophically it fails to recognize the essential difference between the possible and the actual, and theistically it detracts from the richness of the divine experience.

The claim that the notion is fantastic and incredible is likely to be answered by theists who wish to affirm it with the argument that it only seems to be such to those who do not properly appreciate the infinity of the divine: no number of possibilities should in principle be regarded as beyond the essentially unlimited scope of God. Even so, it is hard to entertain the idea that all the myriad possibilities that may follow from any state of affairs in the universe has always been envisaged by God. More acceptable is Wolfe Mays's suggestion that in this kind of understanding ' "to be" is to be the value of a variable' (Mays 1977: 65). In that case God's envisagement of the eternal objects is to be regarded as being somewhat like the entertainment of a propositional function with variables to which a range of values can be assigned.

This emendation — or interpretation — of Whitehead's doctrine of the eternal objects envisaged in the primordial nature of God meets Hartshorne's philosophical objection that the doctrine crucially fails to recognize that it is of the essence of a possibility to be less definite than the quality which actualizes it: 'the distinction between possible and actual is that between the relatively indefinite and the relatively definite' (Hartshorne

1978: 32). According to Hartshorne 'the "pure potentials" are not definite entities, they form a continuum which is without definite parts' (1970: 128; cf. 65f; also 1973: 101 (C3), 103 (E6)). There are also theistic reasons for preferring Hartshorne's position on this point. It is at least arguable that the notion of God's primordial envisagement of all possibilities in their precise definiteness seriously detracts from the possible richness of the divine experience. If God precisely envisages each possibility, the actualization of some seems able to add little or nothing to the divine experience beyond the recognition that state *a* rather than state *b* or *c* or . . . has come about. The process of actualization then ceases to be fully creative. It becomes a rather uninteresting sorting between determinates.

Nevertheless, whether the primordial nature of God is conceptually prehended by each concrescing entity as a list of precisely defined possibilities from which it decides upon its synthesis or as continua within whose ranges it fixes its actual form, the primordial nature of God is the ground of the creative potentiality of the processes of reality. Apart from it nothing creative would come to be. In *Modes of Thought* Whitehead thus describes 'Deity' as expressing 'the lure of the ideal which is the potentiality beyond immediate fact' and as 'that factor in the universe whereby there is importance, value and ideal beyond the actual' (Whitehead 1938: 139f).

There is, however, another facet to Whitehead's understanding of deity. God is not only the origin of all possibilities. The divine experience includes the reception of all actualities: God 'shares with every new creation its actual world' (Whitehead 1978: 345). It is this aspect of the divine reality which Whitehead calls 'the consequent nature' of God. According to this notion the actualization of God's being involves the physical prehension of all concrescent creatures as they come to be; the actualization of all those entities, that is, necessarily involves their complete 'objectification' as 'novel' elements in God (ibid.: 345). Negatively this means that what is not prehended by God does not exist; positively, that everything that occurs is embraced by the divine and for ever contributes to the character of the divine being. 'Each actuality in the temporal world has its reception into God's nature' where it is transformed into 'a living, ever-present fact' (ibid.: 350).

Whereas, therefore, it has been widely assumed that a correct appreciation of the essential perfection of the divine entails that God is impassible in every respect and utterly simple, Whitehead maintains that in important respects God is both passible and complex. Absolute impassibility in every respect is ruled out by the combination of the doctrine that God is the chief exemplification of all metaphysical principles and the principle that to be actual is to be socially related. While, that is, to become an actual entity is to become an object for all other subjects, it is also to be a subject which prehends the universe composed of all other objects (cf. ibid.: 56). Since, then, as actual God physically prehends all other actual occasions, each one affects the divine being. Whitehead speaks of the 'prehension *into* God of each creature' (ibid.: 345; my italics). Furthermore, since God is perfect, the divine consciousness of each actual occasion as a novel contribution to the divine being is complete. God is not simply passible: God is pre-eminently so. The divine being, without in any way ceasing to be the perfectly divine, is affected by every quality of every drop of experience that is an actual occasion. 'The relativity of all things' hence implies among other things that 'there is a reaction of the world on God'. In this respect part of the quality of the divine reality is 'derivative': it is 'consequent upon the creative advance of the world' (ibid.: 345).

Thus to understand God entails the negation of the doctrine of divine simplicity, at least as often interpreted. Whitehead maintains in contrast that 'the consequent nature of God is composed of a multiplicity of elements with individual self-realization' (ibid.: 350). Each item of experience as an actual occasion is incorporated as itself into the consequent nature of the divine. It does not lose its individual identity by being merged into the ocean of a cosmic punch. On the contrary, as will be considered in the final chapter, it is the divine preservation of the memory of each individual entity in its objective distinctiveness that is the basis of its ultimate significance — and the character of its immortality.

Although each possibility is conceptually prehended in God's primordial nature and each actual occasion is physically prehended in God's consequent nature, the divine reality is not to be thought of as a disordered collection of items. Reference to God is not to a lumber-room in which every possibility has always resided and into which every actual occasion is indiscriminately tossed on the appearance of its successor! While the divine fully grasps and preserves each actual occasion in its novel individuality, Whitehead holds that what is thus 'derived from the temporal world' is prehended in the light of God's 'all-inclusive primordial valuation'. It thus 'acquires integration' in the divine being as it is seen both for what it is and for what it can contribute to 'a perfected system' of universal harmony (ibid.: 345). According to Whitehead, furthermore, God's primordial nature is not prehended by each concrescing entity as an undifferentiated range of possibilities. Taking account of all that is now the case, God grades the eternal objects according to their relevance for producing 'vivifying novelty' in the ongoing process of creative concrescence (ibid.: 164). God thus acts in the creative process of reality negatively as the principle of limitation and positively as 'the eternal urge of desire' (ibid.: 344).

The underlying model for this understanding of the divine relationship to the world is a personal one. Just as 'an enduring personality in the temporal world' creatively combines its constituents into a more or less unified self, so God combines the 'multiplicity of actual components' provided by the world according to a vision of their creative harmonization. The ultimate value and completeness of this vision, which is achieved without 'any loss ... of individual identity' by what is therein united, then constitutes the character of God's response to the next stage of the process of reality (ibid.: 350f). This harmonization is what Whitehead considers to be the present reality of the kingdom of heaven and of the actuality of the love of God for the world as a 'particular providence for particular occasions'. He summarizes his understanding of the relationship between God and the processes of reality thus:

> What is done in the world is transformed into a reality in heaven, and the reality in heaven passes back into the world. By reason of this reciprocal relation, the love in the world passes into the love in heaven, and floods back again into the world.

> (ibid.: 351)

Accordingly the Creator may be described as 'the great companion — the fellow-sufferer who understands' (ibid.).

As Whitehead recognizes, he understands the divine nature as being 'dipolar' in a way that is analogous to the nature of all other actual entities. References to the primordial nature of God are to that side of the divine reality which is 'limited by no actuality', 'infinite', 'free, complete, ... eternal, actually deficient, and unconscious'. On the other hand, discussions of the consequent nature of God concern what in the divine reality is 'determined, incomplete ... "everlasting," fully actual, and conscious' (ibid.: 345). While the result is a doctrine of God which indicates how the divine may be conceived as aware of and responsive to the processes of reality, it is not clear that it provides a way of talking about God which is both completely adequate to the divine and yet avoids the kind of intrinsic problems that were discussed in Chapter 2. Whitehead's comments on God are suggestive rather than a thoroughly worked out system. According to Hartshorne, Whitehead himself recognized this: he 'said once that his thought about God was "very vague," but that others would be able to clarify the matter' (Hartshorne 1978: 145). Indeed it is to Hartshorne that one must primarily turn for the development of a process theism — with the warning that the ways in which Whitehead and Hartshorne present their theistic understandings do not coincide conceptually. While there is fundamental agreement in substance, it is expressed in ways that are subtly different. Whitehead's dipolar view of God, for example, is not the same as Hartshorne's. What the former distinguishes as the primordial and consequent natures is not the same as what the latter means by the distinction between the existence and actuality of God. Failure to recognize these conceptual differences has led to no little confusion and some nonsense in expositions — both supposedly appreciative and obviously hostile — of the concept of God in process thought. In the remainder of this chapter, therefore, we will consider how Hartshorne expounds his understanding of the 'dipolar' structure of the concept of God.

Hartshorne's major contribution to philosophical understanding in general and to theistic understanding in particular has been to show how it is possible to have a concept of God which is at once coherent (i.e. not self-contradictory) and adequate both to rational understanding of the nature of God and to actual theistic faith in the reality of God. In several books and many articles spanning half a century and using various conceptual models, he has combined his extensive knowledge of past philosophical thought, and especially of the ideas of Peirce and Whitehead, with his own considerable insights to show how a self-consistent concept of God may be developed which recognizes the intrinsic ultimacy properly demanded by thought about the divine and the personal character required by theistic faith, at least as found in the Judaeo-Christian-Islamic tradition. According to his understanding of the notions involved, it is possible — and indeed necessary for any adequate theism — to conceive coherently of God as both necessary and contingent, as both utterly absolute and totally related, as both unchanging and changing, as both infinite and finite, and as both eternal and temporal, in appropriate aspects of the divine reality. Indeed, far from these pairs of attributes being a threat to the coherence of the concept of God as ultimate and perfect, they are required by it.

As was mentioned in the previous chapter Hartshorne considers that the proper method of metaphysical argument is by conceptual analysis in which the options are exhaustively identified and then all but one of them is shown to be rationally untenable, preferably because careful inspection reveals that the rest are intrinsically incoherent. It is in this way that he approaches the problem of the concept of God. For example, in an early study of theism, *Man's Vision of God*, he classifies and examines 'the formally possible doctrines of God' in terms of the notion of perfection (Hartshorne 1964: 8f), while in *Creative Synthesis and Philosophic Method* he uses the categories of necessity and contingency to analyse 'an exhaustive division' of the 'ideas of God' (Hartshorne 1970: 266). In spite of the many subtle arguments that are found in theology, he argues in the Preface to *Man's Vision of God* that he is justified in adding to the existing mass of writings on philosophical theology since there is a need for 'exactitude, logical rigor' (Hartshorne 1964: vii). In an article published a few years later he complains that

> it would be hard to find a philosopher who does not deal in some way, even if only by calling them meaningless, with such terms as 'absolute,' 'perfect,' 'relative,' 'imperfect,' 'God,' 'Supreme Being.' Yet is is also difficult to find a philosopher who defines these terms with the care and precision that reason requires.

(Hartshorne 1953: 110; cf. 1964: 6ff)

It is a complaint that he has never ceased to make and a need which he has persistently sought to meet. How has he done it?

Basic to Hartshorne's analysis of the concept of God is a distinction which he makes by using the terms 'existence' and 'actuality'. He summarizes the distinction in this way: ' "Existence" is merely a relation of exemplification which actuality (any suitable actuality) has to essence' (Hartshorne 1965: 131; cf. 38ff). What he means by this, at first sight somewhat obscure, remark may be clarified by an illustration.

Consider, for instance, the statement 'A table exists in the next room' (a rather odd way of putting what would more normally be expressed as 'There is a table in the next room' but not a way which alters the meaning of the statement). This statement is true and only true if there 'exists in the next room' (a phrase whose meaning is presumably clear to those who understand English and which will not be examined further) something which has the 'essence' of being 'a table'. Again, on the basis of a knowledge of English it is possible to specify what is connoted by talk about something being (i.e. having the 'essence' of) a table: for example, to be a table may be held to be something that has the qualities of being a solid object with a flat top, supported by one or more legs, and large and strong enough for articles to be placed on it. The presence of an object in the next room which meets such a specification would mean that it is correct to state that 'A table exists in the next room.'

Hartshorne's distinction, however, draws out something that is often overlooked in such analyses, namely that since there are many different kinds of tables, a wide range of actual objects can make this statement true. Among the possibilities are that this solid object may be made of wood or of iron or of plastic . . . — and if it is made of wood it may be made from oak or pine, or mahogany . . .; its top may be square, oblong, circular, or oval; it may have one, two, three, or more legs; it may be a delicate side-table or a sturdy dining-table or . . .; it may be highly polished or rough and pitted. Thus while the true statement that 'A table exists in the next room' tells us that there is in that place something which is describable as a solid, flat-topped object with one or more legs, large and strong enough to hold articles, we cannot tell from this statement what precisely is in the room. Only by examining the actual table that is there can we discover in which of the various possible ways does this particular entity satisfy the description of being a table.

To say, then, that an *a* exists is to say that an abstract essence (the essence of being an *a*) is somewhere and somehow instantiated in an appropriate concrete form. The essence of being an *a*, however, is an abstraction which only specifies more or less broadly the range within which any particular existing *a* must be concretely exemplified. It does not specify its concrete actuality. Furthermore, no *a* can exist wholly and simply as actualizing its essence: as existing it must actualize that essence in some determinate way. A table, for example, cannot exist simply as 'flat-topped': it must have an actual flat top which is of one configuration, specific dimensions, and a particular degree of flatness. While, then, to state that an object 'exists' is to affirm that there is a reality whose characteristics lie within a certain range of variables, that object only exists as a particular actuality

67

which is a combination of totally determinate points within that range.

When we consider any real entity apart from God, we find that both its existence and its actuality are contingent, relative, changing, finite, and temporal. Whether, for example, the object of our reflection is a human being, a table, or a manuscript, its existence is not necessary, not absolute, not unchanging, not infinite, and not eternal. There is no necessity that it should ever have existed at all, and that it does happen to exist is due to forces prior to and other than itself (for example, if a table exists in the next room it is because of decisions to make it and to place it there); it cannot prevent its essential character being affected and even destroyed by others; it changes by the effects upon it of internal processes (e.g. the natural processes of decay) and external forces (e.g. the effects of the environment and of decisions about its fate — for instance, to restore it or to scrap it); it is in one place at one time and cannot simultaneously be elsewhere; there was a time when it was not and it is regarded as beyond doubt that there will come a time when it no longer exists. Furthermore, what is true of the 'existence' of such objects must also be true of their actuality. If an object's existence (i.e. its instantiation of an essence at some point within the range of variables connoted by that essence) is contingent, relative, ..., its actuality as the particular, specific form in which that essence is realized must also be contingent, relative, ...

God, in contrast, is uniquely the individual whose mode of existence is necessary, absolute, unchanging, infinite, and eternal. Nothing can prevent or bring an end to God's existence (i.e. God's existence is necessary); nothing or no one other than God causes God to be (i.e. God's existence is absolute); God is never anything other than fully divine (i.e. God's existence is unchanging); everything is immediately present to God (i.e. God's existence is infinite); there was no beginning and there will be no end to the divine (i.e. God's existence is eternal). A being whose existence did not have these properties would not satisfy the defining characteristics of being 'God'. For instance, it would not be 'that than which a greater cannot be conceived' because a 'greater' could be conceived, namely a being whose existence was necessary, absolute ... What this means is that God, as God, must be thought of as existing always and everywhere and for ever, as one who can never be destroyed, as one who can never be prevented from being divine, and as one who cannot be made to be other than divine. One of the characteristics of this unique mode of existence to which Hartshorne draws attention is that the divine is 'omnitolerant': God's existence is compatible with and cannot be destroyed by any possible event. Whatever happens to any human being, to humanity, to the earth, or even to the present cosmic epoch, God will continue to exist as the divine.

The qualities of the divine existence distinguish God from all else. In this respect Hartshorne's understanding of the divine may be considered to agree with the views traditionally expressed in theism. His great insight is to perceive that the nature of the divine existence does not entail that the divine actuality must have the same formal properties. The actuality of what exists contingently, relatively ... must also be contingent, relative ... It does not follow from this, though, that the *actuality* of what *exists* necessarily, absolutely ... may not be contingent, relative ... All that follows for the divine actuality from the nature of the divine existence is that some actuality must exemplify God's existence in some appropriate form. Thus God's actuality may be held to be contingent, relative ... if and so far as this understanding of the divine actuality is consistent with the nature of the divine existence as it has been described and is an appropriate exemplification of that mode of existence.

Indeed, for God to exist as God in a way that satisfies the theistic understanding of God as an actual object of worship which is self-aware, conscious of others, purposive, and agential (i.e. as 'personal' and not simply as a cipher for supreme value), the particular form of the *concretion* of that existence (i.e. the divine *actuality*) must be contingent, relative.... For example, God's actuality as creator is *contingent* upon God's choice to be the creator of this particular cosmic order rather than of some other possible cosmos; the actual scope of God's gracious relationship to the creation is *relative* to what it contains to be related to — God cannot be gracious to what is not there to be a recipient of divine grace; the concrete form of God's grace in practice *changes* as the situations to which it is addressed change — the precise form of the divine response to Saul at the stoning of Stephen was presumably not the same as that to Paul in Rome; God's scope for actual influence is *finite* in that God can only influence what is available to be influenced – God cannot now influence choices that I made twenty-five years ago (although God can now influence my current attitude to those decisions); similarly God's actual enjoyment of the values enriching our experience is *temporal* in that God cannot now share my joy at having a pleasure which I am not now experiencing.

By this dipolar analysis of God's existence and actuality, Harts-horne provides a formal structure in terms of which the material qualities of the divine are to be understood. It shows that two sets of 'qualifiers' or 'operators' (to use I. T. Ramsey's notion (cf. 1957: 49ff)) are involved in descriptions of the divine reality. These formal terms act adverbially to modify the adjectival attribution of material characteristics to the divine. When this is grasped it is seen to be somewhat misleading to speak of God as such as being necessary, absolute ... in some ways and contingent, relative ... in others. It is much clearer and more accurate to speak of God's knowledge or God's love or God's reality as being necessary, absolute ... in some respects and contingent, relative ... in others. Furthermore, because these terms are dipolar, any description of a material quality of the divine which uses one of these qualifiers is liable to be seriously inadequate unless it also takes account of its polar opposite.

Another way of delineating the significance of the dipolar structure of the concept of God is to point out that the set of qualifiers which are appropriate to the nature of the divine existence clarify the character of God's material qualities *in principle* or *abstractly*, while the other set indicates in what manner they are actualized *in practice* or *concretely*. As with the distinction between existence and actuality, the significance of these methodological comments becomes clearer when they are illustrated by reference to various qualities of the divine. We shall, therefore, consider briefly how Hartshorne's dipolar under-standing elucidates what is meant by attributing to God the material qualities of knowledge, love, and reality.

In the case of divine knowledge, it is correct to say that *in principle* God's knowledge is necessary. This is because a being who may be regarded as in any way ignorant is inferior to 'that than which a greater cannot be conceived'. It is absolute because God cannot be thought of coherently as being unaware of any-thing that is knowable: reality may hence be defined as what God knows to be such. It is unchanging in that at each moment God knows all that is then knowable. It is infinite since nothing is outside the range of God's knowledge; and it is eternal for God never forgets anything.

Granted, however, that to be actual is to be in process, *in practice* the concrete actualization of the divine knowledge is contingent since God can only know what happens to be know-able. God, for instance, knows the ten billionth digit in the decimal determination of π (since there is such a digit) but does not know the number that is the sum of the infinite series $1 + 2$

+ 4 + 8 . . . (for as infinite the series has no end); God knows the name of the Queen's sister (since she has one) but God does not know the name of the present Queen's brother (since she has never had one); God does know my daughter's blood-group (since I have a daughter) but not the age of my second son (since I have not got one). This does not mean that God is any way ignorant. Only what is knowable can be known and it is no mark of ignorance not to know what is not (and never has been) there to be known. Similarly God's actual knowledge in practice is relative to the state of its objects — for example, God's knowledge of the number of pieces of paper on my desk at this moment is relative to the number of pieces of paper that are now on it. The concrete state of God's knowledge in practice is also changing because as novel events occur they add to the sum of what God knows to have happened. It is finite because the divine knowledge of what has happened, for example, includes only(!) every event that has actually happened; and it is temporal because God does not know events as determinate until they have become determinate by happening.

The dipolar interpretation of God's love is similar. Hartshorne (1967: 15) argues that the compelling object of worship must be loving since of the three and only three choices for the quality of the divine relationship to the world, namely, hate, apathy, and love, the first is intrinsically self-destructive, the second is intuitively deficient, and therefore only the third is coherently attributable to the divine. On such grounds it is affirmed that God must be held to be *in principle* necessarily loving. The divine love, furthermore, is absolute in that it is never adulterated by other passion. As a pure and total concern for others which is never marred by any selfishness, imperfection, or reserve it is also unchanging. The divine love is infinite in that nothing at all can be outside its range. It is also eternal. The story of the Deluge and the threat of the three 'Woes' (cf. Revelation 6ff) are libels which ascribe to the divine a truculence which is sadly typical of human impatience. In contrast God never has been and never will become tired of loving. Whatever, then, the state of affairs to be found in reality, *in principle* God's relationship to it is always of total love.

As in the case of knowledge, though, *in practice* the divine love is expressed — and has to be expressed — in concrete ways which are contingent on what is there to be loved and relative to the state of the object of the love. God, for instance cannot love my grandson since it happens to be the case that I do not have one but God can — and does — love my daughter since it is also a contingent fact that I have one. More interestingly, while the divine love is always absolutely pure love, the actual form in which it is expressed in each case at each moment is relative to what in that situation will be the most enriching relationship. The concrete form of divine love for Lesley in an outburst of impatient anger may be an understanding sympathy whereas for Arthur in a bout of self-indulgent indignation it may well take whatever is the divine form of coolly raised eyebrows! Furthermore, the concrete expression of the divine love changes as situations change. In order to be utterly loving in practice God must respond appropriately to each situation as it arises and develops. Just as Katharine's boyfriend knows that love for her requires different responses to her when she is worried about her rabbit's health and when she is euphoric about her examination results, so the concrete expressions of the divine love for her and for all others change according to what is most appropriate in the circumstances for the well-being of the beloved. In practice, finally, God's love is finite in that its concrete expressions are for particular goods for particular cases (even though they are all the particular cases) and is temporal in that, as already has been indicated, its expressions are relative to and change with the processive constituents of reality. What was the loving response to Robert yesterday when he had come in from laying fixed ropes in a blizzard is not the loving response to him today when he needs to get a pack up to the next camp!

As a third example of the dipolar treatment of God's material attributes, we may consider the general notion of the divine reality — the very being of God as God. Although what can be significantly apprehended of the godness of God is very limited — and the way in which some theologians discuss doctrines like that of the Trinity provides grounds for suspecting that they lack critical self-awareness! — something needs to be grasped if theistic understanding is not to be vacuous. It is perhaps most clearly to be discerned by considering the relationship of God, as holy, ultimate, self-conscious, personal agency, to the world of nature and of history. That God *is* as the God of whatever is to be found in the world has always been true and will always be true. The being of the divine reality has, however, dipolar aspects.

While, for instance, *in principle* God's reality must be necessary as the underived ground of whatever else exists (and thus the existence of the divine reality is explicable only by reference to Godself), what *in practice* God is ground of is a contingent matter which depends upon what happens to be there — as result of divine choices (so far as the divine chooses what to create) and creaturely decisions. God's reality as God is *in principle* absolute and unchanging: being 'God' is a state which admits of no degrees (being God is not like being a philosopher which one can do more or less well!) and which can neither be acquired nor abandoned. In this respect God has never been and can never be other than God, the holy and ultimate in being, rationality, and value. *In practice*, however, so far as God is significantly a personal agent, the actualization of that reality is relative and changing according to what is the appropriate form of the divine for the present state of the processes of reality. Unless, for example, God is to be thought of as self-worshipping (which seems intuitively questionable), God's being as the proper object of worship is only actual to the extent that there are others with modes of awareness which make them capable of worship. Similarly, while God's reality *in principle* is infinite and eternal since at any moment God is God of whatever is, *in practice* it is confined to what is now — God is not actually the God of what has no reality although it is true that whatever in the future may come to be will finally be ordered by reference to God just as whatever has existed was so ordered.

Consideration of these examples of the application of Hartshorne's dipolar view of the formal structure of the concept of deity to the material attributes of God indicates a considerable amount of overlap between the characteristics of each aspect. This is to be expected. Each of the metaphysical notions of necessity, absoluteness, unchangeability, infinity, and eternity seems to entail the other four; the same is the case with their polar opposites. Although there is no need to provide analyses of the notions to demonstrate the point, the result is that what is correctly discerned to be the case with the necessary aspect of the divine knowledge, if fully elucidated, would cover what is to be held, say, about its absolute and unchanging aspects; what is to be held about the eternity of the divine love can only be coherently maintained if it also at least implies what is meant by its necessity and absoluteness; what is contingent about the divine reality entails its relativity and temporality in this respect, and so on. It is, therefore, for the sake of clarity and convenience of exposition that the five sets of polar opposites are used. Strictly only a full elucidation of one of them — and so presumably of any one of them — is required to identify the formal structure of the concept of the divine.

In view of certain criticisms that are made of it, it is important in considering the dipolar concept of God to remember that what is being put forward is a *formal* scheme in terms of which the *material* attributes of the divine are to be interpreted. H. P. Owen, for example, accuses Hartshorne of presenting 'a self-contradictory piece of anthropomorphism' in a 'logically sophisticated form' (Owen 1969: 107). This is no petty charge! His successor at King's College, London, shares his unhappiness with the theistic understanding found in process theology (cf. Gunton 1973, 1978). Leaving aside Owen's apparent failure to appreciate the inherent unsatisfactoriness of traditional concepts of deity (cf. Owen 1971), examination suggests that his criticisms of Hartshorne are based on a crucial failure to understand the logic of the latter's dipolar position and, in particular, Hartshorne's explicit distinction between existence and actuality. It is a kind of error which, as will be indicated in the next chapter, also lies behind Gunton's criticism of the notion of divine activity in process theism.

Hartshorne calls his understanding of the concept of God *dipolar* because it uses both of various pairs of opposites (i.e. contrary terms), the application of each of which requires also the appropriate application of its correlate (i.e. they are *polar* opposites) to create a formal structure for interpreting the material qualities of the divine being. Once the logic of this formal structure and the distinction between formal and material qualities are understood, it is evident that the resulting concept of the divine is intrinsically neither self-contradictory nor the product of an arbitrary affirmation of different notions.

In particular there is no justification for the charge that the principle of dipolarity in the case of the divine means that the opposite of whatever quality is to be attributed to God is also to be attributed to the divine. According to such a charge, since God is to be held to be both necessary and contingent, infinite and finite, and so on, then in order to be consistent the predication to God of being loving, knowing, and just must be accompanied by the predication of being hating, ignorant, and unjust. Such a position would result in a concept of God that is theistically absurd. A being that in this way embraces all possible predicates (i.e. in this total sense is the *ens realissimum*), whether those qualities are admirable or disgusting, could not be an object of unreserved worship. It also produces a rationally incoherent concept: to hold that God is, say, both loving and hating, both knowing and ignorant, is to return to the contradictions and vacuity of theistic understanding from which the notion of dipolarity is intended to free thought about God.

The fundamental mistake which gives rise to this charge is to treat the material qualities of the divine in the same way as the formal, metaphysically determined characteristics of the concept of God. Correctly understood, the dipolar nature of the concept of God is a matter of the interpretation of the material attributes of God — such as those of being personal, conscious, active, passive, knowing, loving, and creative — according to a formal scheme which clarifies what they refer to in the divine being both *in principle* (i.e. in relation to the nature of the divine existence) and *in practice* (i.e. in relation to the divine actuality). Each of God's material attributes is thus held to have a necessary and a contingent, an absolute and a relative aspect, and so on, in the divine.

Furthermore, the choice of which material qualities are to be attributed to the divine (e.g. love, knowledge, compassion) and which are not (e.g. hatred, ignorance, apathy) is not made in a methodologically arbitrary manner. The guiding criterion is that suggested by Anselm's perception that, as 'the supreme Good through which every good is', God must have every good and so be 'whatever it is better to be than not to be' (Anselm 1962: 11). The material qualities of the divine are, that is, to be determined by principles laid down in the defining characteristics of God as holy, ultimate, and a proper object of worship. Although this may lead to disputes about individual qualities — is, for example, the capacity to enjoy fragrances (cf. Genesis 8: 21; Ephesians 55: 2) or to indulge in scornful laughter (cf. Psalm 2: 4; 37: 13) to be attributed to God? — there seems to be no disputing that love but not hate, knowledge but not ignorance, compassion but not apathy are to be considered to be material qualities of the divine and, hence, to be interpreted according to the dipolar character of the concept of God.

Having considered how a coherent concept of the God of theistic faith is possible, the question arises of how the relationship between such a God and the processes of reality is to be conceived. The discussion of this begins in the next chapter — and continues to the end of the book!

5 Panentheism

Hartshorne sometimes uses the term *panentheism* to describe his understanding of God. Whereas the term 'dipolar' points to the way in which he grasps the intrinsic structure of the concept of God, the notion of 'panentheism' focuses attention on the character of God's relationship to the world. As the form of the word suggests, 'panentheism' is a way of considering the divine which is to be distinguished from what may be called 'theism' and 'pantheism'.

The phrase 'what may be called' is important in this respect. Both terms, 'theism' and 'pantheism', have in practice a broad range of uses and each of them is sometimes used to refer to what Hartshorne technically distinguishes as 'panentheism'. Since, furthermore, what he so denotes is the most adequate way of understanding God as the proper object of faith in the Judaeo-Christian-Islamic tradition, it is arguable that 'panentheism' is the authentic form of 'theism' proper (since θeos = God) and that what is explicitly distinguished from 'panentheism' as 'theism' is an inadequate form which is better called 'classical' or 'absolutist' or 'immured theism'. Accordingly when in the earlier and later chapters of this study the word 'theism' is used without qualification, it should be understood as including and, when most adequately apprehended, as specifically referring to what those who delight in technical terminology may prefer to call 'panentheism'. When the word 'panentheism' is used, it is to draw attention to the intimate and all-inclusive relationship between God and the world.

What, though, is the 'panentheistic' position? The term itself seems to have been coined by the early nineteenth-century German thinker, K. C. F. Krause, to describe his own theological position. According to Krause all finite realities are in the divine being but do not wholly constitute that being. On the one hand God, as the 'One Supreme Being, infinite and eternal', is essentially prior to and independent of any particular finite being: 'no being *is* God except God alone.' On the other, while as created each finite and limited being has its own appropriate degree of independence, it 'exists and lives in, with, and through God' as 'one universal life'. Everything 'that is, is in God'. As such it is influenced by God and contributes to the divine reality (Krause 1900: 5, 60; cf. 5ff).

Although there are differences in their metaphysical positions, Hartshorne's use of the term is basically similar. In the 'Epilogue' to *Philosophers Speak of God* (1953), an extensive study of different forms of the concept of God which he produced in collaboration with W. L. Reese, he describes 'panentheism' as the understanding which 'affirms God as containing both an all-independent all-causative factor *and* the totality of all effects'. Whereas 'classical theism' considers that the affirmation of the causal independence of God requires the denial of any dependence of God on the world, and while 'classical pantheism' contrariwise considers that the affirmation of the total receptivity of all events in the divine involves the denial of God's genuine independence of the world, 'panentheism' maintains that it is coherent to affirm what is positive in each of these positions without the denial which each is characteristically also held to involve (Hartshorne and Reese 1953: 505). It is a view of the relationship between God and the processes of reality which accords with the somewhat enigmatic antitheses which Whitehead presents towards the end of *Process and Reality*. He states, for example, that 'it is as true to say that God is one and the World many, as that the World is one and God many' and that 'it is as true to say that God transcends the World, as that the World transcends God' (Whitehead 1978: 348).

While, however, these remarks accurately summarize the panentheistic view of God and the world, they may not be readily apprehensible. In order, therefore, to clarify and develop the panentheistic understanding, it will be elucidated first by contrasting it with its alternatives, 'pantheism' and '(immured) theism', and then by considering some of its major characteristics.

According to pantheism the divine being is constituted by the sum total of all that truly is. God does not simply include the world within the divine: God is the real world and the real world is God. There is no distinction between the two. Where there seems to be reality which is external to the divine, or a divine reality which is distinct from anything else that is, it is an illusion.

In *Philosophers Speak of God*, for example, Sankara is quoted as affirming that 'perfect knowledge' recognizes that it is 'sense-less . . . to maintain that the individual soul is different from the highest Self'. The 'manifold world with its objects of enjoyment, enjoyers and so on has no existence apart from Brahman'. What are apprehended as different and changing objects in the phenomenal world are in reality forms of 'the fundamental cause of all . . . just as an actor appears in various robes and costumes' (Hartshorne and Reese 1953: 172). In modern western thought the classical presentation of the pantheist position is given by Spinoza's elucidation of the doctrine that God is the *ens realissimum*. For example, in *The Book of God* (which was written early in the 1660s although unknown for a couple of centuries) he argues that since 'all attributes are predicated' of God, it follows 'that all other things can by no means be . . . apart from or outside Him' (Spinoza 1958: 12). Hence all the constituents of 'Nature are but one single being, and by no means different things' (ibid.: 8; cf. 88f). Furthermore, according to the a priori argument of his *Ethics*, whatever truly is in the order of nature not only is a determinate expression of the divine attributes (cf. Spinoza 1959: 60) but also is a necessary expression of the infinite and perfect nature of God (cf. ibid.: 63). Accordingly, when 'Natura' is understood to refer not to the interrelated connection of supposedly contingent entities but to that which exists of necessity and infinitely (and only such truly exists), 'God and 'Nature' are equivalent terms — *Deus sive Natura*.

Although pantheism can be understood in various ways and many of its expressions are much less sophisticated than the views advanced by Sankara and Spinoza, its defining characteristic is the assertion of only one autonomous reality. Either it is maintained that God is the only autonomous being and that the apparent independence of the constituents of the world is an illusion or 'God' is treated as a cipher for the aggregate of independent entities which happen to exist. In neither case is there any possibility of affirming a significant relationship between God and the world. In the former case the 'world' is an emanation of the divine; any God–world relationship is a relationship of God to Godself. In the latter there is no divine reality; the relationship of the world to 'God' is the relationship of what happens to exist to the agglomeration of all such existing beings.

By 'theism' is meant, in contrast, the position which affirms both that God and the constituents of the world have each an appropriate degree of autonomy and that the nature of the divine is such that no significant reciprocity is possible between them. Necessity, absoluteness, and perfection are held by this analysis to be essential characteristics of the divine which result in categorically asymmetrical relationships between God and the world. For example, God is wholly cause and in no way affected by the world whereas in relation to the divine the world is wholly effect and in no way cause; the divine being is utterly unchanging while the world changes as it responds to that being; God is in a state of bliss but the world contains suffering and so cannot be experienced as such by God; God's perfection is a state of total completion and hence nothing that occurs in the world can contribute to the divine being. Whereas, therefore, pantheism denies any final distinction between God and the authentic reality of the world, theism recognizes that God and the world are external to each other but holds that there cannot (because of the logic of the 'theistic' view of God) be any way of linking the two in *mutually* enriching ties. God gives, the world receives: but while God's being influences the world, the world's processes cannot affect God. Consequently nothing that the world achieves can have significance *coram Deo* (before God).

The classical roots of this theism are to be found more in Aristotle's deduction of the existence of an Unmoved Mover as the ontologically ultimate than in Plato's affirmation of the Good as the Form of the forms. According to Aristotle it is 'evident . . . that there is a primary being, eternal and unmovable and separate from sensible things' which necessarily exists and cannot be 'otherwise than as it is'. This being is the divine. The divine 'life' is utterly 'self-sufficient' and the divine knowledge is changeless knowledge of 'the supreme excellence' of the divine being (Aristotle 1960: 259f, 266). It is a view of the divine which is deeply embedded in traditional theological understanding. As was noted in Chapter 2, Aquinas maintains, for instance, that 'in God there is no real relation to creatures' whereas 'there is in creatures a real relation' to God (Aquinas 1964: 6, 27). Moses Maimonides similarly argues that since 'God has absolute existence' while all else has 'only possible existence', to posit a relation between God and all else would be to envisage God as 'subject to the accident of relation'. He therefore instructs the bewildered that 'there is no relation whatever' between God 'and any other being' (Maimonides 1956: 71f).

The difficulties which this 'theistic' view of the divine creates for Christian theology may be illustrated by E. L. Mascall's attempt to affirm both 'the reality of God's concern with the finite order' and the rational conclusion that 'we cannot validly assert that the finite either adds to or detracts from God' (Mascall 1949: 141). On the basis that reflection on the divine perfection requires that God be conceived as 'unchanged and unchange-able', Mascall tries to reconcile the impassibility which this entails with the divine compassion (which the Christian faith maintains) as 'the union of omnipotence and love'. He does this in terms of what he considers to be the 'real consolation' of knowing that God is 'not entangled' in the predicaments of our contingent states. He thus maintains on the one hand that God knows us in our fragility and ephemerality better than we know ourselves, and on the other that human suffering is not 'contained in God'. Consequently, although God's 'unruffled beatitude' is not to be criticized as a matter of luxuriating in 'self-centred detachment' since the divine will is that we should share it, God is 'the strength and stay upholding all creation' as one 'who ever doth himself unmoved abide' (ibid.: 142f).

Mascall — like Anselm (cf. 1962: 13f) and numerous other Christian theologians — deserves credit for ingenuity but in the end the problem for which he seeks a solution is insoluble in the way that '(immured) theism' poses it. Such theism presupposes a monopolar understanding of the divine which, as has been noted in the previous chapters, is irreconcilable with claims that God is intrinsically caring, loving, and compassionate and not merely externally experienceable as such. 'Theism' may thus be judged to be defective as a way of understanding the relationship between God and the processes of reality. This is because while, in contrast to pantheism, it recognizes the relative autonomy of two ontologically distinct modes of reality, that of the divine and that of all other entities, it understands the essential nature of the divine to be such that the divine can in no way be aware of the changing states of the genuinely contingent world nor, therefore, be responsive to them in a conscious manner.

According to the view of God at the heart of 'theism', the unchanging divine may beam with pure love but it is like an automatic lighthouse which is totally unaware of the ships that pass by — and of the triumphs and the wrecks that they actualize. The result is an understanding of faith that may be said to appreciate that God 'makes his sun rise on good and bad alike, and sends the rain on the honest and the dishonest' (Matthew 5: 45). At the same time it is an understanding which is at least uneasy and, if taken strictly, apparently incompatible with the implication that God 'makes' or 'sends' anything as a deliberate response to the contingent states of the world. This view of the divine nature implicitly contradicts the faith that God is consciously aware of the contingent events of the world to such an intimate extent that we can be assured the fall of a sparrow and the number of our hairs are noticed (Matthew 10: 29ff). While, then, theism may properly be held to recognize a distinction and a relationship between God and the world, its conception of the intrinsic perfection of the divine fundamentally undermines any faith that suggests that the divine is aware of, incorporates, and responds to the contingent events of the world. It thereby denies the validity of any faith which suggests that the divine is consciously concerned about the contingent events of the lives of individuals and gives their being ultimate significance.

Most views of God in the Judaeo-Christian-Islamic tradition of faith, however, do not in effect strictly adhere to the 'theistic' position as thus outlined. Although they may affirm, more or less strongly, its basic understanding of the divine nature, so far as they respond to the actuality of that tradition of faith they attempt to combine it with a recognition of mutual consciousness and interaction between God and the world. The results are theologies which struggle to maintain that uneasy compromises are not hiding fundamental contradictions. The advantage of the self-conscious adoption of 'panentheism' is that it provides a conceptual structure which meets the needs of adequate recognition both of the unique perfection of the divine and of the relative autonomy of the world in a way that allows each to be conceived as able to affect the other in significant and appropriate ways. Consequently, as was suggested at the start of this chapter, panentheism is not a new position but a new appreciation of the proper conceptual structure of a dominant tradition of religious faith in God.

Hartshorne's analysis and development of the panentheistic position is an application of the dipolar concept of God to the question of the relationship between God and the processes of reality. Basically this understanding holds that God incorporates within the divine being all the experiences which constitute the world while having an identity as a self-conscious being which is significantly separate from and accordingly able to respond to the contingent processes of the world. Knowing the world wholly and intimately, God is consequently influenced by its states; as a self-conscious being God is not determined by the world but can make decisions about it.

One model for this understanding of the God–world relationship is that of the human self–body relationship. On the one hand all that happens to 'my' body happens to 'me'. If I touch a hot pan or bite a chilli or look at a page, what occurs is more than the stimulation of a localized group of cells that are part of my body. I consider that 'I' feel, taste, see. These are 'my' experiences. My selfhood is as a holistic being which embraces the events that happen in any part of my body as my own. On the other hand, though, I can distance myself from any of these parts and the physiological processes which they undergo. This is not in the sense of denying that they are happening to me (even if in some deluded state I protest 'This cannot be happening to me', the very protest shows that it is!) but in the sense that I can reflect on them and, in some cases, decide what I wish to do about them. Not only, for example, may I be consciously aware that I am enjoying the taste of a peach and try to prolong the experience by taking another one: I may become aware that this or that part of my body is malfunctioning and so needs to be treated, even radically excised as in the case, say, of a gangrenous finger.

In the case of human beings, the awareness of what is happening to the self is limited. We are not consciously aware of most of what impinges upon us and so is part of our experience and we are generally even less aware of almost all of the physiological processes of our bodies. Attention isolates for notice only a minute fraction of what is occurring around and in us. Our capacity to respond is also restricted — I may take measures to enhance my awareness of what happens to me and I may manage to improve the performance of my heart by taking exercise. I may even have bits — a cancerous tumour, say — removed. In the end, though, there are limits to how much I can develop myself and to how many pieces I can afford to lose and yet survive as a self. However, while our awareness (and hence our ability to respond intentionally) is minute in relation to the processes that are occurring, God's awareness and responsiveness are not so limited. Nothing happens of which the divine cannot be conscious and is not conscious. Nothing happens, furthermore, to which the divine cannot and does not respond in the most adequate way possible.

An illustration of the panentheist view of the divine was unwittingly provided by a child's picture used on the dustwrapper of Ronald Goldman's *Readiness for Religion.* Out of a cloud-shaped but presumably solid object (the world?) emerge the trunk, arms, and head of a figure. Above the picture is written 'ThiS IS Cod' and below it 'Cod is The Wold'. The spelling and the artistic skill may be somewhat lacking but the vision is good. It pictures what Grace Jantzen has recently expounded — quite independently of process thought — in *God's World, God's Body* (1984) and what Hartshorne sums up as the panentheist view of the divine reality when he writes of God's

> wholeness as always self-identical, but self-identical as self-enriched, influenced but never fully determined by (and never fully determining) others — in short, a living, sensitive,

free personality, preserving all actual events with impartial care and forever adding new events to his experience.

(Hartshorne and Reese 1953: 514)

Whereas, therefore, 'the absolute is the One merely as One; the superrelative' (which is one way in which Hartshorne analyses the panentheistic character of the divine as the perfect) 'is the many as also one, or the one as also many'. Apart from God 'the many' — the diverse constituents of the contingent processes of reality — are 'merely' many and the notion of 'the world' is 'an abstraction' which refers to no real whole; in God the many constitute a whole as they become 'one, as the integrated, active-passive content of omniscience' (ibid.).

In *Philosophers Speak of God* Hartshorne and Reese classify the concepts of God presented by a wide range of thinkers according to their answers to five questions: 'Is God eternal? Is he temporal? Is he conscious? Does he know the world? Does he include the world?' (ibid.: 16). Panentheism is represented by extracts from, among other, Plato, Schelling, Fechner, White-head, Iqbal, and Radhakrishnan. Whereas other views of God provide only 'truncated' doctrines since they explicitly or implicitly deny of the divine one or more of these factors, panentheism is held to be the most adequate concept because it answers all these questions affirmatively.

Panentheism, that is, maintains that God is 'eternal' in that 'in some aspects of his reality' the divine is 'devoid of change, whether as birth, death, increase, or decrease'. The divine has never come into being nor ever been other than purely God and never will cease to be such. Whatever happens to occur, whether by the will of God or by the acts of the creatures, God is. On the other hand, God is also 'temporal' in that in some aspects the divine reality is 'capable of change, at least in the form of increase of some kind'. This does not mean that at any time God is less than fully divine or needs to be augmented in order to become truly God but that as events occur within the processes of reality, they are incorporated within the divine reality. On coming to be, they become constituents of the divine synthesis which embraces and integrates all occasions of experience.

The divine reality is also 'conscious' or 'self-aware' and 'knows the world'. God, that is, is neither oblivious of the qualities of Godself nor ignorant of any non-divine reality. As aware of all that is and of what may creatively be produced from it, God can accordingly be predicated with qualities of appreciative enjoyment and deliberate intentionality. Finally, in his outline of the panentheistic position, Hartshorne emphasizes that God is 'world-inclusive, having all things as constituents'. Without annulling any of the divine freedom or creaturely autonomy and without preventing reciprocal interaction between the divine and the creaturely, the world is embraced within and finds its final significance as part of the divine. God is thus internally as well as externally related to the world — and the world is, in an appropriate way, externally as well as internally related to God (Hartshorne and Reese 1953: 16).

The resulting concept of God as Eternal-Temporal Consciousness, Knowing and including the World (ETCKW) thus provides a coherent way of recognizing the deity of God emphasized by '(immured) theism' and the intimate relation between God and the world affirmed by 'pantheism' without the denials that each of these positions have been considered to require. While, then, the phrase 'dipolar panentheism' may appear to be offputtingly technical terminology, what it refers to is an understanding of God and processes of reality which combines a proper appreciation of the divinity of God with a way of perceiving God's awareness of and responsiveness to those processes. The terminology may be unfamiliar but the 'God' which it is describing is the God who is witnessed to in the sacred writings of Judaism, Christianity, and Islam (and perhaps, though I am not competent to judge, of other faiths) and whom believers in those traditions of faith have typically considered that they worship, trust, and serve.

In order to clarify further this understanding of the divine nature, we will consider in the remainder of this chapter how a panentheistic view of God conceives the attributes of omniscience, passivity, activity, and power as they refer to the nature of the relationship between God and the world.

The dipolar structure of divine knowledge was mentioned in the previous chapter. So far as the intrinsic character of the divine being is concerned (i.e. the aspect of divinity which is particularly illuminated by an appreciation of its 'diplolar' character), in principle God knows necessarily and absolutely all that is to be known but in concrete actuality what God knows depends upon — and so is contingent upon and relative to — what is there to be known. In practice, therefore, God knows all that has been the case and all that is now the case anywhere. It is therefore legitimate to speak of God as being 'omniscient'.

Does the divine omniscience mean that God also knows all that is going to happen on any future occasion? Many theologians have considered that to deny this would be to make God less than 'that than which a greater cannot be conceived' and so less than fully divine. They have consequently maintained either that God's being is a timeless one where all events are simultaneously co-present to the divine (and so distinctions of past, present, and future are not applicable) or that God's knowledge is such that at any moment God is as completely and precisely aware of what will occur as of what has occurred. There are, then, no surprises for God — either because there is no future for God or because what will happen, in however remote a future moment, is already patent to the divine.

Both these attempts to reconcile divine omniscience with the temporality of the processes of reality make nonsense of claims that there is a significant and reciprocal relationship between God and the world. The former solution implies that what appear to be the *processes* of reality are in fact an illusion. In reality — that is, in the ultimate state of reality as known totally by God — all events are simultaneous. At one and the same moment (and 'moment' here must be conceived as a non-temporal notion for it has no prior and no subsequent moments) every event in the cosmic story is now. When, for example, God is aware of Robert, he is aware simultaneously of Robert as embryo, baby, schoolboy, playing cricket, climbing in Baffin Island, looking for a job, middle-aged parent, pensioner, grandfather and senile wreck. It may be compared to the knowledge we have of a historical character — as I think about Oliver Cromwell I am aware more or less of the story of his life from birth to death — or of a living contemporary's past. Such knowledge, though, is only possible in cases where there is no opportunity to enter into personal relationships with the events so known by having intentions which influence what occurs in them. I may rejoice over or regret what is known to have happened but the fact of knowing it as such means that I can do nothing about it beyond value it for what it was. If, therefore, all occasions are present to God, God cannot — logically cannot — do anything about them. They are what they are. When completely generalized, this view of the divine makes a nonsense of the notion of God as purposive and creative providence. God and every event just is. God can neither intend anything nor respond to anything for both intention and response presuppose a futurity in which novel states may be brought about. To defend divine knowledge of future events by asserting that all events are timelessly present to God is to render notions of divine creativity and providential care pointless and, indeed, meaningless.

The alternative solution which holds that God knows what will occur in all future events even though they have not yet happened similarly makes a nonsense of claims that God is lovingly responsive to what occurs. It renders God either totally impotent or totally responsible — and paradoxically there is no significant difference between these states so far as God's relationship to the processes of reality is concerned! If God knows not only what has happened and what is happening but also what will happen, God must thereby know what will be the effectiveness or ineffectiveness of whatever is the divine (or any other) response to any present event. Divine involvement in the passage of events would thus be like the frustrated state of people in some science-fiction scenario reliving their past while being conscious that they are reliving it. Faced with a present problem, they not only make a decision about what to do but as they make it they know what will happen, whether or not it is what they intend. To hold that this is the divine state is to raise all the spectres of foreknowledge. Although it is arguable that it does not entail preordination, it leaves God with the nightmare of knowing what is going to occur and knowing that no one, not even God, can prevent it because what each agent will do and how others will respond is already completely known and hence unalterable.

The solution to this difficulty lies in considering again what is meant by omniscience. As was suggested in the previous chapter, God's actual knowledge, while perfect, is limited to what is knowable. It is no defect in the divine that God's knowledge of the past, for example, does not include knowledge of what never happened — such as the places that Jesus travelled to in Tasmania or the 'O' levels that Plato passed. Nor does perfect knowledge include knowledge of what is necessarily unknowable — such as the identity of the being that is greater than God or the shape of a round square. Furthermore, on analysis it appears that the future is not symmetrical with the past in relation to the present. The past is composed of events which have occurred and, since they have thereby a precisely determined form, are knowable. The future refers to ranges of possibilities within which the final determinations of particular actualizations have not yet occurred and accordingly are not yet precisely knowable. Since, therefore, future possibilities are only reduced to particular determinate forms which are knowable as actual objects when whatever was future becomes present and moves into being past, it is not coherent to talk about the future as containing determinate — and so knowable — events.

Although it may be possible to speak about knowing the range of possibilities out of which successive 'presents' will be determined, this is not the same as holding that what will actually occur is itself foreknowable. Accordingly, while God may be held to know at any time the range of what is possible at future times and also which among those possibilities are the more probable, the divine knowledge cannot be held to include foreknowledge of what will occur. Such foreknowledge, as opposed to predictions about what is likely to occur, is an incoherent notion since the concept of the future necessarily refers to what has not yet been determined and so cannot be known.

To ascribe perfect knowledge — 'omniscience' — to the divine thus does not contradict panentheistic understanding that there is mutual interaction between God and the processes of reality. Granted that to be involves having temporal aspects (a quality of the divine which will be discussed in the next chapter), the essential absoluteness of divine awareness is thus compatible with holding that God has an open future which makes it possible to speak coherently of God as responding to events and having purposes.

As panentheism considers the divine, God's knowledge of all that occurs is not merely an external relationship of registering what is the case, comparable to a computer mindlessly recording the data fed into it. It involves appreciative sensitivity and concerned responsiveness. God is thus understood to have internal relations with and so to be affected by awareness of the constituents of the world. Consequently, in holding that the divine knows and responds to all that occurs, panentheism rejects two ways of regarding the relationship between God and the world which have been advanced by some theologians. These are, first, that God is to be thought of as intentionally affecting and being affected by some but not all events in the world and, second, that God intentionally affects and is affected by no events in the world.

The first of these options may seem to be attractive because it allows God to be said to enjoy and incorporate within Godself the good that is actualized in the processes of reality without being sullied by the evil that also occurs. The divine awareness, for example, might be considered to include the joy of sharing with a friend but not the pain of rejection, the delighted energy of a healthy child but not the wasted lethargy of a starving one, the beauty of a garden but not the squalor of a dump. Such limited or negative prehension, however, would mean that God's supposed bliss is preserved at the cost of ignorance of a large

God and the processes of reality

proportion of social and (for all but rare saints) individual life. The absurd result would be that God might enjoy the devotion of a Mother Teresa but be unaffected by the plight of those for whom she cares. If accepted, this position would imply that God cannot be held to be authentically compassionate because the divine cannot be aware of suffering, nor deliberately salvific because the divine cannot be aware of the evil from which people must be redeemed. The divine relationship to the world would thus be as hollow as a state visit which is carefully shielded from all slums and demonstrations. So far as divine awareness is concerned, it would be an imperfect state and therefore it is not appropriately attributable to the divine.

The second option may be warrantably held to be a kind of perfect state. It describes the radical form of the God of 'theism'. As so understood God is unchanging and unchangeable in every respect. Intentionally to affect and to be affected by no contingent events within the world is, however, to have a mode of being that is ideally applicable to a foundation stone or a standard of measurement — unaltered by and unconcerned about influencing whatever impinges upon it, it remains exactly as what it is. It is to be an absolutely unmoved mover. Such a mode of perfection, however, is not appropriate to a being that is to be described in significant respects as personally purposive, caringly responsive, and consciously loving. It is therefore not appropriately attributable to the God with whom believers trust that they are in reciprocal relationships.

In contrast to these options, panentheism maintains that God is both eminently passive and eminently active. It conceives of God as affected by and consciously affecting all events. Nothing whatsoever can occur without being totally embraced in the divine experience and becoming part of all subsequent divine responses to what is coming to be. As will be considered in the final chapter, so far as the non-divine is concerned this dual responsiveness to actual occasions does not devalue their integrity and proper autonomy but is the salvific basis of their ultimate significance.

As for the character of the divine reality, the utter passibility of the divine means that God is not a distant, cut-off, impassible, and impassive deity. Whatever else may be held to be entailed by the divine perfection, panentheism maintains that it is not to be understood as existence in a state of bliss whatever happens, self-centredly content and oblivious to all that would disturb that bliss. Instead, taking radically seriously the view that God's nature is primarily to be understood in terms of unreserved love, it holds that God shares intimately in all the joys and sufferings that are experienced in this world. As one who is lovingly aware of every actual entity, however trivial, God incorporates the feeling of each occasion within the divine reality. In this way the non-divine contributes its own states to the life of God.

It is thus appropriate that Hartshorne whose scholarly work embraces birdsong as well as philosophical theology quotes from 'On Another's Sorrow' by William Blake at the front of *Man's Vision of God* (1964):

Can I see another's woe
And not be in sorrow too?. . .
Can a father see his child
Weep, nor be with sorrow fill'd?

And can he who smiles on all
Hear the wren with sorrows small,
Hear the small bird's grief and care,
Hear the woes that infants bear,

And not sit beside the nest
Pouring pity in their breast?

Those who find problems with such notions because they contradict the image of God dwelling in an absolutely painless heaven may be confusing their own self-centred desires with the character of the divine being as love. Their response shows that either they have not perceived or they are unwilling to accept the implications of what are widely claimed by theists to be formative insights into the nature and activity of God. At the heart of Judaism, for example, is the story of the Exodus which is held to show God as one who takes note of the suffering of the people. Islam affirms God as 'the all-compassionate'. Christianity not only remembers the teachings of Jesus about the lost and his practical concern for the outcast but, furthermore, maintains as a foundational belief that the character of God is normatively revealed in the suffering of Jesus who is the Christ. The notion that God does not suffer is an interpolation into belief about God of a mixture of philosophical mistakes about the nature of the perfect state and natural desires to avoid pain in all its forms. It is not a correct inference from the perfection of the divine as loving.

As was mentioned earlier, panentheism understands God to be eminently active as well as eminently passive. This accords with the witness of Exodus to a God who delivers the people from their suffering, of Jesus to 'the Son of Man' coming 'to seek and save what is lost' (Luke 19: 10), of Muhammad that 'God is powerful over everything' (Koran 16 (The Bee): 75), and of traditional Christian belief that in some unique way God acted in the person of Jesus and, as the Holy Spirit, continues to act in the world. While people may worship God as the embodiment of the highest ideals, as the Good which elicits adoration, the faithful put their trust in God as their 'deliverer' and saviour, as the one who can and does respond effectively to their deepest needs. Thus, as Blake's poem puts it, God does not only 'sit by us and moan', sharing in our griefs: God also seeks positively to give 'to us his joy' so that our griefs may be destroyed. Furthermore, as eminently active as well as eminently passive, panentheism holds that God influences every concrescing occasion. The divine activity in the World is not the occasional interference of a miracle-worker who dramatically changes a few courses of events — and thereby leaves believers bewildered at the apparent niggardliness of the aid that is effectively given — but a universal and unremitting grace.

How the divine activity is to be understood in practice in relation to creation, evolution, history, and salvation will be the topics of later chapters. At this point, it is important to emphasize that the 'dipolar panentheistic' concept of God, such as is developed by Hartshorne, includes a notion of authentic divine activity. Hartshorne, for example, does not consider that highly abstract statements about God's existence cover everything that can coherently be said about the divine. Although, according to the dipolar analysis, God's *existence* is necessary, God's *actuality* is contingent in part on God's decisions and in part on the actuality of the world which God embraces (and there can be nothing actual which is not embraced in the divine reality). Thus, while Hartshorne affirms that 'God is bound to exist, no matter what his decisions' (cf. Pailin 1968, 1969 for an evaluation of Hartshorne's understanding of the necessary nature of the divine existence), he also states that it is 'legitimate' to demand that 'the acts or decisions of God make a difference (and be contingent)'. Indeed he describes this demand as posing 'the essential religious question' — namely, 'what do I (and my friends and enemies) do about God, and what do I (we) suppose him to be doing about me (us)?' (Hartshorne 1966: 29, 33).

These remarks about the contingent activity of God are interesting in view of criticisms that this form of theological understanding is inadequate because it lacks a significant understanding of divine agency. In *Becoming and Being*, for example, Colin Gunton asserts that Hartshorne's concept of God 'actually precludes the taking of initiatives by God' and that 'as cause God can (*logically* can) only be the essence of passivity.' According to his analysis the God portrayed in dipolar panentheism (sometimes called by Hartshorne 'the neoclassical God') is unable to be 'anything other than a receiver of impressions' and acts only 'by means of passive influence' (Gunton 1978: 43, 81, 46; cf. 223). The result is that what Hartshorne describes is in effect not creator but the supreme creature.

Gunton's justification of his judgements, though, reveals that he has failed to appreciate the logic of Hartshorne's position and in particular the crucial distinction between the *formal* character of the dipolar structure of God-talk (which identifies the nature of the abstract and the concrete aspects of the divine reality) and the *material* attributes of God (which include both activity and passivity as well as love, knowledge, and so on) which are to be understood in terms of that structure. Gunton writes, for instance, that 'according to the logic of the position, it is passivity that is concrete and therefore ontologically prior, and activity that is an (abstract) aspect of it' (ibid.: 40). He consequently concludes that 'the only sense in which action may be ascribed to this [Hartshorne's] God is an abstract one' (ibid.: 45). This, however, is not 'the logic' of Hartshorne's position. That 'logic' does not regard activity and passivity as polar opposites in the sense that abstract and concrete are: they are different material attributes of the divine which are to be interpreted according to the dipolar structure.

Contrary to Gunton's error (cf. Ogden 1980), then, it is not the logic of the position that God's passive awareness of all must be concrete and hence God's activity by the rules of dipolarity must be thought of as abstract — and so effectively as non-existent. The correct use of the dipolar logic treats both God's passivity and God's activity as having abstract and concrete aspects. The abstract aspect of the passivity, as has been suggested above, is that in principle God is aware of all that it is possible to be aware of — of the actual as being actual and of the possible as possible. Whatever is is embraced by God. The concrete aspect of this passivity is that what God in fact embraces depends upon what is actually there to be embraced. Similarly God's activity has an abstract aspect in that in principle nothing has ever occurred nor could anything ever occur in the future outside the divine sphere of influence. Every concrescing occasion, whatever it may be and wherever it may be, must occur within that sphere and be subject to influence by the divine. The concrete actuality of God's activity, however, is dependent in part upon what in the particular case of a concrescing occasion God may choose to be its proper goal among equally valuable but incompatible possibilities for it — and what happens also depends upon how the concrescing occasion responds to that goal.

The universality of the divine influence on events does not, however, entail that all that happens is determined by God. Panentheism develops an understanding of divine power which indicates that it is no necessary threat to the autonomy, freedom, and significance of the non-divine.

Traditionally God has been held to be 'omnipotent'. Power in the non-divine — and so the possibility of activity which can give significance to the non-divine — has then had to be understood either as an expression of God's power (so turning the creature in effect into an emanation of the divine without an integrity of its own) or as only made possible by an act of divine self-limitation. In the case of a being who is regarded as essentially impassible and hence unaware of contingent beings, it is difficult to make sense of the notion of such self-limitation; but in the case of the panentheist notion of the divine as totally aware of all that is and totally responsive, such a notion seems quite coherent. Although in principle God's power is supreme, God's creative purposes may be held to restrain that power so that the creatures may enjoy a limited degree of autonomy.

Furthermore, the notion of power is relational. Hence the notion of omnipotence in the sense of having an absolute monopoly of power is intrinsically incoherent. A being which had all power would be related to nothing real — except in so far as it could be said to be related to its own being. In effect it would be no different from a being that was utterly powerless because there would be nothing with power of its own with which it could have relations and over which it could exercise power. In such a case the processes of reality would be an emanation of God rather than the activity of a creation which has some, if limited, independence of its own and so is able to enter into authentic relations with the divine. As will be discussed more fully in Chapters 7 and 8, however, it is arguable that God is to be thought of as essentially the creator and that the basic idea of creativity implies that as such God is not involved in acts of emanation whereby the divine being finds further modes of self-expression. As an actual creator God is necessarily involved in bringing about the reality of that which has an integrity and hence a value of its own over against the divine as well as for the divine.

What, then, is to be made of the notion of divine 'omnipotence'? So far as it suggests that the divine is potentially, if not
at present actually, an overwhelming threat to the significance of
the non-divine, a power that may destroy the earth as myth
claims happened in the Deluge, an irresistible force that always
is capable of getting its own way, whether by blatant force or
devious manipulation, then the notion is to be given up as an
inappropriate quality of the proper object of worship. It implies
that God is capable of being a despot and that we may believe
that the divine does not act despotically at present either because
we are ignorant of the strings that are pulling us like puppets or
because God is at present not sufficiently bothered to take
control. This is a position which poses an enormous problem of
evil which probably renders belief in God incredible. If God is
capable of deflecting agents from effecting the evils experienced
in the world and does not, the divine is guilty of those evils by
omission if not by commission. In that case there may be a being
with transcendent power in the universe but there is no God.
Neither the activity of a cosmic tyrant nor the carelessness of a
supreme indolence are characteristics compatible with being the
proper object of worship.

Such views of divine power probably owe more to human
limitations than to insight into the divine nature. When we find
ourselves frustrated we are tempted to react like children and
think that 'if only' we had the power then we would not put up
with such nonsenses. Utopia would be forced to appear: dissen-
ters would not be allowed to stand in the way of what was clearly
for the best. Thus we in effect approve for ourselves images of
the reformist dictators whose magnificent policies have resulted
in social disasters. We then go on to think of God as similarly
motivated and are puzzled that the processes of reality indicate
otherwise. Indeed some people are so convinced that if there is
a God then God must act as an irresistible force, compelling and
coercing conformation to the divine will, that when they do not
find such a power at work in the world, they conclude that there
is no God.

More careful reflection, however, suggests that the being with
what is finally the most effective as well as the most awesome
power is not one which uses irresistible might to coerce other
agents. Such might can only enforce outward subservience to its
will. Far more impressive is the power of one who is prepared
with endless patience to attract and persuade until other agents
are drawn into willing conformity by recognizing the unsurpassable goodness of what is asked of them. As the proper object of

worship God's activity is accordingly to be conceived as the luring influence of a love which respects the proper integrity and intrinsic value of all others. In *Process and Reality* Whitehead makes this point when he contrasts 'the brief Galilean vision of humility' which has 'flickered throughout the ages' with 'the doctrine of an aboriginal, eminently real, transcendent creator, at whose fiat the world came into being, and whose imposed will it obeys'. With the latter doctrine Caesar conquered Christ as the source of the traditional image of God. Whitehead calls for a return to a view of God which 'dwells upon the tender elements in the world, which slowly and in quietness operate by love' (Whitehead 1978: 342f). A few pages later he puts it that

> God's rôle is not the combat of productive force with productive force, of destructive force with destructive force; it lies in the patient operation of the overpowering rationality of his conceptual harmonization. He does not create the world, he saves it: or, more accurately, he is the poet of the world, with tender patience leading it by his vision of truth, beauty, and goodness.
>
> (ibid.: 346)

Hartshorne similarly argues that the only tenable understanding of divine power sees God as influencing but not determining the actual form of all that happens according to the divine purpose that each creature make its own unique contribution to the experienced beauty of the world (cf. 1984: 25).

Although it is arguable that lures might be made so attractive that they are effectively irresistible, there is no necessity to consider that God would so act since this would undermine the purpose of creation, namely the appearance of significantly independent, value-producing agents. Bearing this in mind, the model of luring allows notions of divine activity and power in relation to the processes of reality to be developed in ways that do not impinge upon the relative autonomy of the non-divine. God may thus be conceived as seeking in loving respect to draw others to ever higher states of aesthetic richness but without the coerciveness which would destroy the very purpose of the divine creativity. How this may be worked out in more detail in relation to the processes of nature and of history will be discussed in later chapters. So far as panentheistic understanding of the all-embracing character of the divine activity is concerned, however, a proper recognition of the 'omni-' quality of divine power is an appreciation of the limitlessness of its scope and the perfect quality of its relationships rather than a perception of the ogre of transcendent determination.

While the term 'panentheism' may with some justification be regarded as adding unnecessarily to the terminology of theological thought, what it identifies is a way of understanding the relationship between God and the processes of reality which respects both the proper independence of each and the intimate relationships between them. In later chapters we shall consider what this may mean in relation to nature, history, and the significance of human being. Before we turn to these issues, however, it is important to consider further how the perfection of God is to be perceived and how it may be coherent to think of God both as essentially perfect (which is a necessary quality of the divine as an adequate object of worship) and as personal (which is essential if the divine is to be regarded as purposive).

6 God as perfect and personal

As the ultimate in value and the proper object of the contemplation, adoration, and emulation that is true worship, God must be conceived as essentially perfect. Otherwise the unreserved quality of faith in God would be impossible. Whatever the awesome superiority of its object, there would always be a temptation to qualify our attitude towards it with the thought that while it is the best that we know about, there might possibly be a better. Thus Anselm came to perceive that it is not sufficient for adequate theistic[1] understanding to describe God as the greatest actual being or even as the greatest being that we can imagine; the only satisfactory way of identifying God is to hold that God is 'that than which a greater cannot be conceived' — or, as Hartshorne puts it, 'the perfect'.

One implication of the recognition of this defining characteristic of the divine is that pure worship has to be seen as inescapably iconoclastic, especially in relation to the material apprehension of what is properly to be worshipped. True worship is directed towards a reality which criticizes our images of the divine as inadequate. And if we replace those images with what we are led — and are warrantably led — to consider to be more adequate ones, it shows up their inadequacy too. The quest for theistic understanding is one that never ends. As Tillich puts it, 'God is symbol for God.' Since 'no finite reality can express' the truly ultimate, 'religiously speaking, God transcends his own name' (Tillich 1958: 44ff). Consequently whatever way God's nature is conceived must be recognized to be an attempt to represent what can only be indirectly (Tillich himself would say 'symbolically') apprehended.

Actual faith, on the other hand, cannot be satisfied by a recognition of the inapprehensible mystery of God. Worship would be empty and faith directionless if they were addressed towards an utterly blank void or to purely formal ideas of ultimacy and perfection as such. However inadequate it may be, some perception of the material attributes of the divine is needed to give substance and orientation to the practice of faith in the

---

[1] Cf. the comment at the start of Chapter 5 that the term 'theism' is generally used in this study to refer to the concept of God most adequately described in technical terms as dipolar panentheism.

world. Thus faith has to find an answer to the question, 'Which of the innumerable symbols of faith is most adequate to the meaning of faith?' According to Tillich the adoption of a particular answer is 'a matter of daring faith, of courage and risk' (Tillich 1958: 47). It need not, though, be a matter of a-rational assertion. As Newman points out in the *Grammar of Assent,* while faith goes beyond what can be demonstrated, rational reflection can and does act as a necessary antecedent by which faith is warranted as a justifiable commitment.

One implication of theism's demand that God be conceived as perfect is that theistic understanding is committed to finding a way along a perilous ridge towards the goal of the most adequate apprehension of the divine perfection that is attainable. It must do this without falling either into the gulf of rendering the notion of that perfection vacuous (for example, by maintaining that 'God is perfect in a totally mysterious way') or into the abyss of giving it content which is manifestly inappropriate for images of that which is ultimate in being, rationality, and value. This, though, is not the only condition of a satisfactory concept of God for theistic understanding. It must also satisfy another requirement, namely that its concept of God's perfection be appropriate to the divine reality as having a personal mode of being, i.e. as having self-conscious and intentional agency. God is not only the ideal by reference to whose nature ultimate judgements of value are to be made: God is also the one who gives ultimate significance to all the processes of reality by being aware of them, appreciating them, and responding to them in a way that is most adequately conceived by analogy with the personal mode of being characteristic of human being. The question that thus arises — and which provides the primary concern for this chapter — is how God may be conceived as being both personal and perfect.

Since God is the intrinsically ultimate, judgements about divine perfection are not to be treated as judgements about the divine satisfaction of certain standards which are independent of the divine reality. This is not simply because human beings cannot justifiably presume to be in a position to compare the divine reality with certain norms so as to determine that the divine reality is the best possible because it precisely conforms to them; as God challenges Job, 'Dare you deny that I am just or put me in the wrong that you may be right?' (Job 40: 8). The primary reason that no such evaluations are feasible is that God is that standard by which all judgements are to be made. To compare God with the essential being of God, though, is not an illuminating exercise. It may purport to show that God is wholly God but it gives no insight into the material character of the divine reality.

One corollary of this is that, as applied to God, the notion of perfection does not announce that God has achieved some independently recognized standard — as happens when we describe the alignment of a bearing or the movement of a ballerina as perfect — but that God necessarily is identical with the appropriate standards for judging the final significance of the products and processes of reality. Since this identity follows from what is meant by 'God', God is not to be congratulated on having achieved 'perfection'. The divine could not, *logically* could not, be anything else. In this respect, therefore, to describe God as 'perfect' is to glorify God by recognizing the nature of the divine. It does not provide material information about God's nature but highlights two definitive characteristics of talk about 'God'. The first is that God has a logically unique status. The second is that attempts to provide material information about the divine reality must be regarded as pointing understanding in particular directions (i.e. it must be in the form of 'directional utterances') rather than as providing straightforward descriptions of the divine nature.

The proposition 'God is perfect', however, expresses more than the formal tautology 'God is God'. It also sums up the way in which God's material characteristics are to be understood. Serious misunderstandings have arisen in theological thought because the significance of the notion of perfection as applied to the divine has been grasped in terms of inappropriate analyses derived from its uses in normal discourse. How, then, is the notion to be correctly understood in relation to the divine?

It is important, to begin with, to recognize that except in the unique case where 'the perfect' is used to denote the nature of the divine as the proper object of worship, 'perfection' itself does not connote a material quality. It is a qualifying term which ascribes the highest possible state of some material quality to something in being what it is or what it is for. To call something 'perfect' is thus to employ what may be called a second-order description — the term qualifies a quality, including the quality of an object's instantiation of the essence of what it is as such a kind of object. If the word is used without an explicit quality to qualify, one is implied. To say, for instance, 'A is perfect' is meaningful as connoting 'A is a perfect case of a-ing' or 'A is a perfect y' — where the context has made it clear that its being a y is what is at issue. Thus 'The table is perfect' is a way of saying things like 'The table is a perfect instance of its kind' or 'of what is wanted' or 'of being unblemished'.

Being 'perfect', then, is not ascribable to an object in the same way that being 'red' or 'oval' or 'loving' may be ascribed to it. Something is not deemed to be perfect as such but in respect to how it is being considered — as a perfect argument or a perfect friend or a perfect lock, for example. From this it follows that the qualities which might be held to be indicated if an argument is said to be perfect (self-evident premises and deductive reasoning from them, for instance) are not the same as those which are likely to be regarded as appropriate in the case of a lock (material strength, smoothness of operation, and unpickability, for instance), and neither of these sets of qualities is relevant in the case of a friend. Furthermore, it is important to appreciate that in order for something to be perfect as what it is, it may be necessary for it to have a particular quality in certain respects and not in others. It is arguable, for example, that a perfect friend needs to be reliable in certain respects, so as to be properly trustworthy, and yet to be unpredictable in others if the friendship is to be a personally enriching relationship.

When, therefore, perfection is held to be the mode of the divine attributes and this claim is intended to connote more than that they are *God's* attributes, what does the use of the qualifier 'perfect' indicate? What precisely is thereby being claimed about the material qualities of the divine reality? To answer this question involves deciding which of the different ways in which the qualifier 'perfection' may be used most appropriately applies to the attributes of the divine being. The failure to recognize the need for such a choice — or an insufficient consideration of the implications of such a choice — underlies the unsatisfactoriness of many traditional views of God.

There are various ways in which the qualifier 'perfect' is properly understood, each appropriate to particular qualities or objects. In the case of a table of the values to the fifth decimal point of the sine of angles, perfection may be regarded as the state of total exactitude and availability. The calculations that have been made are correct and their results accurately transcribed. The table never needs to be checked nor is it to be altered. It is just to be used. Unchanging and exact sphericity would presumably be an essential characteristic of a 'perfect' ball-bearing. Such an object would preserve its shape no matter what pressures were exerted upon it. Here, though, the perfection is a matter of physical form rather than of intellectual correctness. A different kind of physical perfection applies in the case of a spring-balance. In this case perfection involves variations that unchangingly and precisely correspond to the different weights placed in its pan.

A more complex notion of perfection is involved in the case of a motor car. Here perfection is not to be thought of as a single quality but as the optimum combination of various qualities such as safety, power, fuel consumption, comfort, lightness, strength, cheapness, style, and workmanship. Furthermore, what is regarded as the optimum combination may well differ according to the circumstances in which the car is to be used. Ruggedness and low fuel consumption are far more significant than elegance for the 'perfect' car for crossing the Gobi but less so for one that is to be a status symbol in Dallas.

On moving from the qualities of the abstract and of impersonal objects to those appropriate to persons, the significance of the qualifier 'perfect' becomes very complex. Personal qualities typically involve sensitivity and intelligent responsiveness rather than actual unchangeability or automatic reaction. Thus, while the perfect loyalty of a friend in principle is a matter of an unchanging and unwearying readiness to assist, its concrete expressions involve a perceptive grasp of what is best in different situations and accordingly varied forms of support. For example, to be a perfect 'friend' to me in practice may mean telling me to stop wingeing, pulling me out of a peat-bog, criticizing my draft, laughing at me, or being ready to go to lunch with me. A computer may be programmed to react in precisely controlled ways to various commands and data but this is not the model for the responsiveness of a perfect friend — or of a perfect teacher, doctor, or ruler. In such cases perfection does not involve automatic reactions to signals but a sympathetic awareness of the situation indicated by the other's signs and a search for the response that will lead to the highest fulfilment in the particular case. Although a perfect ball-bearing would never distort, whatever forces were placed upon it, a parallel unresponsiveness in every respect in friends, teachers, doctors, or rulers would reveal serious imperfections in them. Hence the limited value of teddy bears, teaching machines, computer diagnosis, and rule-governed bureaucracy. The very nature of its predictability and programming makes the machine unable to cope with individuals in their essential uniqueness. It has to convert them — and depersonalize them — into specific determinations of preconceived variables.

In the case of a fully personal relationship such as friendship, the notion of perfection involves a complex interaction of qualities of reciprocity, constancy, changeability, and unpredictability. Consider two friends: whereas such relationships as those of teacher to pupil and of doctor to patient can be regarded as largely asymmetrical since the teacher rather than the pupil, and the doctor rather than the patient, seeks to appreciate and respond to the needs of the other, the relationship between partners in a perfect friendship is fully reciprocal. Ideally each is constant in his or her loyalty to and concern for the other; each changes by being affected by and responding to the states of the other; each contributes to the flourishing of the relationship by introducing unanticipated actions that prevent the relationship from stagnating.

The significance of the notion of 'perfection' thus varies according to the character of the different qualities to which it is applied. In what ways, then, is 'perfection' to be appropriately understood in the case of the attributes describing God's reality? There is a wide range of models to choose from. Which ones are chosen will depend upon what is considered to be the most appropriate way of explicating the concept of God.

Traditionally God's perfection has been understood in terms of total unchangeability *(impassibilis)*, completeness *(actus purus)*, and the possession of all possible values *(ens realissimum)*. On reflection, though, the third of these notions of perfection appears to be intrinsically incoherent and the first two, while possibly reconcilable with the worshipfulness and ultimacy of God, are inconsistent with the personal character of the divine being as maintained in theistic understanding. The alternatives, however, may seem equally unpromising. The concept of a being that is describable as inconstant, incomplete, and deficient in some values hardly seems to be a serious candidate for apprehending the nature of the proper object of worship and the source of the ultimate significance of the processes of reality.

What is needed is a reappraisal of the proper significance of the forms of perfection as they apply to an understanding of the divine as personal. In such a reappraisal it is important to bear in mind the second-order character of the notion of perfection as well as the dipolar and panentheistic structures of the concept of the divine which have been discussed in the previous two chapters. Just as the awareness of the dipolar character of the material attributes of the divine reality indicates that what God is in principle is unchanging but that how God actualizes that nature involves appropriate changes, so the form of perfection appropriate for one quality of the divine may not be appropriate for another. Furthermore, just as a perfect teacher would respond in one way to a student who had failed to grasp the point and in another way to one who was not paying attention, so the perfect form of the divine love may have to be thought of as patient in relation to our faltering attempts to perceive the divine will but unrelentingly demanding in relation to our attempts to evade its categorical demands. That the divine love (which is the determinative characteristic of all divine relationships) has a particular form and corresponding mode of perfection in one set of circumstances must not mislead us into thinking that it must have that form and mode of perfection in all.

The notion of total unchangeability has traditionally been regarded as entailed by the perfection of the divine nature. In certain respects this conclusion seems warrantable. If for instance, God is perfect, it appears that any change in the divine must either be to some degree of imperfection or imply that the divine was previously not perfect and has become so. To predicate either of God is absurd. God is unchangingly never more nor less than the absolutely divine (for such 'more' and 'less' can have no reference in the case of what is intrinsically and definitively ultimate in being, rationality, and value). From this it is maintained by some that God must be in every respect unchanging and unchangeable. Even the possibility of such movement cannot belong to a reality whose qualities are necessarily perfect.

This view of divine perfection agrees with the view of change that associates the latter with disintegration and decay. Remembering how last year's heroes have hardly won a match this season, how one-time wizards with the ball now hobble rheumatically, it is fitting that the crowd at an English Football Association Cup Final should sing: 'Earth's joys grow dim, its glories pass away; Change and decay in all around I see: O Thou who changest not, abide with me!' The view also fits in with classicist prejudice for the past. The golden age was long ago; history is the movement away from the perfect state.

It is by no means obvious, though, that such a view is the correct way to determine the nature of the perfection appropriate to the personal aspects of the reality of God. Change need not always be a movement towards or away from a perfect state. It can also be a necessary condition for being unchangingly perfect in relation to the processes of reality. Consider the state of perfect consciousness, including awareness of the present and memory of the past, in the case of a temporally ordered world where novel events continue to occur as successive presents come to be and then perish into pastness. If this consciousness is never to cease to be perfect, the actual contents of its awareness of what is the case must continually change as moment by moment it is aware of what has now come to be, succeeding for a moment a previous state and about to be in turn succeeded by a further novel determination of possibilities. As a corollary the contents of its memory must continually increase (and so in that sense change) as it registers what becomes past. In terms of its concrete actuality, therefore, a consciousness that did not change would be seriously deficient, if not a contradiction in terms. Hence God's perfect consciousness of the processes of reality requires in the divine a changeability that is coextensive with all change. Only as having such changeability in practice is it unchangingly true that in principle God is perfectly aware of whatever happens and never forgets anything that has happened.

This dipolar appreciation of the divine awareness is not as odd as it may first appear. Whereas, for example, perfection as a checker on the till at a supermarket would require a person to be in principle unchanging as having completely adequate awareness of each article as it passes before him or her, the instantiation of that awareness would require in practice different appraisals of, and appropriately changing responses to, those different articles in accordance with their actual states and prices. In the case of the divine consciousness of the contingent events of the processes of reality, perfect awareness involves both the unchanging existence of total awareness of whatever occurs (i.e. each moment God knows exactly what has happened and is happening, whatever those events might happen to be) and changing actual awareness correlative to the changes of events in practice (i.e. the contents of God's awareness of what has become past and of what is now present alter as previously present events perish and novel events are actualized).

The identification of change with decay may similarly be countered by pointing out that the difference between the living and the dead is the difference between the ability and inability to respond to events in the environment. Change need not lead towards disintegration. It may be a continuing activity of integration in the context of a changing situation. As such it is the mark of life. From this perspective, change is also to be seen as a necessary condition of the production and appreciation of novel values. The unchanging is stagnant, the changing creates. In this respect, therefore, modes of changeability are appropriately ascribable to the concrete actuality of the divine as living and creative. Such attribution, though, is balanced by unchangeability in the abstract existence of the divine: God unchangingly quests for the proliferation and integration of value in the processes of reality.

The unchangeable–changing dipolar nature of the divine as personal and living stands in opposition to even a qualified version of the view that change is either to be regretted because it means movement away from some supposed golden age in the past or is sad because it is an attempt to reproduce glories that have been lost. The force of this myth is contrary to notions of God as having a personal and hence creative mode of being. Instead of recognizing that a genuinely living God is one for whom the past is a store of memories of values which the future provides the opportunity to use and to augment, it suggests the Nietzschean caricature of God as sitting beside the fire like a weary crone, grieving for lost youth (Nietzsche 1954: 373).

This is to conceive the divine in terms of middle-age disillusion and old-age exhaustion which characterize those who have accepted death as a way of existing. It is not to appreciate God as one whose energy, imagination, and zest are limitless. To think of God as the source and inspiration of value involves a positive view of the future. As for the myth of a golden past, its limited validity may be that it provides a (largely misleading) expression of the truth that whatever has been achieved never finally perishes. All its values are preserved and treasured in the divine.

Another way in which the perfection of the divine reality has traditionally been understood is as a state of total completion — as *actus purus,* pure actuality without any element of potentiality. As with the mistaken attribution of unchangeability, there appear to be sound reasons for interpreting the divine nature in this way. For instance, it may be argued that a being which has potentiality must lack something which may or may not be later actualized. As one whose reality is perfect, though, God cannot lack anything. Therefore the divine must be considered to be without potentiality. Again, as has already been suggested, it is maintained that unless God is now complete, the divine must be moving either towards or away from such a state and therefore is not truly God. Finally the notion of potentiality in God is attacked on the grounds that it implies that God is open to influence by others and that believers cannot be sure that God will remain for ever the same. Such implications are claimed to be incompatible with the blessedness and reliability that are to be attributed to God.

These arguments, however, mistakenly absolutize and universalize as a quality in itself what is properly to be seen as a second-order quality of certain aspects of the material attributes of God. In terms of abstract existence, God is always complete — in the sense that the divine is always actualizing in some appropriate form the fullness of what it is to be 'God'. We do not have to wait for 'God' to emerge from some process nor can we observe something developing into 'God' through the activity of external or internal forces. The nature of the divine reality means that God has always been there, never less than or other than existing as the completely divine. Indeed, it is odd to speak of God as being 'completely divine' because the qualifier 'completely' is redundant. Talk of a being that is incompletely God is incoherent.

On the other hand, the notion of God as complete in all respects rules out any significant talk of the divine as personal and so, in some important respects, as living. A being that is in all respects complete is finished and replete. There is no difference between describing it as such and as dead. It has reached the pointless, valueless state of having nothing further to achieve. Such a description might be appropriate for an ideal. It is incompatible with a personal mode of being, for this involves being directed by the search for values, responding to situations, enjoying novel experiences, and developing relationships with what else exists. Above all, personal being involves the creation and appreciation of novel forms of value. This does not, however, mean that God must be thought of as being *either* personal *or* complete. Rather, a proper notion of the divine completeness indicates that God is to be conceived as the one who in certain respects is eminently and completely personal, always present as the individual with an unrestricted capacity for consciously seeking value, responding to events, and evoking novelty.

Potentiality in the divine, then, is not a mark of imperfection but a necessary implication of the personal aspects of God's reality. In this respect the difference between human states and God's perfect state is not the presence of potentiality in the former but not in the latter. The difference is rather between the limitations of human and the infinity of divine potentiality. From this it follows that God is to be thought of as having not yet experienced everything that is possible as actual. Only if God is conceived to be in some such state can personal being be coherently attributed to the divine: absolutely finished objects are impersonal and lifeless.

Reflection, furthermore, suggests that it is the human experience of weariness rather than the experience of creativity and fulfilment that leads to doubts about potentiality in God. We become weary. As a result a state where nothing more needs to be done — no more hedges to trim, rooms to decorate, books to review, students to teach, mountains to climb, writings to explain, problems to solve — may sometimes seem attractive. A good rest, however, soon persuades us otherwise. Joy and satisfaction are found in creative activity. They reach their peak at the moment of achievement but immediately begin to decline and to give way to a sense of boredom until a new venture is engaged upon. Once a problem is solved it becomes uninteresting unless its solution leads to further problems and insights. The not-yet-done also disturbs us because we know that a time is coming when we will not be around to do it. Consequently our temporal finitude tempts us to regard potentiality as frustrating. The divine, in contast, is not subject to weariness nor will there be any end to the divine activity. While, then, God may be said to know the 'frustration' of the sense of the 'not-yet', it is not genuine 'frustration'. It is a condition of the enjoyment of creativity and of the possibility of personal life.

There remains the objection that the attribution of potentiality to the divine means that God may be open to influence by others and so may not be trusted to be one who will remain the same forever. As was suggested in the previous chapter, though, if the divine is to be held to be conscious (and this seems required if personal being is to be attributable to God), this implies that God's perfection in this respect includes an unrestricted capacity for consciousness of the states of all others. God's actual experience is then a complete awareness of all that is. Nevertheless, while completely aware of all that occurs, God is not controlled by those events. In the divine reality potentiality is combined with constancy. Whereas in human beings potentiality means that they may change for the worse, become unreliable, and act inconsistently, potentiality in the divine being is always actualized in ways consistent with the defining characteristic of the divine as ultimate in being, rationality, and value.

Since, then, the personal mode of being appropriate to God's reality involves changeability and potentiality, it is not surprising that the most adequate model for grasping the nature of the perfection of God's attributes comes from human experience of personal being rather than from analyses of the kinds of perfection appropriate to impersonal objects and ideal values. In the case of impersonal objects perfection is unchanging conformity to some independent standards. Even if this involves varying responses in the object (as in the case of a heart-beat recorder), the object itself stays as what it is. Similarly the regulative ultimacy of a perfect ideal means that it does not have potentiality to change. What is wanted in the case of the divine, however, is a model of perfection that shows how it is possible for the realizations of potentialities — and so changes — to affect God without in any way questioning the unqualified 'godness', including the ultimacy and worshipfulness, of the divine. Such a model is provided by reflecting on the nature of human being as personal.

By 'personal identity' is not meant simply a constant expression of certain qualities in different situations. A well-designed machine could have this kind of identity. In the case of people, identity involves intrinsic development as, by their awareness of and responses to situations, they change in what it is to be themselves. These changes do not involve dissociation from previous states but their incorporation into successively larger wholes which may or may not continue to indicate domination by the values that controlled earlier states. Personal being is thus a series of states, each of which transcends the previous one by uniting its contents with further experiences and appraisals.

The existentialist slogan 'Existence precedes essence' has only limited validity. So far as what we become is determined by our decisions, it is correct; so far as those decisions involve responses to our past as well as to our present experience, it is too sweeping. Furthermore, while we can change how we regard our past and in this sense change what our past is for us, we cannot deny the reality of the happenedness of our past as ours without losing our identity as persons.

In the case of our experience, though, personal development is marked by forgetfulness and aberration. So far as we are consciously aware of ourselves, we have forgotten most events that constitute our past. Even if we are told about some of these events, we may find it difficult to identify ourselves with the person reported to have been acting in them. More seriously, at different periods we may adopt radically different principles of conduct so that our past seems more like a succession of performances by different persons, although with a massive amount of overlap in the transitional stages, than an integrated development of a single person. But while the ability to break the continuity of personal development, to be 'converted' into a 'new person', is a valuable characteristic of human being, such breaks are with the previous pattern of personal development and not with the past as such. A total break with the past would involve loss of identity as a person. God, in contrast to human beings, never needs to renounce past forms of the divine and find new ways of being God. While, therefore, the model for the perfection of God's reality may be taken from human experience of personal transcendence, it is without the forgetfulness, aberrations, and domination by bad qualities that mar our forms of it.

The resulting model is one which Hartshorne has described as that of 'dual transcendence' (cf. 1970: 227ff; 1983: 314ff). According to this principle God cannot be surpassed by any other, but the divine state at one time is surpassable in certain respects by the divine states at later times. The perfection of God's relation to the processes of reality, for example, means that in principle at any moment God remembers everything that has happened up to then, is aware of everything that is then the case, and influences everything that is coming to be. In this respect no being can surpass the divine since the divine embraces everything that there is to embrace. On the other hand, what in practice God remembers as having happened and what thus constitutes the material quality of the divine being at one time surpasses what was the case at any earlier time since in the intervening time novel events have occurred. This is necessarily the case since, on the one hand, the divine incorporates all that comes to be and, on the other hand, the difference between two points in time is essentially that between those points certain potentialities have been realized and others thereby have been rendered unrealizable. If nothing happens, there is no time. If something happens, there is time and what has come to be augments the divine reality.

God is thus to be conceived on the model of personal being as the unsurpassably self-surpassing. No other can ever surpass God although later states of the divine being surpass earlier states in certain respects (e.g. in their incremental content but not in the quality of their awareness of the actual processes of reality). This does not simply mean that as the processes of reality bring new things into being, God simply comes to know, influence, and eventually remember them as objects. Such a self-surpassingness of successive states of the divine could be a mechanical response to events that did not affect the reality of God. The divine reality itself is affected because God's relationship with all is a matter of internal as well as external relations. As was suggested in the previous chapter, God's incorporation of all in the divine means that God really does rejoice with the happy and feel miserable with the sad. More than our limited capacities ever make possible for us, God shares completely in our experiences.

To ascribe a personal mode of being to God, however, raises the question of how the divine may be appropriately conceived to develop. A personal entity that does not develop has not just become stagnant. It has lost its value. Its state is comparable to that of individuals who have been so totally obsessed with a particular problem that it has become for them the be-all and end-all of existence and who then find a solution to it. Unless they can find other things by which to give goals to their existence, their continuation will be an empty, valueless persistence. Human finitude, however, ensures that no human being ever covers every possible mode of personal being. In practice there is always room for new developments. Senility and death cut us short of such exhaustion. With God, however, such a fate is not conceivable. But is it possible to think coherently of the divine as endlessly developing, in view of the fact that God cannot deviate from the defining principles of the divine? What is needed is a concept of the divine as personal, worshipful, and instantiating what is ultimate in value. The concept which meets this requirement is that of a restlessly creative God who is exciting and stimulating rather than peaceful.

Traditionally God has often been envisaged as existing in a state of bliss, untroubled by unpleasant feelings. As such the divine has been considered an object of envy and believers have been promised a post-mortem share in the divine state: 'Soon, soon to faithful warriors cometh rest; Sweet is the calm of paradise the blest.' Such beliefs, however, fit uneasily into a Christian theism which finds its central symbol of the divine in the love that goes to the cross. More generally, they suggest that God does not experience much of what happens in the world — suffering, disappointment, misery, frustration, and despair. Granted that unpleasant experiences occur, bliss is only attributable to God at the cost of ruling out the attribution of sympathy (or compassion), since this is the quality of sharing in the feelings of others. Either, then, God is in bliss or God sympathizes: not even the divine can be what is mutually contradictory and instantiate both qualities.

The incompatibility of bliss and sympathy is one case of the general problem for understanding the nature of the divine posed by the non-compossibility of values. To realize some values is necessarily to make it impossible to realize others. Other cases which have relevance to decisions about the concept of God are self-sufficiency and openness to reciprocal relationships with others, controlling others and encouraging them to be autonomously creative, embracing all experiences and being unaffected by evil, and foreknowledge and the enjoyment of novelty. In some cases, such as perhaps the values of mercy and justice or of loving compassion and peace, careful analysis of the apparently conflicting ideas may allow us to regard them as conjointly possible without losing their essential characteristics. In other cases apparent conflicts may be removed by producing a fresh understanding of one or both of the terms under consideration. In *Adventures of Ideas*, for example, Whitehead develops an understanding of 'Peace' which treats it as 'a positive feeling'. According to his analysis it is an active state which 'crowns the "life and motion" of the soul'. While 'difficult to speak of', it is not to be thought of in terms of 'the negative conception of anaesthesia'. Its actuality, that is, does not depend upon ignorance of the grim events of life. Instead the sense of ultimate peace is based on a fundamental 'trust in the efficacy of Beauty'. It is a confidence which is justified by what Whitehead says elsewhere about the universality of the divine awareness of and response to all events. On the basis of this confidence the feeling of peace combines the zest of creativity with the awareness of tragedy in an 'immediate experience' of the reality of final satisfaction in a divinely envisaged 'Harmony of Harmonies'. It is an experience which then shows in practice the final efficacy of beauty as it influences 'the World' by persuasively luring its actual constituents to realize 'such perfections as are possible for its diverse individual occasions' (Whitehead 1933: 367, 381; cf. 368ff; cf. also Dean 1972: *passim*). Nevertheless, while Whitehead's analysis of 'peace' corrects many misunderstandings of what may be meant by that notion, it does not overcome the incompatibility of the apparent 'good' of the absence of unpleasant feelings with the 'good' of being sympathetic. There remain important cases, then, where the attribution of some values entails either the absence of others or, at best, their presence in attenuated forms.

One implication of the non-compossibility of all values is that it is logically impossible for any actual being to possess all values. If it has any use the idea of an *ens realissimum* can only be as an intrinsically incoherent concept of a combination of values that can never have a correlate in actuality. While, therefore, the notion of the divine as possessing all values (as *ens realissimum*) may seem an appropriate way to think of the divine as perfect in value, reflection shows that the notion affirms nothing since it is self-contradictory as a description of a particular entity. Although it may be used to bestow a metaphysical compliment upon God, it leaves unanswered the question of which qualities are correctly to be attributed to the divine.

Since, therefore, the non-compossibility of values rules out Anselm's solution to this problem — which is that as 'the highest of all beings' God must lack no good but be 'whatever it is better to be than not to be' (Anselm 1962: 11) — some way needs to be found of deciding which one of the incompatible values, or which set of incompatible sets of values, is instantiated by the divine. Discounting suggestions that the answer may be discerned through God's self-revelation (on the grounds that a prior understanding of God's nature is needed in order to decide what is a revelation from God), what is required is the discernment of some principle by which the divine nature must be determined in itself as well as in its activity. Aquinas, for instance, holds that God's 'goodness' is the reason for the divine willing those things which are different from Godself (Aquinas 1975: 268). The same principle, however, must apply to the determination of what God is in Godself as well as what God, as the highest good, creates as other than Godself. How, though, is this 'goodness' to be interpreted if it is not to be a formal cipher for the highest value, whatever that be, but to have specific material implications?

The answer lies in recognizing that the highest goodness must be what is valuable in itself and not for the sake of anything else. This rules out pragmatic, rational, and moral notions of goodness because their value is in what they make possible for others. For example, the value of pragmatic goodness, as intended when a piece of machinery is said to be 'good', is a matter of what it enables us to produce with it; the value of rational goodness, as found in true understanding, is that it enables us to be conscious of, and to respond to, what is the case; the value of moral goodness, as actualized in honesty and benevolence, is that it enables us to develop personal relationships and community. In such cases what is called 'good' is valuable not in itself but because of what it leads to. The highest goodness, in contrast, is to be sought in what is rightly regarded as the final goal that justifies these instrumental goods. The form of goodness that has this quality is what may be called the 'aesthetically' good. It is supremely valuable in itself. To hold that aesthetic goodness is another form of instrumental goodness because it gives pleasure is to confuse the satisfaction that characterizes the appreciation of aesthetic value with some further goal for which the aesthetically good is sought. This is mistaken. The aesthetically good is good for no other reason than that it is satisfying in itself. Its value is intrinsic and ultimate.

If this is so, the goodness which determines the nature as well as the activity of the divine is aesthetic goodness. Which of non-compossible qualities or sets of qualities must be attributed to God is, therefore, the one which will result in the greatest possible flourishing of aesthetic value. Whether, for example, God is to be considered to be in bliss or sympathetic, self-sufficient or personally related, controlling others or encouraging them to be freely creative, sharing all experiences or being unaffected by evil, knowing what is to happen or enjoying novelty, is to be decided according to which is found on reflection to have the greatest potential for producing aesthetic value. When we make such judgements, though, we must bear in mind that they are made from our limited perspective and that things may well seem different from the universal perspective of the divine! Even so, the underlying principle of the judgement is valid.

The recognition that the intrinsic, self-justifying good is aesthetic is doubly disturbing. So far as the divine being is concerned it is disturbing because it means that the divine is never satisfied. Creativity never ends. So far as faith in God is concerned, it is disturbing because it means that no believer can ever rest content with what has been achieved: faith calls for exploration of the unknown to create riches not yet actual. If, though, the appreciation of aesthetic value can never be finally satisfied, the divine — and hence the creative influence of the divine in the world — is always restlessly seeking new experiences and novel forms of aesthetic value. Søren Kierkegaard makes the point powerfully in his treatment of the aesthete in *Either/Or* with such pieces as 'The Rotation Method' and 'Diary of a Seducer'. The crucial difference in God's case, though, is that the divine never forgets, disowns, or devalues past experiences of value. What once provided authentic satisfaction in the past is never spurned. It is preserved as a treasure in the divine and contributes its value to further aesthetic adventures. God has thus the historical continuity of personal being which Kierkegaard's aesthete lacks.

If, then, God is understood to be forever seeking the maximization of experiences of value, it is possible to produce a concept of God which is capable of satisfying the demands that the ultimate be thought of as both personal and perfect. There is, however, a corollary of this view of the divine. To conceive the divine as in certain essential respects changeable, having potentiality, and seeking experiences of aesthetic value presupposes that the divine actuality is temporally ordered. Many theologians, however, have opposed suggestions that there is a temporal dimension in God. They have preferred to try to make sense of the divine reality as being in a state of timeless eternity in which all events are simultaneously present to God (*totum simul*). Before closing this discussion of the concept of God as perfect and personal, therefore, it is important to consider this fundamental objection to the view of God being advanced.

When its implications are considered, the view that God does not have a temporally ordered mode of being, since all temporally distinguished events are simultaneously present to the divine, is found to be a view which makes nonsense of any talk about the divine as creative, personal, responsive, and purposive. It also renders the processes of reality pointless. Their processiveness and the apparent openness of future possibilities at any moment only seem to us to exist because we do not share the divine perspective. It is as if we were making our way along a huge mural. We see only a bit at a time and wonder what may come next: God, though, sees it all at once and knows. For the divine, that is, all the events of the cosmic story are 'now' — in a 'now' that has no before and no after. The processes of personal development and the whole story of cosmic evolution are alike illusions. We may think that there is a temporal structure to reality, that each 'present' has emerged as a specific contingent determination out of a range of possibilities and is set between the pastness of previous determinations and a future of open possibilities awaiting determination. For God, though, there is no story, no open possibility; all events are present. There is, therefore, no coherent way of conceiving of God as having purposes, making responses, and acting creatively for all such notions imply a distinction between potentiality and actuality and the move from the former to the latter is essentially temporal — indeed, it is what defines the essence of temporal orderedness. In that case it is as ludicrous to think of God responding to the processes of reality as to think of a child at a film-show changing the story by shouting warnings to the images on the screen.

In view of these absurdities — for it seems over-generous to accept them as 'paradoxes' — why has theological understanding been resistant to the view that God is to be ascribed a temporally ordered mode of reality? The answer seems to be that theologians have generally failed to analyse what is meant by such attribution and what is not meant by it. At least five considerations are involved. When they are examined it appears that there is no

113

sound reason to reject the view that the divine reality is to be regarded as temporally ordered.

The first is the argument that to ascribe temporality to God is to deny the ultimacy of the divine. According to this argument, if God is not outside time, God cannot be the creator of time; if God is not the creator of time, time must be a reality which is independent of God; in that case God cannot be the ultimate ground of all things. The basic error in this argument is the view that time is a kind of reality that exists independently of the events that occur 'within' it. Instead it should be recognized that time is the way in which changes are observed, essentially the change from possibility to actuality. So far, then, as the notion of divine creativity (a notion which will be considered in the next chapters) may be coherently held to envisage God as bringing into being the processes of reality, it may be argued that in their processiveness time also comes into being — but only as an abstraction from those processes and as the way in which those processes are ordered. God cannot, however, be coherently thought of as 'creating time' separately from such processes. Temporality, therefore, is neither prior to God nor created by God: it is the way in which the successiveness of the divine thoughts, actions, and experiences are distinguished by God. The dichotomy, then, that *either* God created time and is ultimate *or* God found Godself in a temporally ordered reality and is not ultimate, is a false dichotomy. There is a third possibility: temporal ordering is part of the creative activity, awareness, and responsiveness of God.

A second consideration sometimes considered to inhibit the attribution of temporal ordering to God derives from the nature of our experience of time. On the one hand there is the rather naïve objection that God is apparently having to wait a long time for cosmic evolution or whatever to reach the goal divinely envisaged for it. However, even if the notion of the processes of reality as having a final goal were tenable (and later this will be questioned), this objection does not seem to carry much weight. The fact that God is aware of the temporal sequence of things does not mean that God experiences 'clock-time' as we do. Furthermore, even that experience is not uniform. The clock may move at one pace but the experience of the passage of time which it records is very different for a preacher who has much to say and members of the congregation who want to get home to lunch! The fact that God's reality is composed of temporally ordered series of events does not mean that the divine is liable to be either bored or rushed. To object on such grounds to ascribing temporality to the divine is to understand God in far too anthropomorphic a manner.

A more sophisticated form of this objection is based on the relative character of our temporal experience. What we now observe as happening on distant stars took place millions of years ago. Inter-galactic communication is impossible for us because the time taken for messages to pass between receivers would be greater than our life-span. All physical events are limited by the speed of light. While, however, this is apparently true of the physical processes we observe (and whether it is or is not is for scientists to determine), there is no reason to maintain that God's mode of experiencing is restricted to the means provided by physical processes. The fact that the laws of physics do not allow us to have simultaneous experiences of all that is occurring now in the universe — or, rather, that they impose a relativistic meaning upon what we mean by 'now' in terms of experiencing — does not mean that God is so inhibited. The 'now' of a moment of concresence, wherever it is occurring in the universe may be coherently thought of as being immediately experienced by God simultaneously with its occurrence. What relativity theory implies is not that such experiencing is impossible for God but that God cannot change what has occurred, even though the knowledge and effects of the occurrence may not be perceived in other parts of the universe for a long time. God may know that some years hence a supernova will be observable on earth. What God cannot coherently be thought of as doing is either making it so that that event did not happen or stopping its effects from being experienced on earth in due time according to natural processes.

A third objection to attributing temporality to God seems to arise from human experience of time as a threat. For human beings, both as a species and individually, time is more than a way of ordering events and experiences: it is a limitation. There were events before we existed and there will be others when we will not be present. Accordingly it is considered that God must be thought of as non-temporal. The fallacy of this objection — which is more often implied than explicitly stated — is that it fails to recognize clearly the nature of the temporal ordering of the divine reality. On the one hand temporality is a limitation for God as it is for human beings in that what is past and the order in which events occurred in the past cannot now be changed. Attitudes to them and evaluations of them may change but not their happenedness and sequence. To claim, though, that this imposes an unacceptable limitation on God is as odd as to claim that the principle of non-contradiction imposes a limitation. It is a limitation, if it can be so described, which is necessary for coherence in experience and responsive action. Without such a structure, even for God, reality would be chaotic and purposive activity impossible.

On the other hand temporal orderedness presents no real threat to God because the divine is everlasting. Just as there never were events to which God was not present, so there will never be events when God is not present, experiencing and responding to all that occurs. Temporality is a threat to human beings because they are mortal. It is not a threat to God because the divine will never perish. Human experience of time, then, is no genuine ground for denying temporality to God.

A fourth objection makes another unwarranted application of our experience of time to God. We get weary. Writing books and, even more, reading them makes us tired. However creative their insights, there is a limit to what we can cope with. We need breaks. The notion of unending activity appals us. We feel sorry for Sisyphus. Thus to ascribe unending activity to God as having everlastingly temporal reality seems to be condemning the divine to a mode of being that is far from perfect. The fallacy of this objection is that it applies our experiences of exhaustion to one whose energies are unlimited. So far as it is legitimate to understand the divine by analogy with human experiences, it is likely that the divine experience of unceasing activity is comparable to a permanent experience of the joy we find when we are so creatively engrossed in what we are doing that we notice neither our use of energy nor the passage of time. The notion of a Sabbath rest is probably a human imposition on God of the sense of needing a day to recover from six days of creativity rather than a proper insight into the divine reality. If God is inexhaustible, there are no grounds for considering God not to be everlastingly temporal.

The fifth objection to holding that God is temporally ordered is that such a state would deny that God has *fore*knowledge. According to this objection — aspects of which were considered in the previous chapter — a God who does not know what is going to happen is less than perfect. One response to this objection is to point out that if God is timeless talk of divine foreknowledge is misleading since there can be no future for God to foreknow. Thus the attribution of foreknowledge to God, if justified, implies that the divine has a temporally ordered mode of being. This, though, is not the decisive objection. The fundamental objection to holding that God has foreknowledge is that it makes a mockery of the temporality of existence. If it is true, while we think we face a future constituted of ranges of possibilities awaiting determination, in fact 'future' decisions and events are already determined and hence are known by God. Foreknowledge, as much as the *totum simul* view of God's eternity, renders temporal existence an illusion. Furthermore, as is clear from the discussions of divine knowledge in the previous two chapters, the essential perfection of divine knowledge does not include a knowledge of what is not knowable and so does not entail having foreknowledge.

On reflection, therefore, it seems that the objections to holding that the divine reality is temporally ordered cannot be sustained by convincing arguments. It is thus possible, by reflecting carefully on the proper material qualities to be attributed to the divine reality and by interpreting them according to the formal structure of dipolar analysis, to conceive of God coherently as having a perfect and personal mode of reality. The question now arises of the significance of the reality of the divine as so conceived for the processes of reality. In the following chapters this will be discussed in terms of the relationship of God to the natural order, to history, and to the significance of human being.

7 God and creation: cosmogenesis

In the early stages of the development of modern science the study of the natural world was held by many theists to provide convincing proofs of the reality of God. The controversial William Whiston, for example, wrote that: 'he who will now be an *Atheist*, must be an absolute *Ignoramus* in Natural Knowledge; must neither understand the Principles either of Physicks or Astronomy.' The size, arrangement, greatness, and gloriousness of the universe give 'many and noble Indications of that Divine Power[,] Wisdom, and Goodness' from which it has arisen (Whiston 1725: 242, 253f). William Derham similarly maintained that astronomical observations of the heavenly bodies show that only '*stupid prejudiced Blockheads*' can deny the universe to be the product of 'an infinitely *indulgent*, as well as *wise* CREATOR!' (Derham 1738: 75, 101). Examinations of 'this lower, and most slighted Part of the Creation' (i.e. the earth) 'plainly argue the Vileness and Perverseness of the Atheist, and leave him inexcusable' in denying 'the Being, and Attributes of the Infinite Creator' (Derham 1723: 426, 428).

At the end of the seventeenth century John Ray (1692) canvassed the realm of natural history to show how its members display the goodness and wisdom of God, their Creator, while at the beginning of the nineteenth the Archdeacon of Carlisle, William Paley, comforted his readers by reminding them of Saturn's rings and of the structure of an earwig. As they lay worried in their beds, they could reflect on that 'intelligent Power' which has constructed a vast ring to overarch Saturn's inhabitants. Closer to home (if less appealingly), they could inspect an earwig: 'the hinges' in its wings and the 'joints of its antennae' witness to the care and benevolence of the stupendous Creator of all things (Paley 1837: iv, 355).

Today such arguments are reminders of an intellectual era long past. Rather than awareness of processes of natural reality being held to provide proofs of the being and character of God as its creator, such awareness is today widely considered to cast doubt on the possibility of apprehending any significant doctrine of divine creativity. There are several reasons for this change. Appreciation of the extent of the cosmos has increased dramatically from the time when Whiston could try to illustrate its dimensions by the distance that would have been travelled by a musket ball fired at the 'Mosaick Creation' some 6,200 years earlier (Whiston 1725: 253). Talk is now in terms of the red shift and of billions of light years. According to one physicist, in a handful of sand there are about 10,000 grains: in the cosmos there are more stars than there are grains of sand on the shores of this planet. Although psychologically it is hard to escape the pre-Copernican anthropocentrism which makes the human the centre of understanding — a form of hubris which currently seeks justification in certain interpretations of the anthropic principle — reflection indicates that human being is but one very recent development in a minute fragment of the cosmos.

As a result models taken from human designing and making and creating appear woefully inadequate to apprehend what it means for God to be creator of the universe. The originating mind and power which could be envisaged as responsible for the universe appear to be so far beyond human experience that it is questionable if remarks about them which are even remotely adequate can have more than formal content. So far as God is held to be the necessary ground of all being, the divine seems increasingly to be that unknown x beyond which in principle no question can be asked but whose intrinsic reality can only be formally defined.

Divine creativity, furthermore, has traditionally been understood as the implementation of divine designs. God's creation of the different creatures has thus been regarded as crudely analogous to the activity of a child with plasticine — except that with superior power God needed no primary 'stuff' and could make the productions 'live'. Modern studies, however, raise serious doubts about the reality of any intelligent and intelligible supervision over the processes of development in nature. In spite of the way that naturalists often use creationist language to describe the objects of their interest, speaking of this or that species as having certain characteristics 'so that' it can crack nuts or probe into crevices or be camouflaged in the desert, the appearance and development of the present state of affairs in nature seem to be the product of the interaction of random changes and chance interactions in particles belonging to structures which generally behave according to the regular relationships called the laws of nature. It is not that ducks, hippopotamuses, oaks, and humankind were designed to be what they are: things seem rather to have turned out that way as the result of a fantastic number of accidental events which led initially to the emergence, and then to long sequences of alterations, of complex biochemical molecules.

119

Although it may not be impossible to hold that some intelligible guiding purpose lies behind these developments overall (cf. Bartholomew 1984), it seems increasingly difficult to maintain this with reference to any particular development that has occurred in the evolutionary process. The understanding of the world suggested by the natural sciences consequently seems to many today to leave no significant place for regarding God as a creative agent, either as an efficient cause involved in the production of particular things or as a final cause exercising a general influence on what occurs.

Whereas, then, theists have traditionally found comfort in the belief that, whatever happens, the actual world is ultimately grounded in the benevolent intentions of God, over the past century perception of the story of evolution, both cosmic and terrestrial, has increasingly cast doubt on the belief that it is directed by any ultimate structure of meaning and value. As they are currently understood, that is, the processes of natural reality appear to offer no support to the basic human hope in the significance and worth of human being. In 'In Memoriam' in 1850 Tennyson remarked that 'Nature' is not only 'careless of the single life': the fossils show her cry to be 'I care for nothing, all shall go' (Tennyson 1912: 392f). More recently, as was mentioned in the first chapter, Monod's reflections on his scientific discoveries have led him to call on humanity to recognize that it is solitary and isolated, existing on the edge of an absolutely indifferent cosmos (Monod 1972: 160). The threat of nuclear extinction may trouble us but an event which destroyed humankind would be a trivial hiccup, probably in the story of the solar system and certainly in those of our galaxy and the cosmos. It would mark the extinction of a production so brief and limited as to be hardly noticeable.

Such understanding, though, is the result of attempting to find intrinsic meaning in reality by considering its observable character and processes. It can be challenged on the grounds that it rests upon three questionable assumptions. In the first place, it may too readily assume that the cosmos constitutes a whole whose significance can be inferred from what we can presently observe of parts of it. Sceptics may even maintain that the notion of a *uni*verse with intelligibility and purposiveness is a rational imposition upon a chaos of random events. If so, apparently adequate models of divine creativity may be dismissed as universal fictions which purport to make sense of the smaller-scale fictions by which we give order to our observed world. On the other hand, if (as arguably we should) we reject such fundamental scepticism about our knowledge of reality, we must not pretend to any other perspective than our own. Consequently we must bear in mind Whitehead's warnings against the inclination 'to take modes of observable functioning of the human body as setting an absolute scale' (1938: 192f) and against 'the self-satisfied dogmatism' which regards 'existing modes of knowledge as final' (1968: 121). Magnitudes appropriate to human experience may be inappropriate for understanding cosmic creativity and the human standpoint may have a distorting effect on attempts to discern what is ultimately significant through considering what can be immediately observed. Attempts to construct a doctrine of creation have to try to avoid unwarrantable pretentiousness while trying to make significant claims.

Second, pessimistic conclusions derived from observations of both macroscropic and microscopic reality may be questioned on the grounds that they rest on an assumed secularism and on the supposition that any meaning in the processes of natural reality must be wholly intrinsic to those processes. Neither presupposition is a necessary condition of understanding. Whitehead, for instance, opposes 'the grand doctrine of Nature as a self-sufficient, meaningless complex of facts'. Instead, he holds, it needs to be recognized that 'all ultimate reasons are in terms of aim at value'. Hence they can only be discerned in terms of life for 'it is the essence of life that it exists for its own sake, as the intrinsic reaping of value' (Whitehead 1938: 180, 184). The life which renders the phenomena of natural reality meaningful may, however, not be directly observable as a part of those processes.

Third, then, it must not be assumed too readily that the only life which could give meaning to the whole must be human life. Upsetting as it may be for human self-esteem, Hartshorne is correct in reminding us that the implied answer to the question 'Does Job serve God for nought?' is affirmative. It is not that the solution to the problem of his suffering in the relation of God to the world is too profound for him to grasp. The divine response brings Job to perceive that 'individual demands are not in order.' The only 'right or reason-satisfying aim' for human life is the service of God, not the pursuit of personal advantage. There is 'no appropriate reward' for such service — but neither is there anything else that a conscious being can wholly live for (Hartshorne 1967: 116f). The ultimate significance of reality, that is, does not lie primarily in what it provides for the peace and pleasure of the non-divine but in the richness of the divine experience which it makes possible.

121

In view of these considerations it is tempting to give up trying to apprehend significant material content in the notion of God as creator. Many theists as well as agnostics maintain that we are not capable of apprehending the creative ground of natural reality. What have generally been offered as descriptions of the creator might have been appropriate for a Ptolemaic or even for an early Copernican view of the universe but they fail to envisage a 'God' who seems big enough for the job of being creator of the cosmos as we now perceive it. The most sensible course is to stop attempting to make sense of what in any case is largely unknown by reference to what is presumably vastly beyond our intellectual capacity. The wise will follow Job's example: they will stop trying to understand (cf. Job 42: 1ff). Cynics may add that in any case if the ultimate meaning of natural reality is not anthropocentrically determined, then so far as human being is concerned there is no real difference between holding and denying that that reality is finally significant. The latter position holds that there is no ultimate meaning; the former holds that there is an ultimate meaning but that it is not centred in human interests. Either way, according to such cynics, humanity is denied that godlike security and status which is the unacknowledged goal of its quest for understanding.

Foolishly or not, however, humanity is discontent with both such silence and such cynicism. As Samuel Alexander points out, Lotze is apparently philosophically justified in asserting that 'to ask the reason why the world was created is a question *mal posée*' since all our notions of 'coming into being, production, causation, willing, decrees, belong to parts of the world and not to the world as a whole'. Nevertheless, while

> the philosopher may expose the unfitness of the question as
> he will; the unregenerate man, and the philosopher himself,
> when he relaxes from his tension of thought, persists in it.
> He is not content to accept the world; it is so mysterious a
> thing that the world should be ... that he finds himself
> unable to dispense with the imagination of a creating agency.

(Alexander 1939: 257)

Whitehead views such questions more positively. He suggests that rather than dismiss them as philosophically absurd, philosophers should recognize that they free their discipline from the suspicion of 'ineffectiveness' when they show how religious concerns and scientific insights can be fused 'into one rational scheme of thought' (Whitehead 1978: 15).

The crucial issue, though, as Alexander goes on to recognize, is not that of determining 'how the world came into being' but that of discerning 'what sort of a thing the world is in its ultimate and simplest nature' (Alexander 1939: 258). That is to say, the important issue is not that of trying to discover the means by which reality came into being out of nothing, like a cosmic rabbit being produced from total emptiness by a supreme magician. As will shortly be suggested, this is an incoherent notion of cosmogenesis through divine creativity. The important issue, rather, is that of trying to determine the structure of reality that ensures its ultimate meaningfulness. This is the question that theism seeks to answer by reference to God. According to its understanding, reality is ultimately meaningful because it is theocentric, grounded on the intelligible and purposive activity of God as creator.

Furthermore, whatever the questions pressing upon human self-understanding, on two counts the credibility of theism depends in part on its ability to give material content to the doctrine of God as creator. In the first place 'If God, then creator' seems a necessary entailment (for a being which is not the creative ground of all reality would not satisfy the definition of what it is to be 'God'); and 'If creator, then continually and universally involved in events' seems a plausible implication (for a God who initiated the creative process and then carelessly abandoned it to its own devices, showing no interest in its productions, is hardly a proper object of worship). Consequently, if both the notion of being creator in general and the perception of the continual activity of the divine are not intelligible, then the basic intelligibility of the notion of God becomes questionable. Second, theology is not an autonomous discipline which exists alongside other forms of understanding: it is essentially committed to the production of an overall understanding which embraces the discoveries of the different sciences in a coherent and satisfying story. Theism, as a form of theological understanding, is thus more than an attempt to identify the activity of one of the agents affecting the processes of reality — the divine agent: it is an attempt to identify that fundamental agency which gives meaning to the whole, rendering it an intelligible, purposive universe rather than a pointless chaos. To cast doubt, therefore, on the possibility of talking significantly about God as creator is to cast doubt on the significance of theistic understanding. Such doubt implies that in relation to the natural world the defining concept of theistic understanding, God as the proper object of worship which is ultimate in being, value, and rationality, is materially empty. It provides no significant and coherent way of perceiving the purpose and character of the processes of natural reality.

What, then, is to be said about God and the processes of natural reality? In *Adventures of Ideas* (1933), Whitehead speaks with some admiration of the theologians of Alexandria because they were concerned about 'the immanence of God in the world'. They wanted to grasp how 'the primordial Being, who is the source of the inevitable recurrence of the world towards order, shares his nature with the world'. For Whitehead himself this 'ultimate question' may be put as that of 'the relation of reality as permanent with reality as fluent' (Whitehead 1933: 166; cf. 1978: 348). Any significant doctrine of divine creativity which attempts to answer that question, though, needs to satisfy five criteria. It must be conceptually coherent in that it describes the creative relation of God to the world in a way that is both self-consistent and appropriate; scientifically tenable in that it fits what current scientific investigations are warrantably claiming to be the character of natural processes; metaphysically significant in that it makes sense of those processes in terms of the ultimate and universal character of reality; theistically important in that it shows that those processes can plausibly be considered to be an expression of divine purposing; and rationally credible in that the doctrine which satisfies the previous four conditions must not seem to be so far-fetched that reflection judges it to be clever but not credible, ingenious but not ingenuous. This is a demanding requirement — but such is the nature of theistic understanding! What can be done to meet it?

In formulating a doctrine of the divine as creative the insights of process thought have much to contribute at the conceptual level. As has been indicated in previous chapters, those insights have to a remarkable degree succeeded in developing a coherent concept of God as 'dipolar' which both recognizes the proper ultimacy and necessity of the divine and, at the same time, permits the ascription of contingent aspects to the divine reality. In particular, by establishing the legitimacy of talking of God as being in certain respects genuinely temporal, all-embracing, aware, responsive, active, and liberating, they make it possible to predicate of the divine verbs expressing temporally ordered activity (such as 'deciding', 'choosing', 'bringing about', 'being affected by', and 'affecting', where each of these refers to a process with a 'before' and an 'after'). Thereby it is possible to present the divine as immediately experiencing all that comes to be (cf. panentheism), and as intentionally affecting all that is to happen in ways that respect the proper autonomy of the created (cf. the notion of the divine power as persuasive attraction rather than as coercive might). A conceptual basis is thus provided for describing the divine as acting purposively to bring into being what was not the case, and as reacting to what has come into being in order to bring about an altered state of affairs.

According to this way of understanding, God may be conceived both as radically immanent within the processes of the natural world and as radically transcendent to them. It makes sense, that is, to consider the divine to be actively creative, self-consciously responding to every actual occasion by seeking to lure its successor towards the realization of the highest aesthetic satisfaction. In place of the widespread notion of the divine as a static ideal absolute, process thought posits the concept of an ultimate being to which intentional activity can be significantly ascribed. A strong doctrine of divine creativity then becomes conceptually possible whereas it is precluded by those views of God which maintain that the divine reality is in all respects a perfect 'unmoved mover'.

In view of these conceptual possibilities, what is to be said about the actuality of the divine creativity? It should be noted in this respect that, at least in contingent matters, while what is true must be conceptually coherent, not all that is conceptually coherent is true. For example, whereas the insights of process thought make conceptually possible a doctrine of creation which envisages the divine as actively engaged in influencing the particular form of each actual event, it does not follow that the divine creativity must be of this order. It is important, therefore, to take account of the other criteria of the doctrine mentioned above and thus to consider what the actual character of the processes of natural reality indicates about the mode of divine involvement in them. As will be indicated, reflection along these lines suggests that the insights of process thought provide the conceptual possibility of a doctrine of creation which is much stronger than the evidence of those processes warrants. In practice the involvement of the divine in the processes has to be considered to be much less precisely directed than believers may desire and some process thinkers have maintained.

In dealing with the divine creativity, though, two issues need to be distinguished, that of cosmogenesis and that of evolution. The first deals with questions about the divine as the ultimate ground of why there is something rather than nothing; the second deals with questions about the divine relationship to the procedures by which the actual states of the natural order have emerged. Although the two issues cannot be totally separated, it is clearest to discuss them in turn. The remainder of this chapter will be concerned with the former issue, that of cosmogenesis.

So far as cosmogenesis is concerned, the traditional doctrine of divine creativity holds that God created the world 'out of nothing' — *creatio ex nihilo*. While this doctrine recognizes the proper ultimacy of the divine, it does so in ways that are open to misunderstanding. The notion of 'creation out of nothing' may be taken to imply, for instance, that in some way the divine primarily existed without a world and chose to create the present cosmos. By affirming the ontological dependence of all things upon God in this way, the notion may be interpreted as implying that creativity is a contingent state of the divine. God in fact does have a world (and so being creative is truly predicated of God) but it might have been otherwise — although if God had not chosen to be creative, no one but God would have been aware of this (or any other) characteristic of the divine reality!

It does not seem possible to deny the contingent status of the divine creativity by referring to the nature of the divine as ontologically ultimate (for this ultimacy seems compatible with holding that it is possible that nothing other than God might exist). Nor is the contingent status of divine creativity contradicted by the combination of the existence of the actual world and the ontological ultimacy of God (for the issue is not whether this world is contingent upon God but whether God could be other than creative and so have had no world contingent upon the divine). It is arguable, though, that being creative must be considered to be a necessary characteristic of the divine existence rather than a wholly contingent quality of the divine reality. Such an understanding may be held, for example, to be entailed by the notion of the divine as essentially personal or as ultimate in value. As personal, so it may be maintained, the divine must be held to be related to what is other than Godself since it is only possible to be personal in relationship to others. Similarly, it may be argued that as ultimate in value God must be considered to be loving (for this is the highest mode of value) and that to be loving requires objects for its expression. Since it is intuitively unacceptable to hold that the realization of the divine love is satisfied by self-love (monotheistic narcissism or a kind of mutual admiration fellowship of the members of the Trinity seems unworthy of the proper object of worship as well as, in the latter case, tritheistically heretical), God cannot be coherently considered to be without a world and so must be regarded as necessarily creative.

Does the claim that creativity is a necessary attribute of the divine contradict the definition of God as the ontologically (as well the valuatively and rationally) ultimate? It may be argued, for instance, that being unable to be without a world is incompatible with being ontologically ultimate since it implies that at all times there must exist both God and the world. Hence the world must be necessary as well as God. Furthermore, so far as Whitehead's remarks on the matter are to be taken into account, it may be added that some of his statements suggest that God may be subject to creativity rather than being the truly ultimate. In *Process and Reality*, for example, he writes of God as 'the primordial creature', and of creativity itself as 'that ultimate notion of the highest generality at the base of actuality' (Whitehead 1978: 31). According to his 'philosophy of organism' the 'ultimate is termed "creativity"; and God is its primordial, non-temporal accident' (ibid.: 7).

Whitehead's statements, however, are not to be understood as denying the ultimacy of God but as elucidating essential characteristics of that ultimacy and of the nature of God's actuality. So far as the divine ultimacy is concerned, it is not that God is subject to creativity as if this existed prior to and independently of God and brought God into being. Rather, the situation is that God is the self-grounded ground of all else, the bare existence of the divine being dependent on nothing other than Godself. To be God, however, is necessarily to be creative. 'Creativity' is neither a force or principle which exists independently of God and to which God must conform in order to be authentically divine (a version of the rationalist misunderstanding of the divine nature); nor is it brought into being by a necessarily arbitrary act of will by the divine (a version of the voluntarist misunderstanding); rather 'creativity' is to be seen as an essential quality of being God. The 'ultimate' may thus be called 'creativity' because God, as the ultimate, is necessarily creative. The issue of God's ultimacy accordingly becomes the question of whether God is to be deemed to be less than ultimate because God cannot be other than creative and hence must always be the ground of some world (and so some world must always exist). When it is appreciated that creativity is the actualization of value, and that the actualization of value is the self-justifying final goal of activity, then to say that God cannot be other than creative is not to diminish God's status but to recognize a necessary characteristic of the divine as personally agential.

Furthermore, when Whitehead states, in connection with the relation of creativity to the divine, that God is 'the outcome of creativity' and 'a creature transcended by the creativity which it qualifies' (ibid.: 88), his remarks must be interpreted in terms of his previous statement that 'in all philosophic theory there is an ultimate which is actual in virtue of its accidents' (ibid.: 7). In other words, Whitehead is not maintaining something called 'creativity' made God exist but that what God *actually* is is the product of the creativity of the divine. God has the actual character of being now the God of this world rather than the God of some other cosmic order because, through the influence of the divine creativity, it is this rather than any other world which has emerged and contributes its own novelty to the all-embracing nature of the divine (cf. ibid.: 349).

Granted that to be God is to be necessarily creative, the issue of cosmogenesis raises the question of whether it is coherent to conceive of God as in any way initially determining the fundamental form of the present cosmic order. In principle, the necessary creativity of God entails that God must always be related to some world; it does not entail, though, that God must be related to any particular order of reality. Although the divine perfection entails that God must always choose the best (i.e. that which will produce the highest value), it is possible to consider that there may be different possible cosmic structures which are equally 'good' and therefore that cosmogenetically God, as creator, initially decides which one is to be actualized, at least for the current cosmic epoch. If so, it may make sense to consider that God primarily determines, for instance, what shall be the cosmic constants and the so-called 'laws' of nature. Hartshorne, for instance, writes of God as having 'adopted certain contingent "decrees" or intentions' which structure 'our contingent cosmic situation and us creatures in it'. These 'acts of God' are identifiable as 'the laws of nature' (Hartshorne 1967: 90, 102; cf. 1970: 137; 1976: 17; 1985: 113). In this way God is conceived as choosing what kind of a universe it is within which the processes of nature occur. In defence of such a view, it may be argued that only as making such a fundamental choice is the ultimacy of the divine properly recognized.

In an article some years ago I advocated such a view of the divine creativity. I argued that it was important to distinguish between truths that are a priori for God and for us (which truths must apply to any possible world as they are necessarily embodied in the divine), and truths which are a posteriori for God and a priori for us (which truths are established by God as a personal agent in choosing to create this particular world) (cf. Pailin 1974: 188f). I am no longer convinced that such a distinction can be sustained. In the first place, it entails that there are at least two equally good cosmic structures beween which God, as the creator of this particular cosmic order, has had to choose. This is because if one structure were better than any other, God, as the worshipful and so perfect, would have to choose it. Second, if God were to have such a choice, it must be arbitrary since there could be no reasons for choosing one structure rather than any other if the options were equally good. Third, it may be held that such a notion of divine selection may be rendered compatible with the everlasting creativity of the divine by holding that if one cosmic epoch perishes, God immediately chooses the order of its successor. The result, however, resembles more the somewhat limited deity of the Noachian story who gets tired of an existing world and moves to replace it with another than the properly worshipful God of infinite patience, care, and resource who unceasingly seeks to save the world by using 'what in the temporal world is mere wreckage' (Whitehead 1978: 346).

There is, however, an alternative — and much more satisfactory — way of understanding the cosmogenetical significance of the ultimacy of the divine. This takes up Whitehead's view that the 'divine ordering' of possibilities according to their 'effective relevance' for the actual world is 'itself a matter of fact' which 'conditions creativity' (ibid.: 31). Accordingly, as he puts it later, 'the primordial nature of God is the acquirement by creativity of a primordial character' (ibid.: 344). What this means is that while creativity in itself is an utterly formless movement of novel syntheses in the processes of reality, the limits of the possibilities for change (and hence the fundamental structures of the cosmos) and the relative ranking of those possibilities are determined by the essential nature of the divine in which they have their reality as possibilities. They are not selected by God but are given in, as, and by the divine reality. God, that is, does not choose that the fundamental structure of the world shall be of this rather than of that order (e.g. that the relationships between the powers of the cosmic constants shall be of this rather than of that order, and that the basic 'laws' of nature shall produce this rather than that pattern of statistical regularity). Rather, the nature of God is such that everlastingly, without beginning and without end, the world that exists is limited by the possibilities which the being of God instantiates. In this respect God is 'that actuality. . . in virtue of which there is physical "law" ' (ibid.: 283).

By denying the coherence of the notion that God once had no cosmos and then initially brought something into being, this understanding of the cosmogenetical role of the divine avoids problems of the incompatibility of maintaining both that the divine is essentially creative and that there was a decision and an event when the divine created the cosmos 'out of nothing'. It also is an understanding which accords with the perception that the ultimacy of the divine includes being ultimate in rationality — being, that is, that which is the final reason of all things and itself, except in so far as the divine being is intrinsically self-explanatory, the a-rational end of the quest for understanding (cf. Pailin 1974: 193f).

So far as the fundamental structure of reality is concerned, Whitehead makes this point when he states in *Science and the Modern World* that

> God is the ultimate limitation, and His existence is the
> ultimate irrationality. For no reason can be given for just
> that limitation which it stands in His nature to impose. . . .
> No reason can be given for the nature of God, because that
> nature is the ground of rationality.

(Whitehead 1927a: 221f)

Later, in *Process and Reality*, he puts it that God does not choose 'the categoreal conditions' which provide the fundamental order of the creative advance of reality; they are both exemplified and established in the 'primordial' aspect of the divine actuality (Whitehead 1978: 344; cf. 344ff). The ultimate determination of the creative character of reality arises, that is, from the intrinsic nature of the divine. It is not a matter of divine selection but of divine being. When, therefore, Whitehead writes of God's transcendent 'decision' as 'the actual entity in virtue of which the *entire* multiplicity of eternal objects obtains its graded relevance to each state of concrescence' (ibid.: 164), his use of the term 'decision' must not be interpreted as implying a selection between possibilities (whether or not consciously made) but as indicating a final determination (cf. ibid.: 43). This determination is given by the divine being.

What in that case becomes of the traditional distinction between the necessity of the divine existence and the contingency of the existence of the non-divine? It is not destroyed but it needs to be more carefully analysed than has often been the case in theological discussions of the relationship between God and the world. Some of the complexity of the relationship is indicated by the list of antitheses which Whitehead presents towards the end of *Process and Reality* when he states, for example, that 'It is as true to say that, in comparison with the World, God is actual eminently, as that in comparison with God, the World is actual eminently,' and that 'It is as true to say that God creates the World, as that the World creates God' (ibid.: 348). The divine necessarily exists whatever may happen; nothing brought the divine into being and nothing can destroy the divine being. Furthermore, God exists as the one who embraces all occasions in Godself and who seeks to lure the processes of reality in the cosmos so that future occasions will actualize the maximum aesthetic richness. What the divine actually experiences and seeks to influence, however, is contingent in part upon what happens in the cosmos according to the free actions of its constituents.

While the essential creativity of God thus means that the divine is never without constituents of a cosmos to embrace and future ones to influence, there is no necessity that any particular constituent should exist. That it has come to be at all (i.e. as a specific actual occasion with precisely that form) — and so how it is experienced by God — is not only contingent upon the possibilities determined by the intrinsic character of the divine — what Whitehead refers to as the 'primordial' nature of God. It is also contingent in part upon the limitations for its own novel synthesis given by its inheritance of the novel syntheses which decided the actual forms of unimaginably huge numbers of previous actual occasions as well by the chance opportunities for interaction between them. A different decision in the synthesis of one of its predecessors, however remote, would have meant that it would not have existed. For example, if one of my ancestors fifty generations back had not mated with another of them, I would not now exist as this particular person having, as every other person has, a 'genetic fingerprint' unique to myself. Alternatively if one of the nucleotides in the DNA chain in one of my cells had been slightly altered last year by a cosmic ray from a supernova millions of light-years ago which had just passed through the earth, the person constituted by the route of inheritance from those and a host of other ancestors might now be dead rather than worrying about whether the notion of divine creativity makes sense!

Whereas, then, the divine must be present at all the actual occasions of the non-divine and while there must always be some such occasions, the distinction between the 'necessity' of the divine and the 'contingency' of the non-divine is such that whereas God cannot not exist, no particular non-divine actual occasion must happen to be. There could be a world without it. Indeed reflection quickly shows that the chances of there being an actual world which includes it are hugely remote. The perception that this is the relationship between the existence of God and the existence of all else is a valid insight of the so-called ontological argument (cf. Pailin 1968; 1969a).

A further problem with the notion that God is essentially creative concerns the possible goal of divine creativity. It seems that creative activity must seek to actualize something if it is not to be aimless. If God's goal in creativity is ever achieved, however, the creative activity of the divine will cease. There will be nothing left for it to achieve. In that case, if creativity is part of God's essential being, God will be at an end. Are, then, theists faced with the choice of holding *either* that God's creative purpose will never fulfil its goal (and so God will be endlessly frustrated), *or* that God's creative activity is aimless, *or* that God is self-directed towards suicide and so towards absolute meaninglessness? None of these options is appealing. The puzzle, though, only arises if God's goal in creativity is seen as a material goal — a particular state of actuality that can be envisaged as achievable. It disappears once it is recognized, as Whitehead puts it, that the notion of 'a final order' is the product of the 'fallacy that all types of seriality necessarily involve terminal instances' (Whitehead 1978: 111). Contrary to Tennyson's 'one far-off divine event/To which the whole of creation moves' (1912: 448), the proper goal of divine creativity is not to be evisaged as the attainment of a particular state of affairs but as the continual pursuit of aesthetic enrichment. What God seeks, that is, is the proliferation of experienced value. Each actual state of affairs is both valued by the divine for its own sake and seen as the basis from which further values are to be sought. The divine creativity is thus unending but not aimless, for its 'end' or 'aim' is the experience of novel forms of value.

By conceiving the divine goal in creativity in formal rather than material terms, the problem of its unendingness is overcome in a way that is theistically satisfying. The notion that God's creative activity is unending raises, however, the question of God's influence on the ongoing processes of the natural order. It is, therefore, time to move from the question of cosmogenesis to that other aspect of divine creativity which was earlier distinguished — the issue of evolution. How is the divine creativity related to the processes by which the natural order develops?

8   God and creation: evolution

In the last chapter it was maintained that the creativity of God is not to be understood as a one-off, distant act of cosmogenesis whereby God came to have a world and determined its fundamental structure. It is, rather, a relationship with the non-divine which always has been and always will be the case. What, though, is the nature of that relationship? In particular, how is the influence of God on the evolutionary processes of nature to be perceived? This is the question of the concrete significance of holding that God is creator. It is also the question of God's responsibility for what emerges. Consequently, as will be considered later, it has considerable importance for the formulation of, let alone any possible answer to, the supposed problem of natural evil in the world.

The traditional doctrine of creation in Christianity is that God produced the world as we find it today by acts of productive 'fiat'. According to the first story of creation in Genesis, people were inserted into a prepared setting as creatures with moral responsibility and a unique relationship to God. The second story changes the order but the basic meaning is the same: things are as they are because God has so made them. Humanity's special significance is assured by God's purpose in creating the world. This doctrine was generally accepted within Christendom up to the end of the eighteenth century and, for many believers, through much of the nineteenth.

It may seem odd so long after the publication of Darwin's *Origin of Species* and other works in this field to have to make the point but the current resuscitation of 'creationism' perhaps makes it necessary to state that such creationist views of the God–world relationship are not compatible with the evolutionary findings of modern science. When today a scientist says that a humming-bird has a long beak so that it can probe into flowers and a hare has protruding eyeballs so that it can watch for enemies approaching from behind, *so that* does not imply a deliberate purposiveness in the benevolent providence of their Maker. It is to be understood as referring to the current function of the organ as it has emerged through the largely accidental processes of evolutionary development.

The current advocacy of 'creationism' in certain quarters may be interpreted as another expression of the intellectual

133

obscurantism found in some forms of religious belief. Not only is it an obscurantism which arises from confusing firmness of faith with the endorsement of an earlier age's views. It may also be condemned as effectively promoting atheism since it refuses to wrestle with the actuality of God. The object of its faith is a religious teddy bear, a figment of pious imagination which has only accidental links with reality, both divine and non-divine. In this respect 'creationists' provide good examples of what Freud identified as the illusory nature of theistic belief. On the other hand, the resort to 'creationism' may have less discreditable aspects. It may be seen as a reaction to the threat of meaninglessness apparently posed by recent discoveries of the character of natural processes. Frightened by what is being discovered, believers are tempted to affirm the old forms of belief in God as creator in order to justify their convictions about the ultimate significance of reality. This, though, is in effect an attempt to affirm that significance by refusing to admit the existence of the understanding which calls it into question. It is the vain, though emotionally understandable, reaction of people dying of cancer who refuse to admit that they have the disease.

Creationists often give the impression that either the traditional understanding of the doctrine of creation must be affirmed or the doctrine has to be dropped and atheism affirmed. This is deceptive. There are other possibilities. One major attempt to present a theistic doctrine of creation which takes account of the understanding of the evolutionary processes in contemporary biology is offered by Arthur Peacocke. He suggests that while God established the fundamental structures and basic natural laws of the cosmos, its present constituents have emerged through the interaction of forces subject to the interplay of chance and order contained within those structures and governed by those laws. Evolutionary development occurs as the resulting process explores the possibilities open to it. According to Peacocke, though, this process is to be seen as the immanent creative activity of God, present 'in, with, and under the very processes of the natural world from the "hot, big bang" to humanity' (Peacocke 1986: 96). But while the divine is involved in all created things, God is not exhausted by the universe but transcends it in a way that is comparable to the relationship between the self and its body (cf. Peacocke 1979: 132, 148; 1986: 96f, 99). Holding, then, a panentheistic view of God as 'all the time creating' (*semper Creator*) (Peacocke 1986: 95), he compares the creative activity of the divine to that of a bell-ringer working through all the changes on the bells, and to a composer seeking to unfold 'fugally all the variations and combinations inherently possible for and derivable from the tune he originally called' (Peacocke 1979: 210; cf. 105f).

When, though, Peacocke describes current scientific under-standing of the nature of evolutionary development, he appa-rently finds no place for divine involvement in the particular states that the process produces. Natural development occurs through a combination of chance and necessity. This is how the divine creativity is to be understood to act. In his Bampton Lectures, *Creation and the World of Science*, for example, he writes that he sees

> no reason why God should not allow the potentialities of his universe to be developed through the operation of random events. . . . Or to change the metaphor, it is as if chance is the search radar of God, sweeping through all the possible targets available to its probing.
>
> (ibid.: 95)

Just before he uses the analogies of bell-ringer and composer, he speaks of the potentialities of the universe as being 'written into creation by the Creator himself' but as being 'unveiled by chance exploring their gamut' (ibid.: 105). Taking up the Hindu image of the play of creation, he suggests that God's enjoyment of the world is in experiencing the varied things that come into being as the different constituents of the universe interact with each other.

In a later work, *God and the New Biology* (1986), he notes the criticism that what he offers is an 'absentee-landlord' view of God. His response is to emphasize that the purposiveness of the divine creativity is to be perceived in the fundamental structures of natural processes. The laws of thermodynamics and chemical kinetics, in particular, are such that 'the interplay of chance and law bring about that increase in complexity' through which novel 'organised forms of matter appear, both non-living and living' — and, it may be added, must eventually appear in some form or another. The 'potentialities' contained in the 'particular "given" properties and law-like behaviour' of the world are thus to be seen — at least by the theist — 'as written into creation by the Creator's intention and purpose' and as 'gradually actualised' through chance events which explore their whole range (Peacocke 1986: 97f).

On the one hand, therefore, Peacocke clearly wants to maintain that the processes so describable are to be seen as the expression

135

of unending divine creative activity. He states, for example, that the Creator may be 'imagined to unfold the potentialities of the universe which he himself has given it, selecting and shaping by his redemptive and providential action those that are to come to fruition — an Improvisor of unsurpassed ingenuity' (ibid.). This is a strong — and theistically attractive — image of God as immanent and creatively active in the evolutionary processes of the cosmos. On the other hand, what follows in the next sentence undermines that image and makes it questionable whether Peacocke is justified in suggesting that God is deliberately active in influencing what happens within the evolutionary process. He writes that God

> appears to do so by a process in which the creative
> possibilities, inherent (by his own intention) within the
> fundamental entities of the universe and their inter-relations,
> become actualised within a temporal development shaped
> and determined by those selfsame inherent potentialities.

> (ibid.: 98; cf. 1979: 104ff, 210)

Rather than support the view that God influences what appears in the evolutionary process (by 'selecting', 'shaping', and improvising), this latter sentence implies that while God initially established the potentialities of the constituents of that process, it develops autonomously.

To understand creation in this way both gives the ultimate creative grounding of the cosmos to God and, granted that because of that grounding there is chance as well as necessity in the interactions of the cosmos's constituents, is readily seen to cohere with what is currently understood to be the character of evolutionary developments within the natural order. It is important, though, also to note that this way of understanding divine creativity suggests that God does not affect what particular forms of being emerge in the natural order. Having determined the basic structures and laws of interaction, God on this view seems to have neither direct nor even indirect influence on what happens — until, perhaps, human beings (and presumably other beings in the cosmos with comparable attributes) appear whose distinctive qualities allow them to be conscious of and responsive to the divine. The natural order is thereby considered to have a theistic ground in a way that is compatible with the belief that it develops to a large extent in what seems to be a haphazardly accidental manner. It is in the historical order that God is considered to be more directly and continually involved by interacting with people in a person-to-person manner — an understanding which will be examined in the next chapter.

This way of perceiving the relationship of God to the world is not restricted to theologians and believers like Peacocke who are concerned to render theistic belief compatible with current findings in the natural sciences. It is a view that is typical of most post-Enlightenment theology even though it is implicit in the structures and emphases of that theology rather than explicitly asserted. Since the time of Paley and Kant, with a few notable exceptions such as F. R. Tennant, theological understanding has in practice treated the historical order as the major locus of theological insight. Having found difficulty with the notion of God as creator, modern theologians have followed both the Kantian location of theological understanding in the practical reason and the historically orientated bias of the biblical witness. The result has been a concentration on the relationships between the human and the divine which preserves what amounts to a pre-Copernican anthropocentricity in its approach to reality. Even those neo-orthodox theologies which stress the 'otherness' and 'absolute sovereignty' of God do so in practice in relation to the human situation before God.

Popular forms of Christianity have, in contrast, never completely given up the recognition of God as Lord of nature as well as of history. However questionable may be the literal meaning of the words, congregations of believers continue to sing:

> All things bright and beautiful,
> All creatures great and small,
> All things wise and wonderful,
> The Lord God made them all.

and:

> I sing the goodness of the Lord,
> That filled the earth with food;
> He formed the creatures with His word,
> And then pronounced them good.

In doing so they witness to a religious conviction that when theology neglects the relationship of God to the natural order it ignores a vital aspect of the significance of theistic belief.

According to such understanding theology needs to conceive God as creator as involved in all the processes of reality. Otherwise the object of its faith will be mutilated. As Lewis Ford puts it, if faith loses its 'cosmological framework' by being confined to matters of human encounter, 'then we have no way of appreciating God's activity and ... concern toward the rest of the created order'. As a consequence faith and theology will be 'in danger of succumbing to a global anthropocentricity' in its 'existential preoccupation' (Ford 1978: 16f). The kind of understanding that believers seek is illustrated by what John Wesley wrote in his tract, *The Earthquake at Lisbon*:

> Let us even dare to own, we believe there is a God: nay, and not a lazy, indolent, epicurean deity, who sits at ease upon the circle of the heavens, and neither knows nor cares what is done below: but one, who as he created heaven and earth, and all the armies of them, as he sustains them all by the word of his power, so cannot neglect the work of his own hands. With pleasure we own there is such a God, whose eye pervades the whole sphere of created beings, who knoweth the number of the stars, and calleth them all by their names: a God, whose wisdom is the great abyss, deep and wide as eternity.

(Wesley 1812: 407)

For those who share such a theistic faith, there are major deficiencies in the view of God presented, for example, by Peacocke. By understanding the divine as establishing the basic structure of reality and then apparently leaving it to run its course, at least until the human appears, it seems to leave us with a lazy and indolent deity. Implicitly, if not explicitly, it denies to God as Creator any significant role in the details of the development of the natural order and it suggests that there is a radical distinction between God's relationship to nature and to history.

Is, however, Wesley's form of theistic belief credible? It may be that here, as elsewhere, believers are trapped by their desire for security into entertaining stories about a reality that does not exist. Faith in an active, immanent, creative God may be an illusion. Is there any intellectually convincing way of combining what such believers have traditionally held to be the activity of the divine with what scientific investigations currently suggest to be the character of the evolutionary process by which natural reality develops? According to some the resources of process thought provide the basis of such an alternative. Charles Birch, for example, holds that the concepts and insights of process thought about reality make it possible to understand creation as incorporating 'the ever present activity of God, without becoming identified with it'. God not only preserves the created order in being but also 'participates in the life and being of his creatures' (Birch 1968: 194). As a result 'the sacred and secular, the natural and the divine, are not uniquely separate divisions of reality'. It is legitimate to seek a synthesis of scientific insights and religious faith in a coherent understanding (ibid.: 194f; cf. 200). On what grounds may such a claim be held to be justified?

Evolutionary developments occur as a result of very long sequences of events. In each of the relevant events, through the exercise of freedom intrinsic to the concrescence of an actual occasion and through the chance interaction of such contingent occasions, the ordering of the constituents of the DNA molecule governing the genetic inheritance of a particular creature is minutely altered. Most of the alterations which occur have self-destructive results. A few, though, are benign, if not at once positively fruitful. In time they may combine with other alterations that occur to lead to perceptible evolutionary changes in the creature's descendants.

According to the understanding of the process of reality developed by Whitehead and Hartshorne, God is involved in each occasion of actuality. The concrescence of an actual occasion involves its own creative synthesis of what it prehends of the divine. This prehension includes both the divine valuation of previous actual occasions, including that of its own immediate predecessor, and the divine envisagement of possibilites (which Whitehead calls 'pure potentials for the specific determination of fact, *or* forms of definiteness' (Whitehead 1978: 22)), including its own initial subjective aim (cf. ibid.: 108, 244). God thus influences each momentary event. But while God's ordering of the structure of reality ensures that to a massive extent each concrescing occasion conforms to its immediate predecessor, the divine presentation of alternative possibilities provides the ground for minute changes in each occasion's self-creation. Each actual occasion composing the enduring object which is a DNA molecule is thus able to contribute to the evolutionary development of that molecule (and so to the creature genetically produced by that molecule) by its own particular synthesis of what it prehends of what Whitehead refers to as the 'consequent' and 'primordial' aspects of the divine reality.

What are grasped as evolutionary developments are the patterns resulting from minute changes in the actual forms of vast numbers of genetically linked occasions. While, though, as the locus of possibility, God is the necessary ground of all changes, the divine influence on the process is not deterministic. God's creative activity is exercised as an influence which seeks to 'lure' or 'persuade' each concrescing occasion to actualize that form which will result eventually in the greatest aesthetic satisfaction overall. This 'luring' is effected by means of the attractiveness of the 'conceptual harmonization' which the concrescing occasion prehends in God (ibid.: 346; cf. 244f, 343ff). God's creativity is hence conceived to be an unceasing activity which is effected through the divine luring of each concrescing occasion. Nothing at all happens without God being involved in it and, in the consequent nature of the divine, being totally aware of it. How specific, though, is the form which God seeks to persuade a particular concrescing occasion to instantiate?

According to Whitehead, each concrescing occasion not only prehends in the divine the range of states which it is possible for it to actualize, graded in importance according to their relevance to its situation (ibid.: 244). It is also given in its constitutive prehension of the divine an initial subjective aim (or basic conceptual aim). When this latter aim is considered in the light of Whitehead's understanding that in the primordial nature of God each discrete possibility is distinctly envisaged, it may seem to follow that what God presents to each individual concrescing occasion is a precisely defined goal. The occasion is being 'lured' to take just this rather than any other concrete form — although, of course, it is open for it to use its creative freedom to actualize one of the other possible states open to it.

Some of Whitehead's statements, however, may be interpreted as suggesting that the goal which is set before each concrescing occasion as its initial aim is not so precisely detailed. It may, rather, be understood to take the form of a more general directivity. While, that is, God is the ground of all originality in the world (cf. ibid.: 108, 244), the specific form to be taken by a particular concrescing occasion is partly left to its own self-determination. Whitehead states, for instance, that 'each temporal entity ... derives from God its basic conceptual aim, relevant to its actual world, *yet with indeterminations awaiting its own decisions*' (ibid.: 224; my italics). Again, 'while the initial stage of the aim is rooted in the nature of God', its 'completion' is held to depend on 'the self-causation' of the subject. The transition from the occasion that has just perished to the actuality of its successor, is therefore said to involve 'self-determination' which is 'always imaginative in its origin' (ibid.: 245). While, however, these remarks may be interpreted to suggest that the initial aim itself requires determination by the concrescing occasion, it is also possible to interpret them as indicating that while God gives as the initial aim a precisely determinate goal (a single eternal object), the occasion has autonomy to decide whether it shall actualize that aim or some other relevant eternal object. On either interpretation, though, God influences the process of reality by luring each concrescing occasion, whether precisely or more generally, in a particular direction.

In *God and the World,* John Cobb similarly suggests that the divine creativity acts as an urge towards greater complexification (Cobb 1969: 64, 67). He writes of God's agency as a 'call forward' (ibid.: 52) which summons each entity 'beyond the mere repetition' of its predecessors to 'finer and richer' states (ibid.: 82; cf. 64, 67, 91f). Evolution is thus regarded as the emergence after billions of years — and inconceivable numbers of successive actual occasions — of enduring individuals which have high degrees of complex order and which are capable of novel syntheses with rich aesthetic value. What Whitehead and Cobb describe as the creative activity of God may be expressed in more scientific terms as that tendency in natural processes which brings it about that there appear areas of intensification and complexification of forces as localized alternatives to the general tendency of the second law of thermodynamics.

How does process thought envisage the manner of the 'luring' or 'persuading' by which God influences acts of concrescence to move in the direction of greater aesthetic enrichment? Basically its understanding of this aspect of the evolutionary process not only uses but depends for its intelligibility upon a psychical (or panpsychic) view of the constituents of reality. According to Whitehead, for instance, the problems of mind–matter dualism are to be overcome by recognizing that each actual entity has internal as well as external relations: 'each actuality is essentially bipolar'. It has a 'mental' as well as a 'physical' aspect (Whitehead 1978: 108). Each concrescing occasion may thus be described as responding to what it 'feels' its environment to be. Consequently the difference between the organic and the inorganic is not that the former alone has internal relations but that it has the capacity to consider more complex ranges of data and to produce richer novel syntheses of them than the latter. Nevertheless, while 'mental activity is one of the modes of feeling belonging to all actual entities in some degree', Whitehead makes it clear that this mentality only amounts 'to conscious intellectuality in some actual entities' (ibid.: 56; cf. 101f; cf. Cobb 1969: 71ff; Birch and Cobb 1981: 134). In the vast majority of actual entities the 'mental' grasp of data is very rudimentary and unconscious; in comparatively rare higher-grade occasions it is conscious; in very rare cases of the highest-grade occasions it is self-conscious.

141

By holding that each concrescing occasion 'prehends' or 'takes account of' the data of its environment (including the datum of its own predecessor in a route of occasions), process thought treats each occasion as a 'subject' which has 'feelings' and makes 'decisions', however primitive and unconscious they may be. Each entity is thus ascribed a subjective aspect. As such it can respond to lures and select the goal for its own self-satisfaction. In this way the psychical understanding of reality makes it possible to apply a notion of final causality to the process of evolution. It also overcomes the problem of how life and mind emerged. The notion that something could be solely matter is a mistake: no actual entity utterly lacks subjective responsiveness and mentality. What may remain as a problem, though, is to discern how the mental activity which belongs to all actual entities developed into the conscious and self-conscious forms which it has in such a complex nexus as the human self.

Attempts are made to defend such a physical understanding of reality by arguing that our view of the nature of things should be based on what we know best, namely ourselves. Instead of seeking to make sense of ourselves in terms of the models by which we conceive of the increasingly obscure realms of physical objects, cells, molecules, atoms, electrons, quarks, and gluons, we should rather see the latter by analogy with our self-awareness of the former. Hartshorne, for example, states that he agrees with Heidegger, Peirce, Whitehead, and 'many others' in maintaining that 'all our best thought is anthropomorphic in the sense that we must take our own reality as sample of reality in general — the sample we most surely and adequately know.' Even in physics, we find that we can make sense of other things only by generalizing from our own experience of our own being (Hartshorne 1985: 116; cf. Peirce 1931–5: 5.46f, 5.212, 5.536; Whitehead 1938: 214). Since, then, this is the character of understanding, it is argued that there is no good reason to object to attributing a pattern of 'feelings', at least in an analogical sense, to each actual occasion and to treating its self-determination as a 'decision' which synthesizes those 'feelings' in a 'mental' act.

The way in which evolution is accordingly understood in process theology has a number of attractive features. God is held to be intimately involved in every event: the divine both ensures that there is general order and acts as a localized lure which exerts an opposite pull to the tendency towards increasing entropy. Life is considered to be a matter of the choice of novelty orientated by the desire of aesthetic satisfaction. Change occurs as the constituents for an enduring object make decisions which alter the genetic inheritance of their successors. Undetermined inter-actions of two or more actual occasions result in chance develop-ments — as when a particle emitted by a radioactive substance strikes a particle in a DNA molecule and both these independent (or, to be strictly accurate in this social universe, both these practically independent) routes of inheritance are accidentally altered as a result. Finally, while God lures all concrescing occasions, the divine creativity is restricted to the influence which can be exerted over the decisions of somewhat auton-omous individuals.

As Lewis Ford suggests, the resulting picture of God and evolution 'sees the future as organically growing out of its past' and divine providence 'manifest in creation' as acting by persuasion. God is immanent in all events, everlastingly seeking to elicit 'the maximum richness of existence in every situation' — though with hugely varying responses (Ford 1978: 23ff). The result is a story which, according to some process theologians, may justifiably claim to be a biologically valid, metaphysically appropriate, theistically significant and rationally credible way of uniting belief in God as universally and actively creative with what current studies indicate to be the method of biological evolution. Unfortunately, when we move from observing the general character of the story to examining its details, it becomes much less plausible.

One problem with this way of understanding God's creative involvement in the evolutionary processes of nature concerns the effectiveness of divine activity. Traditional ways of reconciling claims about divine power and creaturely freedom depend upon postulating some kind of divine self-limitation. Although poten-tially irresistible, God's power is held in practice to be restrained by the creative purpose of bringing into being creatures with limited autonomy. This solution, however, still leaves problems. Is it compatible with the divine love and purpose to restrain the divine power as much as seems to happen? The enormity and destructiveness of some forms of evil raise questions about the justification of such divine restraint. Should not a good God who potentially has the power to protect creatures from apparently pointless destruction be expected to actualize that power to ensure that they can fulfil the divine purpose in creating them? To be a good father means that I give my children freedom to develop their potentialities in their own way. It is far from obvious, however, that this means that I should stand idly by when my failure to intervene will result in their destruction by factors beyond their control and outside their anticipation. So to 'respect' their autonomy would be self-defeating.

It is on these grounds that Hume criticizes the standard free-will solution to the problem of evil. He suggests that

> a being ... who knows the secret springs of the universe might easily, by particular volitions, turn all these accidents to the good of mankind and render the whole world happy ... and yet would no more seem to disturb the course of nature or confound human conduct than the present economy of things where the causes are secret and variable and compounded. Some small touches given to Caligula's brain in his infancy might have converted him into a Trajan.

> (Hume 1935: 254)

Even today, when the regular procedures of nature are much more finely understood than in Hume's day, a similar protest is possible. By minutely altering the code given by the sequence of the nucleotides in a DNA molecule, it is arguable that God could halt the career of a Hitler or prevent the development of a malignant tumour. What evils could thus be stemmed! That God fails so to act makes it seem reasonable to doubt the divine goodness if the divine wisdom and power to be able to do such things have been correctly appreciated.

Does the view of God's creative activity in process thought offer a way forward? As has been noted, its understanding of divine activity strongly emphasizes that the purpose of God's creative activity is to produce beings with a large degree of autonomy and that the divine relationship to those beings is one of loving persuasion rather than of coercion. It therefore suggests that the supremacy of divine power (or divine 'omnipotence') is not to be conceived as God's power to do whatever God wants but as the recognition that the creatures can never overcome God, either by destroying God or by stopping God seeking to lure them towards states of greater aesthetic richness. On this basis it is arguable that process thought shows that the supposed 'problem of evil' is a mistake because it rests on the presupposition that God's power over all creatures is either potentially or actually deterministic. Instead, natural evil, while undesirable and undesired by God, is to be recognized to result from several factors, acting either individually or in combination.

Natural evil may be the product of the non-compossibility of several values — 'the nature of evil is that the characters of things are mutually obstructive' (Whitehead 1978: 340), or the

outcome of random chance conjunctions, or the result of unsuit-
able conditions — 'insistence on birth at the wrong season is the
trick of evil' (ibid.: 233). Furthermore, it is arguable that what
may seem to us to be evil may in fact be a side-effect of the
fulfilment of divine cosmic purposes to which we contribute but
of which we are not necessarily the end. Above all, evil as we
experience it may be attributed to the free decisions of individual
entities not to actualize those values which God sets before them
as their initial conceptual aim. Whitehead describes these 'revolts
of destructive evil' against the wisdom of the divine aims as
fated eventually to be 'dismissed into their triviality of merely
individual facts' to the extent that they fail to contribute to the
harmony and advance of 'universal feeling' (ibid.: 346). In
the meantime, though, their effects can be highly unpleasant.
According, then, to the understanding of process thought, the
possibility — and hence the actuality — of evil does not constitute grounds for denying the reality of God's activity. Its possibility is entailed by the nature of that activity being one of
creative love which deals with partially autonomous creatures.

It is questionable, though, whether this view significantly
undermines the force of the argument that the presence of natural
evil in the world is a huge objection to the goodness of God so
long as God's power is considered to be a capacity to influence
(even though by lure rather than by force) what occurs in the
world. While there may be much to say in favour of regarding
the divine influence on the created world as being exercised by
the attraction of realizable values rather than by compelling
force, it is not clear that the difference is very significant. In
practice a sufficiently attractive 'lure' may be as compelling,
perhaps even more compelling, than coercive might. The lure of
a great value may bring us to accept privations which no amount
of brute force would make tolerable. In that case, so far as the
actualization of evil states is due to decisions being made which
are out of harmony with the ideal aim presented by God, it is
arguable that the result is God's responsibility. A different result
could (perhaps inevitably would) have ensued had the divine
lure been sufficiently attractive — 'sufficiently attractive', that
is, to prevent agents making 'self-regarding' decisions which
result in evil. In this respect the change from the 'willed limitation
of power' of the standard free-will defence to the 'lure' of process
thought is of doubtful advantage in solving the problem of evil —
although, it must be allowed, the fact that the process position
offers no improvement on the former 'solution' does not make
it inferior to it.

The discussion of the problem of natural evil bears directly upon the question of God's influence on the evolutionary process for it indicates that in practice it is not at all clear what is to be attributed to God in that process beyond a general urge to creative complexification in the combination of the basic constituents of actuality. If divine influence is not to be expected to prevent the actualization of particular destructive entities, it does not appear that it may be held responsible for the emergence of particular beneficent ones. Piety may feel compelled to put the blame for all evil on creaturely freedom and to ascribe all good to God but this ascription of responsibilities does not seem to be at all justifiable by reference to the evidence of things. It is a form of the worship which pays compliments without substance.

When, therefore, we consider the specific case of evolutionary processes, we find that although Birch and Cobb state that 'Life' (their term for 'the central religious symbol' (1981: 195) — i.e. God) is an 'enormously powerful' 'cosmic principle that works for higher order in the midst of entropy', they recognize that in 'vast areas of the universe' this 'Life' has 'little effect'. It can elicit the kind of 'spectacular transformations' which are found on earth 'only when very special conditions exist' (ibid.: 189). What they say seems indisputable. In that case, then, it does not seem appropriate to describe this 'cosmic principle' as an intentional creator who exercises effective influence over the formation of the particular genera and species, let alone individuals, which occur in the natural order and therefore, to a significant extent, can be judged to be materially responsible for what emerges in it. In reality reference to 'God' appears to add nothing significant to the claim that by chance some changes very occasionally occur in fundamental biological structures which turn out, by accident, to be beneficial in the sense that they lead to the appearance of beings with higher aesthetic potential.

Ian Barbour attempts to counter the scepticism about divine creativity implied in the last statement by arguing that 'chance' alone does not give a satisfactory understanding of what happens: it is also necessary to refer to 'law' to produce a credible understanding of how complex and relatively stable combinations of particles, atoms, and molecules have appeared in the cosmos. Furthermore, he maintains, the 'dice' which decide the chances of interaction and combination must be held to be 'loaded' (Barbour 1966: 387). Nevertheless, even when such 'loading' and 'natural laws' are taken into account, the restrictions on changes happening by pure chance which they indicate do not seem to be sufficiently materially important to justify being described as the way in which a divine creator is intentionally active in forming the natural order.

The major problem with the process understanding of divine creativity, however, is that it apparently presupposes a psychical (or panpsychic) view of reality whose significance is fundamentally questionable in spite of the arguments mentioned earlier in this chapter which can be advanced in its favour. So far as the concrete form of an actual occasion is regarded as the product of various constituents, there seems to be little difficulty. Its actual form emerges out of the mutual interaction of various factors — it is 'the product of the interplay of physical pole with mental pole' (Whitehead 1978: 308). Doubts about the sense of what is being asserted begin to arise, however, when it is recognized that this 'interplay' is a matter of internal resolutions which are described in such terms as 'choice' and 'decision'. According to Whitehead, for example, 'the concrescence of each individual actual entity is internally determined and is externally free.' In its self-determination each actual entity is a subject which comes to a 'final decision' that is a 'modification of emotion, appreciation, and purpose' (ibid.: 27f; cf. 24, 43, 46f). This decision is not a simple resolution of those factors. It involves a creative evaluation of them (cf. ibid.: 47). Each actual occasion is thus said to be a subject which is 'the autonomous master of its own concrescence' and whose self-determination is 'always imaginative in its origin' (ibid.: 245).

At the level of human being, such language makes sense. As Whitehead puts it, the self's 'unity' consists of 'the process of shaping' its 'emotions, enjoyments, hopes, fears, regrets, valuations of alternatives', and 'decisions' into 'a consistent pattern of feelings' (Whitehead 1938: 228). This description rings true. Indeed, the use of concepts such as 'choice' and 'decision' to describe our self-actualization is warranted because it is from our awareness of this process of internal relations in ourselves that they are derived. Furthermore, as Whitehead also points out, 'we find ourselves living within nature' and there is no observable justification for a rigid distinction 'between mentality and nature' (ibid.: 214). There is, therefore, some reason for holding that the process of self-constitution which we find in ourselves is an appropriate way to understand all forms of reality. Finally the defenders of psychicalism may argue that we are faced with only three possibilities: materalism, dualism, and psychicalism. The first is to be rejected because it is not consistent with our self-awareness; the second involves unnecessary complications and unsolved problems; the third is therefore to be entertained because it can account for all forms of being.

It is not clear, however, that physical notions can be meaningfully used to describe the process of actualization which produces the nexus that is now a single living cell or a molecule or any one 'of the happenings on an infinitesimal scale, disclosed by the minute analysis of modern physics' (ibid.: 215). R. G. Collingwood, for instance, thought that such a way of understanding was 'only a dodge to evade the question, how does anything generically new come into existence?' (Alexander 1966: I, xviii). The question of the meaningfulness of psychicalism is made more puzzling, furthermore, by Whitehead's frequent reminders that not all experiences and mental operations involve consciousness (cf. Whitehead 1978: 23, 56), let alone self-consciousness. The problem in that case is to discern the content of the language about 'choice', 'decision', and 'self-determination' as applied to the internal relations of the actual occasions which make up by far the greater part of nature. It appears that concepts which are derived from our awareness of our personal being are being applied to types of reality which lack the fundamental characteristics to make such descriptions significant. If, for example, 'mentality' is 'merely latent' at the level of the 'activity studied by physicists and chemists', and if 'the lowest stages of effective mentality' involve only 'the faint direction of emphasis by unconscious ideal aim', how can each occasion be held significantly to constitute itself by an 'aesthetic process' acting on its prehensions (Whitehead 1938: 230f; cf. 1978: 245)? The result is that on analysis the psychical description of reality as a whole seems to be either meaningless, misleading, or deeply obscure.

Turning to the specific matter of the course of evolution, the difficulty with the story told by process thought focuses in this respect on the question of what is to be understood by the language of 'lure' and 'persuasion' used to describe God's creative influence on what emerges. At issue here is both the primary emergence of and then subsequent changes in the information patterns constituted by the ordering of the nucleotides in the DNA and RNA macromolecules.

One problem facing any attempt to identify significant and specific divine influence on evolutionary developments is, as Barbour puts it, that at the 'lower levels' of reality 'physical patterns predominate over mental ones, law over freedom, and efficient causes over final causes'. Another problem is that since God is one of many factors affecting the becoming of an actual occasion, the divine contribution to the emergence of any novelty may be undetectable (Barbour 1966: 450). To what extent, then, is it both meaningful and rationally justifiable to regard God as purposively affecting the development of particular patterns of nucleotides in DNA and RNA molecules? Only if such an influence can be judged credible can the divine creativity be regarded as more particular in its guidance than a general determination that the basic structure of nature involves a tendency to develop stable combinations of particles together with the possibility that sometimes an actual occasion will not accurately replicate its predecessor but will actualize a very slightly changed form.

Lewis Ford, for example, uses the psychical understanding of reality developed in process thought to argue that divine creativity is not limited to the 'cosmological function' of supplying an 'impetus towards greater complexification'. He asserts that God also 'serves as a lure for actualization, providing novel possibilities of achievement' which are intended to achieve that 'modicum of spontaneous response' that is 'possible even on the atomic and molecular levels'. Consequently, although atoms and molecules are for the most part 'traditional in their habits', God may so lure them with 'the urge to maximize the possibilities' in the situation that they actualize 'some evolutionary advance' (Ford 1978: 59).

The credibility of such a conception clearly depends upon the acceptability of a psychical view of the realities involved. In an attempt to make such a view acceptable Barbour emphasizes that we should recognize that Whitehead's language in this respect is somewhat metaphorical and that 'events in a cell have only an incipient mental aspect whose contribution is negligible in practice'. Both their inheritance of their predecessor's form and their response to their environment involve at the highest nothing more than 'an exceedingly attentuated form of aim or purpose' (Barbour 1966: 451). Such a defence of psychicalism, however, attempts to make it palatable by so restricting its characteristic notion that it is doubtful if it can any longer serve as a distinctive way of understanding the character of evolutionary (or any other) events.

It has already been noted that Whitehead holds that the self-determining 'decision' of an actual occasion does not imply conscious deliberation (Whitehead 1978: 43). When, however, all elements of awareness and introspective choice are eliminated from the decision-making, it is questionable whether what is then called the self-determining 'decision' of an actual occasion is distinguishable from an automatic resolution of the factors which it prehends, with a small amount of randomness also possibly involved. By employing terms like 'decision' to explain what happens in evolutionary development, process thought uses ideas whose basic meaning comes from self-conscious mental activity. Even if the application of such ideas to non-conscious levels of reality is not nonsensical, its meaning is very puzzling. As the Swansons ask, 'What could it mean to say that an amino acid [perhaps we should say 'this particular molecule of amino acid'] . . . has subjectivity? . . . Does it really make sense to say that an electron entertains abstract possibilities and decides among them?' (Swanson and Swanson 1978: 48).

A further problem with this way of understanding evolution — and one which follows from the previous difficulty — is that it is doubtful whether it makes sense to describe God as attempting to 'lure' or 'persuade' a particle, an atom, a molecule, or a nucleotide to modify its form or its situation when such an entity is not conscious. Such notions, and complementary expressions like 'responding to' and 'freely embracing' a novel aim prehended as a divine lure (Ford 1978: 59), lose their distinctive content when predicated of non-conscious entities. In such cases God's 'lure' or 'persuasion' seems to be just one force among the many which interact together to determine what comes about. Consequently, since evolutionary changes are due to alterations in the structure and relationships of the components of a DNA molecule, it does not seem meaningful to conceive of those alterations as the result of 'lures' or 'persuasions' which 'attract' the actual occasions of the relevant enduring object to 'decide' to take forms which occasionally result in fruitfully novel patterns. On the other hand, if talk about divine 'luring' or 'persuading' turns out to be a rather misleading way of describing one factor among the many whose unconscious interaction 'decides' what happens, God is not exempt from responsibility for the result. In the case of non-conscious entities no 'freedom' is preserved by God choosing not to determine what occurs. The failure of divine influence to secure its own ends simply shows that God is not exercising sufficiently potent 'luring' to be overwhelmingly effective. Whatever happens, God is responsible: either God has acted powerfully enough to effect the divine will or what has happened varies from the divine will because God has failed to exercise sufficient power. But the fact that the divine apparently does not so act may not be evidence that God is unnecessarily ineffective but rather evidence that this model for understanding divine activity is misleading.

Finally, genetic developments come about when nucleotides alter their positions or are replaced by different ones in a DNA molecule. According to process thought, furthermore, a nucleotide is an enduring object which may be treated as a series of nexus of actual occasions. It does not seem appropriate, though, to conceive the route of succession of a nucleotide as subject to divine influence in the same way as the history of a human being may be so conceived. Speaking of human being Cobb states, for instance, that God 'entertains a purpose for the new occasion, differing from that entertained by the previous human experience. He seeks to lure the new occasion beyond the mere repetition of past purposes and past feelings . . . to finer and richer actualizations' (Cobb 1969: 82). In contrast, the divine will for the lower levels of reality may be considered to be almost wholly for accurate repetition.

If, though, God is to be regarded as having a specific influence on what evolutionary developments produce, the divine must presumably be conceived, by analogy with what is said about the divine influence on human beings, as occasionally 'luring' nucleotides to swop places or to drop out of a DNA chain or to insert themselves into one at a particular place. Consideration of the changes that are known to have occurred in nature suggests, however, that if God has been creatively active in this way, then either the divine influence has been exercised extremely rarely or, as seems more likely, it has been hugely ineffective. Biological studies indicate that far more abortive changes occur than potentially fruitful ones. Of the latter most genetic variants are stored until in a few cases suitable conditions arise for their use. Consequently, even if some sense could be made of the notion of divine persuasion in the case of such entities as nucleotides, the ineffectiveness and vast wastefulness of the process undermine the credibility of regarding it as an expression of a divine creativity which purposefully guides evolutionary developments in specific directions. Birch and Cobb (1981: 193) accept that the evolutionary method of relying on 'random mishaps' to bring about changes seems enormously wasteful but they hold that it is not 'extraordinarily inefficient' since this way of producing variations seems to result in 'the maximum value' (ibid.: 47). For others the conclusion is different. The resulting picture of God bears more resemblance to a pathetic park keeper feebly whistling at a barking, scrabbling, rampaging pack of dogs to get them to come to heel, or to a yachtsman fussily trying to push aside an ore-carrier, than to the intentional agency of the proper object of worship affecting the course of evolutionary developments.

In view of these criticisms, does process thought offer any alternative to the notion of divine creativity in evolution as a series of specific lures which attempt to make specific alterations in chains of nucleotides? There is such an alternative position. It finds expression in a number of works on process theology. Interestingly, it also largely agrees with the position developed by Arthur Peacocke which was discussed earlier.

According to this view evolutionary changes occur by chance at the level of the DNA. Some DNA molecules accidentally mutate in ways that are not immediately self-destructive and eventually turn out to have been potentially fruitful. Hartshorne, for example, holds that while some 'chance variations' occur as the result of the fortuitous combination of the parental genes, other more important ones — 'mutations' — are due to 'chance encounters between particles (such as cosmic rays) and the genes' (Hartshorne 1984: 68). Birch similarly describes evolutionary changes as the product of 'random mutations' and suggests that when the vast length of the genetic series and the influence of selection are borne in mind, what first might appear 'improbable' becomes 'probable' (Birch 1968: 212). More recently in his joint study with Cobb it is stated that 'once in a few million or a few billion times the replication of the multiplying cells is not exact'. Very rarely this accidental error in copying the DNA may code 'a message that confers characteristics that enhance the chance for survival and reproduction' (Birch and Cobb 1981: 46).

If particular evolutionary mutations happen fortuitously rather than through the influence of specific divine intentions, is there any significance in the notion of divine creativity? There is, but what the notion connotes is much more general than has been maintained by traditional views of God as creator and is desired by those believers who want to have the assurance that all is fundamentally well because it is as God constructed it. As creator, God is to be understood as affecting the fundamental processes of nature throughout the cosmos so that they have, at least in certain regions, a tendency towards increasing complexification and novelty. God's creative activity, that is, is to be conceived as ensuring that the constituents of reality belong to a process which combines stability with an appropriate degree of openness to novelty, and which contains an intrinsic urge towards combination in increasingly complex patterns. What particular things evolve within this cosmic structure depends, however, on the accidental interactions of the individual entities within it. God is not to be thought of as attempting to direct, lure, or persuade the evolutionary process to develop any specific forms. Nevertheless, having determined that the process has a bias towards complexification, God may be regarded as enjoying the value of whatever emerges from the process. It is also arguable (see Bartholomew 1984) that God knows that the in-built tendency of the structure of reality will eventually produce some kinds of higher-order nexus which are self-conscious, free, significantly autonomous, and capable of contributing to the divine experience corresponding degrees of aesthetic enrichment. Human being is the highest order of such nexus of which we are aware.

This way of understanding the creative role of God will not be congenial to insecure souls who want the comfort of believing that everything is as it is because God has so planned and made it. On the other hand, the view that God as creator establishes the structure within which actual occasions are drawn into complex nexus by chance interactions within an overall order of natural laws and that God appreciates and preserves the value of all that thereby comes into being can justifiably claim to be an understanding which is biologically tenable, metaphysically significant, theistically important, and rationally credible. If so, it provides an understanding which gives some material content to the notion of God as creator and to the world as a significant product of divine purposing and a significant object of divine enjoyment.

It also, incidentally, exposes the supposed 'problem' of natural evil to be an illusion. In asking of earthquakes, droughts, viruses, and cancer, 'Why did a benevolent God make such things (or allow them to exist)?' the question presupposes a view of divine responsibility for what happens in nature which is radically mistaken. If God did not plan or make the specific entities which have emerged in the natural order, there is no theological problem about their emergence and activity in the natural order. Some of them may be unpleasant and need to be avoided or eradicated as far as possible in the interests of human flourishing but that they are here at all with their particular characteristics is no more God's fault than it is due to divine intention that we exist with the capacity to see and hear within certain wavelengths. At this point, though, we move to considering the significance of history and human being. This is the subject of the remaining chapters.

9 God and history

Since it is difficult to identify specific activity by God in directing the course of natural evolution, some theologians turn to history — and to human beings as the agents of historical events — to find the location of God's personal activity. Human beings, so they allege, are both conscious and self-conscious. Hence it is coherent to conceive of them as being influenced by 'lures' and open to 'persuasion'. They also have a sensitivity for the divine. Accordingly, God may be expected to be more directly and continually involved in events through interacting with people than through influencing nature.

This divine involvement does not entail that God must be considered to determine human actions. It does suggest, though, that it is plausible to think of God as able to exercise a guiding influence on human decisions, perhaps by something analogous to person-to-person relationships. It is a view of the relationship between the divine and the human which is apparently congenial to the ways of understanding developed in process thought.

This last claim may seem surprising when it is remembered that in his contribution to *Faith and the Philosophers,* Hartshorne describes 'the positivist demand that the mere existence of God make a factual difference' as 'the unwitting demand that God be a created demon, and not the universal creator' (Hartshorne 1966: 29). The justification of this remark lies, of course, in his distinction between existence and actuality and in his recognition that statements about divine existence report what is common to every possible state of affairs. Their content is thus highly abstract and identifies no particular state.

Such statements, however, are not likely to satisfy those who want to discern the significance of theism for human being in the world. What such people want to discover is what practical differences God makes as to how individuals live. What, to put it crudely, does God *do* for and with people? If Hartshorne is correct in maintaining that the only satisfying purpose of 'an ideally powerful and everlasting being' is 'to love the creatures which are dependent upon him' (ibid.: 29), their question asks theists to identify what God's love means in practice for life in this world. By answering this question theists will establish that when they refer to 'God', they are not merely speaking in a pictorial way about the being (perhaps Being) that is the necessary ground and recipient of all events, perhaps also using 'God' as a cipher for the ultimate source of possibilities and hence of the processes of reality. They will show, to use Gordon Kaufman's terminology, that the word 'God' can warrantably claim to carry 'important material connotations' as referring to what is 'personal or agential in character' as well as to have 'highly formal meaning' as designating 'the ultimate point of reference' which relativizes all else (Kaufman 1975: 14).

Some critics, though, argue that process theology is unable to provide a satisfactory answer to the question of God's activity in history. Langdon Gilkey, for instance, suggests that it cannot deal satisfactorily with 'God's redeeming activity' since 'it is hard for one decisive act, let alone an ontologically unique act, to enter the system intelligibly' (Gilkey 1973: 25). More recently John O'Donnell has argued that the 'perspective' of a 'God who raises the dead' is properly 'alien to that of the process world-view' since the latter requires a metaphysical conception of 'God's relation to the world'. For such a conception what is to be described as divine activity is 'according to metaphysical necessity'. According to O'Donnell this places 'severe restrictions on the kinds of divine initiatives that Christians have tradition-ally wanted to affirm' (O'Donnell 1983: 106f). In addition, as was mentioned earlier, Colin Gunton critically misunderstands the logic of Hartshorne's position to claim that it 'actually precludes the taking of initiatives by God' (Gunton 1973: 294; cf. 1978: 81).

Leaving aside for the moment the issue of what theists may warrantably affirm about divine activity, examination of Harts-horne's understanding of God (which presumably is to be accepted as a standard example of process theology) strongly suggests that these criticisms are unjustified. Although as a metaphysician he is predominantly interested in the necessary aspects of the divine reason and as a critic of 'classical' theolog-ical thought in emphasizing the passive aspects of that reality, and although he does sometimes indicate that claims about divine activity are empirical or theological matters involving faith as well as reason (Hartshorne 1966: 33), throughout his works there are passages which recognize the contingent agency of divine activity. In *Man's Vision of God* he writes of 'God's choice ... in deciding at what point to check or encourage or redirect this or that' (Hartshorne 1964: 291). In *The Logic of Perfection* he argues that the concrete nature of God's love for me as an individual is a matter of 'empirical fact': it cannot be deduced from a 'concept like "perfect love" plus the fact of my existence' (Hartshorne 1962: 109). In affirming the contingent activity of God in human history, however, Hartshorne is careful to make it clear that the divine agency is not coercive. While affecting every event, God does not absolutely determine what actually occurs. The divine will influences rather than controls human decisions (cf. ibid.: 143; 1967: 58f).

Hartshorne's remarks about contingent divine influences on human activity fully accord with his theistic conceptuality. As was discussed in earlier chapters, what is necessary and absolute in God are qualities of the abstract existence of the divine. As such God can never in principle be other than perfectly knowing and perfectly loving. The concrete actualization of that nature, however, is relative to and contingent upon both what happens to be there and what God chooses from among non-compossible alternatives to be the divine aim for that situation.

Hartshorne's understanding of divine activity in history applies to human being the same concept of divine influencing which was discussed in the previous chapter with reference to evolution. Whereas, however, there are fundamental problems in using psychical notions of lure and persuasion in the case of entities like nucleotides, it is not prima facie implausible to use them in the case of personal being like our own. Judging Whitehead's insight that persuasion is the 'divine method of world control' to be 'one of the greatest of all metaphysical discoveries', Hartshorne suggests that God 'molds' us through 'molding himself'. Each moment God presents each of us with 'a partly new ideal or order of preference which our unselfconscious awareness takes as object and thus renders influential upon our entire activity'. We are thus changed by God as God inspires us 'with novel ideals' (Hartshorne 1948: 142).

At the same time, Hartshorne is uncertain about the extent to which we may justifiably claim to be able to perceive — and hence, presumably, deliberately to harmonize with — the particular form of the divine will for us at any moment. He states, for example, that:

> With regard to the contingent actuality of deity, wishful thinking is not only possible, it is only too probable and pervasive. How do I and my motivations appear to the divine love? Here every kind of self-serving, self-indulgent or masochistic error is possible. For we are no longer, in raising this question, dealing with necessity. We are dealing with contingent possibilities, not all of which, and not necessarily the most desirable of which, are actualized.

> (Hartshorne 1966: 30)

When, therefore, we seek to identify God's will for us and to decide our response to that will, we 'need faith as well as reason' for we are dealing with concrete questions to which any response 'must be partly intuitive and pragmatic, if you will — existential' (ibid.: 33).

The difficulty of reaching specific apprehensions of the contingent aspects of divine agency raises, however, the question of whether references to it in process thought have in practice any substance. Can they be shown to do more than express a general conviction that somehow, for some good ends and with some effect, God influences human actions although we are very much in the dark about the actual character, goals, and effectiveness of that influence? Unless such references can be made more specific and justified as such, it may be argued that they do not offer any significant improvements on either the comforting illusions of fanatics that they are doing God's will or the irritating affirmations of a Dr Pangloss that 'everything is for the best' (Voltaire 1947: 35). Against the charge of illusoriness, process thought may properly claim to be affirming metaphysical truths; and, against Pangloss's naïve Leibnizianism, to be taking seriously the freedom of creatures to frustrate the divine will. Is it able, though, to go beyond abstract affirmations of value by providing specific guidance for individuals struggling to identify and then to realize the divine will in their own lives?

These questions gain rather than lose their force when the treatment of divine activity in other expositions of process thought are considered. Schubert Ogden's investigation of what is meant by 'God acts in history' concludes, for example, that the phrase refers to 'certain distinctively human words and deeds in which his [sc. God's] characteristic action as Creator and Redeemer is appropriately re-presented or revealed' (Ogden 1967: 164). This 'action', though, is not to be understood as 'an action in history, but as action that *transcends* it' and so 'cannot be simply identified with any particular historical event or events' (ibid.: 179). Since God's decisions provide some, but not all, of the influences that are involved in what happens, divine activity is realized in history as and where human individuals perceive the divine will and then re-present it through their words and deeds (ibid.: 180f). In response critics have argued that such talk about God's agency in history is to be interpreted as a matter of giving a final stamp of approval to certain human actions (Griffin 1971: 352-4). They maintain, that is, that according to this way of interpreting them, statements about divine activity do not give information about what God does as an agent but about which human actions which are taken to conform to what God wills.

Daniel Day Williams similarly suggests that 'the divine action need not be thought of as a matter of super-causality behind the scenes through which everything happens' but as 'the continual divine self-communication' which presents to people both goods to be attained and the support of a 'loving reality' in 'the depths of all things' (Williams 1968: 129; cf. 1964: 161–80). What this means for Christian faith at its highest is seen in the incarnation for there 'God has won man's response without destroying his freedom': the life of Jesus is the life of a free, finite, and dependent human being whose fulfilment was found 'in obedience to the will of God' (Williams 1968: 165). But when we try for ourselves to identify 'what God is doing now, or precisely how he has acted, or how he will act', we are in difficulty since 'we have no way of extricating the acts of God from their involvement in the activities of the world' (Williams 1964: 180). Having, then, no clear procedure for determining the will of God in particular cases, we are always in danger of mistaking the divine intention.

John Cobb's analysis of divine activity likewise seems to lose its significance when we attempt to apply its general principles to actual practice. He too claims that God is to be understood as the source of novelty who 'entertains a purpose' for each new occasion of human experience and seeks to lure it 'to finer and richer actualizations' (Cobb 1969: 82). The attractiveness of his presentation of God as 'the One Who Calls' begins to fade, however, once we begin to investigate what God is specifically calling us to do as individuals in particular situations, and how we experience, apprehend, and authenticate that call. Having learned that the divine Logos is immanent in all things as 'the power of creative transformation', readers are likely to be disappointed to be told then that this Logos 'is effectively, if unconsciously, present and felt in all events' (Cobb 1975: 77). It is the 'unconsciously' which is the trouble. It implies that while God calls we may have no sure ways of discerning the particular calls to us.

What Cobb and others describe accords with what many people find to be their experience. Whatever religious tradition suggests, there are no clearly identifiable calls of God that can be apprehended from moment to moment. This means that it is hard to distinguish between a situation in which we are called 'unconsciously' and one in which there is no such divine call. If

God's agency is held to occur through our unconscious experience, can we ever be confident that there is a genuinely agential God who influences human beings in specific ways for particular ends and, if there is such a God, that we know what we should do to conform to the divine will? These are questions which arise when the process view of divine activity is explored. Perhaps some critics are not so far from the mark in suspecting that in practice, whatever may be said about its principles, the view of divine activity in process thought is far from traditional belief in a God who really does act in and with and through human beings. What seems to have happened is that process theologians have felt compelled by their basic understanding to hold that God acts in the world and hence in history but at the same time they have been confronted by the apparent absence of any unambiguous signs of the divine will and by the need to respect the limited autonomy of human beings. In consequence they have adopted a notion of 'unconscious' influencing in order to present a credible view of divine activity.

It is possible, though, that traditional beliefs about divine activity in humanity and so in history are incorrect. It is also possible that the process view of God as responding each moment to each individual, providing a specific aim for that particular situation, is as mistaken in the case of human being as it is held in the previous chapter to be of the processes of non-human nature. On the other hand, such a conclusion ought not to be adopted without careful reflection. The process view just mentioned preserves something of traditional understanding of God as an agent who acts in human individuals in particular ways to achieve finite goals as well as in general ways for universal ends — that is, as one who brings Abraham to do this, Paul to experience that, Anselm to perceive this and John Wesley to feel that in individual, specific ways, as well as one who wills that all people should 'act justly, love loyally, and walk wisely before God'. In process thought, furthermore, in order to avoid any deterministic implications, the divine activity in respect of human beings is presented as a case of luring, persuading, or calling. Its affirmation, though, is kept credible according to the standard of widespread self-understanding of contemporary human experience by holding that these specific divine calls are rarely, if ever, indisputably recognizable as such. Whatever religious traditions may report about Moses at the burning bush or Isaiah's vision in the Temple or Paul's summons to Macedonia, reports about divine calls today tend to be accepted as the more credible the more they are described as occurring 'unconsciously' and 'ambiguously' — and so in accordance with current believers' puzzlement as to how divine agency is to be identified in human existence.

History does not exist, except as an abstraction, apart from the experiences and activities of individuals any more than an army exists independently of the soldiers who compose it. Constituted by the actions of persons, history also provides the context in which they attempt to perceive the significance of their being. The identification of meaning in history as the process whereby the indeterminations of the future become the determinations of the past is thus a condition of any affirmation of the meaningfulness of human existence. If events happen as a random sequence of 'one emergency following upon another as wave follows upon wave' and without anything that can be regarded as 'a plot, a rhythm, a predetermined pattern' (Fisher 1936: v), then human being, as essentially historical, is likewise to be considered to be a pointless meandering through successive presents. It may be, though, that the plot or rhythm or pattern that renders history meaningful is not to be 'discerned in history' simply by studying its events since it is not a harmony or picture or purposive sequence which is to be found by linking together numerous presents like plots upon a graph and projecting them. The desired discernment may, rather, be a matter of seeing events in history in the light of divine purposes which transcend the particular moments and sequences of the historical order while they are to a greater or lesser extent expressed in them.

The fundamental question, then, which needs to be tackled by theologians who wish to understand the relationship between God and history (and hence the basis for determining the significance of human being) is whether the divine should be regarded as an agent who acts in a particularized, even if in a consciously non-perceptible and non-ascertainable, manner, in that part of the process of reality which is concerned with individual human activity and is directly experienced by individual human beings. Plausible as it may initially appear, it may not be justifiable to hold that without such divine agency history — and hence the lives of persons within history — becomes a pointless sequence of events produced by a myriad uncoordinated wills acting within a natural order constituted by the interplay of chance and necessity. On the contrary, it will be argued in what follows that so far as humanity and the activity of God are concerned, theologians generally (and those influenced by process thought in particular) are not obliged to attempt to make sense of a notion of specific divine purposes and acts in order to maintain the meaningfulness of history any more than they are to affirm the significance of divine creativity in the natural order.

What, then, is to be understood by the notion of the meaning-fulness or purposiveness of history as divinely grounded? In what sense may it be held that there is an agential God who gives meaning to the course of history by guiding it according to some envisaged end, and what may then be conceived as the nature of such guidance and of its intended end? In order to deal with this general question, the rest of this chapter will consider in turn the possible components of a divine ground for the meaningfulness of history, the credibility of the notion of divine agency as involved in each human event in a particular way, and how history may properly be judged to be meaningful without a notion of God acting as such an agent.

First, then, what is required for history to be deemed to be meaningful? According to some this claim is satisfied if history can be shown to have a directivity whose goal is finally satisfying. To reach this goal, if it is a material end, or to seek it, if it is a formal end, is intrinsically self-justifying. Plato, for example, speaks of the Good as such an 'end of all endeavour, the object on which every heart is set' (Plato 1955: 269). Theists have frequently used such notions to describe the nature of God as instantiating that perfection which alone provides the unreserved end for all human endeavour. It may consequently be maintained that history is meaningful because it is made up of the needs of individuals whose lives are confronted by and fundamentally attracted towards this ideal nature, whether it be dubbed 'the Good' or 'God'. Even though everyone is free to some degree to choose how far to conform to this reality, its persistent and universal presence, whether or not it is consciously acknowledged, produces a general bias in the character of what occurs. Overall, the course of events tends towards the realization of the qualities of this ideal, even though in practice the path towards it takes in disastrous detours and the exploration of fruitless blind-alleys.

When, though, Aristotle develops the notion of the good as 'the primary object of rational choice', he maintains that the ultimate must be 'a being purely actual' which cannot be other than as it is. While it affects others 'as an object of love', its influence on them is as a final cause. It is itself absolutely unchangeable (Aristotle, 1955: 258). This is an understanding of the ultimate which finds expression in Aquinas's exposition of Christian belief when he states that while all creatures are related

God and the processes of reality

to God, 'being related to creatures is not a reality in God' (Aquinas 1964: 3, 75).

Whether or not this latter view is acceptable as an interpretation of Christian belief, it may well be judged to be an inadequate basis for affirming the meaningfulness of history. Its inadequacy lies in the fact that while it holds that there is a final end which gives overall directivity to the sequence of events in history, it implies that no historical event has more than temporary significance. So far as human beings are concerned, the significance of an event persists consciously only so long as it is remembered and in effect only so long as there are subsequent events which are importantly influenced by it. Eventually its contribution to the present will become trivial and then undetectable, and even the record of it will disappear. As for the Good or God, according to this view no event makes any impression whatsoever. The ultimate which gives directivity to history is never affected in any way by anything that occurs in history. For a time human beings are aware of some of the achievements of their predecessors and, by appreciating their value, give them some importance. God — or the Good — is never aware of them. Consequently it appears that by conceiving of God as the realization of (or a symbol for) an absolute to which nothing can be added, this form of theological understanding on the one hand affirms that history is meaningful (because it is given directivity by the ultimacy of the divine) and on the other denies that any event has lasting significance (because God is unaware of everything that happens). The reality that gives meaningfulness by directivity to history simultaneously radically disvalues all that happens in history.

A contrasting view of history regards it as a process in which the divine comes to be fully actualized. According to this conception God is not an ideal being, co-present with all that happens and attracting it in a particular direction: the fullness of the divine emerges through what happens. Hegel, for instance, speaks of the intended goal of history as the realization of the Ideal in the 'true existence' of the Spirit (Hegel 1956: 110). A more radical position considers that the ideal is not a guide which pre-exists the process but something which emerges from it. Samuel Alexander thus describes deity as a quality superior to mind 'which the universe is engaged in bringing to birth'. Although 'the universe is pregnant' with this quality, it neither can be contemplated from the human standpoint nor can it ever be fully actualized. Every moment it 'looms ahead, awfully', as a novel quality to be attained. The 'actual existence' of God is

162

thus to be conceived as 'the infinite world with its nisus towards deity' (Alexander, 1966: II, 347f, 353).

Such a view of history may be reckoned superior to that which finds its meaningfulness provided by an unaffectable ideal because it not only sees the process of history as having directivity but also grants significance to each event as a contributor to the outcome of the process in the divine being. What has happened does not perish into oblivion. It is permanently embraced by God. Hegel (1956: 79), for example, writes of the life of the Spirit as one of 'progressive embodiments' in which its form each moment 'possesses' in its depths 'all earlier steps'. Alexander's view is that while 'God is something higher than man or man's creations, knowledge and beauty and goodness', the divine 'absorbs and presupposes them' since it is 'their outcome and they are a preparation for it' (Alexander 1933: 294).

Thus to hold that whatever happens contributes to what emerges may, however, still be judged in itself insufficient to warrant the claim that history is a meaningful process. It may be argued, for instance, that this view gives too trivial a significance to individual events and that the events occur in too random a fashion to justify such a claim. There are, however, ways to counter these objections.

The dipolar panentheistic concept of God developed in process theology and discussed in earlier chapters provides the basis for an effective response to the first objection. The heart of this problem is that when individual events are considered in terms of the whole, their separate contributions to it are so tiny that they are in practice undetectable. To this it can, of course, be replied that every physical object in the cosmos, however large, and so the physical cosmos itself, is made up of 'particles'. While each particle is an utterly minute proportion of the whole, unless there were these constituent particles, there would be no constituted whole. Similarly each historical event that is embraced by the divine reality is important because it contributes its quality to the divine whole which would not be as it is without it.

Such an argument, however, is unlikely to satisfy self-conscious contributors that it establishes their significance as individuals, especially when they appreciate that for the divine each of their contributions is accidental. While the existence of God as all-embracing wholeness is necessary, there is no necessity that the constituents of the divine reality include any particular actual event. Tennyson's 'wild and wandering cries' (1912: 359) thus echo deep human doubt when they recognize the story of 'Nature' to be that not only individual lives but even species are ephemeral: 'I care for nothing, all shall go' (ibid.: 393). In spite of this, he does not close *In Memoriam* in despair. He confidently affirms that the one whom he mourns 'lives in God':

> That God, which ever lives and loves,
> One God, one law, one element,
> And one far-off divine event,
> To which the whole creation moves.

(ibid.: 448)

Nevertheless, whatever may be the case about subjective immortality as the fate of human beings, confidence in the significance of the individual (as contrasted with the meaningfulness of the process of history as a whole) seems only to be justifiable if the divine is credibly to be held to be more than an unconscious recipient of whatever happens — more than a kind of cosmic dixy into which all actions are tipped and in which they lose their distinctiveness as they merge into some divine soup. It requires the divine to be evaluatively aware and consciously preservative of each contribution to the whole in its distinct individuality.

As has been indicated in earlier chapters, the concept of God developed in process thought shows that it is possible to think coherently of God as so aware and preservative. Whitehead, for example, describes God's consequent nature as 'composed of a multiplicity of elements with individual self-realization' (1978: 350). The relation of God to history and humanity finds its best image as 'a tender care that nothing be lost' (ibid.: 346). According to Hartshorne the combination of 'cognitive adequacy' (which means that everything actual and possible is included as such in the divine knowledge (Hartshorne 1948: 120ff) with limitless love means that God cares for us 'as we are' — and 'immortally so, for nothing escapes being woven into the imperishable and living texture of deity'. The resulting unity with God, however, is not an impersonal 'absorption' where individuals lose their particular form, but a personal relationship where 'particulars in their particularity' are 'everlastingly cherished' (Hartshorne 1967: 110f). The 'superrelative' nature of the divine means that just as the many become one so also the one becomes many (Hartshorne and Reese 1953: 514). Individuals thus contribute their own experiences and achievements to the divine reality and there they are for ever distinctly remembered.

It may be argued, though, that the affirmation of conscious divine reception and preservation of all that occurs is not, by itself, enough to establish the meaningfulness of history. What is needed is not only the incorporation of events into the divine but also some overall guidance of the course of events. The nature of such guidance, however, may be conceived in different ways. As has been mentioned, some understand the directivity of history in terms of the attraction of the ideal of the Good — or of God — as the supremely desirable object of adoration. Thus Anselm suggests that human beings are created to 'seek God' as the highest being (Anselm 1962: 20; cf. 3ff). Hegel (1956: 57), on the other hand, writes of the 'perfect' towards which 'actual existence' progresses as 'a *germ* or impulse' which serves as a source of 'instinctive movement' in the imperfect states from which it will eventually emerge. Alexander takes up the notion of artistic activity to argue that creative novelty within the world is not the implementation of material plans by a purposive creator. Just as an artist is inspired by 'his excitement' to discover through artistic activity what gives 'the consummation of his desire', so the directivity of history is the product of an intrinsic 'nisus' which blindly 'impels' its constituents 'forwards' to unknown higher modes of being (Alexander 1939: 276ff).

Others, however, consider that history can only be properly meaningful if it is subject to a more particular form of divine guidance. This view is often linked to the claim that the divine power, awareness, and personal purposiveness must mean that God controls human affairs and hence the course of history. It is a belief which affords much comfort. According to Isaiah God uses kings to implement the divine will (Isaiah 45: 1) and according to Calvin 'the minds of men ... are subject to the disposal of God' as they administer human affairs (Calvin 1953: I, 269f). At times when the future for human survival may look bleak, such claims are reassuring if they can be believed: all will be well, for God is in control of events.

In contrast to such notions of divine domination, process theologians attempt to make sense of divine influence on the course of history in ways which are less threatening to human autonomy. According to Whitehead, for example, God is not to be thought of as a 'ruling Caesar' but as slowly, quietly, and tenderly influencing events by 'his own vision of truth, beauty and goodness' (Whitehead 1978: 342f). Hartshorne similarly affirms that God's guidance preserves the limited autonomy of human beings. God affects human minds by being the 'self-determined ... object of our awareness', changing us 'by inspiring us with novel ideas for novel occasions' (Hartshorne 1948: 139, 142). God, that is, gives purposeful direction to history by presenting each moment to those who are to constitute the next moment the divine vision of their optimum actualization — a vision, though, from which each individual has freedom to deviate. Because of this autonomy the course of events is likely never to conform completely to the divine desire but the ever-present influence of the divine gives ground for presuming that the overall pattern of events will move in the direction which God envisages.

This mode of theological understanding may be held to warrant the affirmation of the meaningfulness of history as having divinely grounded goal, direction, and preservation. God as the proper object of worship provides the final end towards which all things are to move, as the active persuader lures all things towards that end by appropriate steps, and as the conscious recipient of all events ensures that no achievement perishes. Unfortunately reflection reveals that there is a fundamental problem with this position. Is the central notion of divine agency as involved each moment in a particular way with each person credible?

In the previous chapter it was maintained that a parallel notion is not to be used for conceiving God's relationship to the processes of nature. Is it any more appropriate for conceiving the divine relationship to history? It appears that this way of understanding meets one criterion of credibility, namely that of coherence: it is composed of self-consistent terms which are appropriate to the nature of the divine as agential. It is arguable, though, that it does not satisfy another criterion, namely that of being in accord with our personal experience of human being and our observation of events. If such a judgement is correct, this notion of divine guidance of history may have to be regarded as a desirable illusion which indicates the human wish for providential control rather than as an accurate description of the fundamental nature of the processes of history. What, then, are the grounds for doubting the credibility of the notion of particularized divine agency in history?

Those who wish to hold in a strong form the belief that God controls the course of events are faced with a huge amount of counter-evidence. The course of events does not suggest underlying providential ordering. The Deuteronomic historians had to manipulate their materials drastically to make it appear otherwise. Believers today are not describing the world in which they actually live when they chant, in the words of *Magnificat*, of God scattering the proud, deposing the mighty, despoiling the rich, exalting the meek, and filling 'the hungry with good things'. It just does not happen that way. If, alternatively, God does control events, then what happens powerfully indicates that divine activity is not guided by morally good values. A supernatural being who brought about genocide — whether of Jericho or of German Jewry — would be a cosmic monster, not the proper object of worship.

As has been noted, however, a more plausible notion of divine directivity of the course events, and one which is developed by various process thinkers, conceives it as a luring or a persuading which exercises an influence upon individuals. Such an understanding recognizes both the purposive activity of God and the significance of human personal being. It is, however, open to objections.

As the earlier discussion of divine creativity in nature indicated, there is no weight to the objection that it is not possible to conceive of a goal for everlasting divine activity. This objection presumes that any goal must be a particular material state of affairs and that the divine goal must be a final material state of affairs. It then argues that the achievement of such a state would mean the end of all processes and so the extinction of all being, including the divine. The result of this analysis is held to be the dilemma that *either* God's activity aims at a fulfilment which brings about the cessation of all being *or* divine activity has no aim — which is incompatible with the perfection and intentionality of the divine as agent. The fundamental mistake here is to consider that God's goal must be a particular material state. This is as absurd as holding that an artist can only make a specific number of pre-envisaged artefacts. Just as an artist may be motivated by the formal desire to produce objects of beauty without being able to indicate beforehand what particular objects are to be produced, so the divine may be understood to have no particular material end in view but to be inspired by a ceaseless quest for the realization of novel experiences of aesthetic good. In that case God has a formal goal which is directional without there ever being a terminus to the divine activity.

A more worrying objection maintains that the supremacy of the divine as agent effectively rules out any significance in human actions and so in history. The only significant agent in the moulding of the human clay is the divine potter (cf. Jeremiah 18: 5f). So far as this objection is based on notions of God as exercising overwhelming might, it can be met without too much difficulty. The exercise of power is governed by the purpose in using it. If, therefore, God intends to enjoy the enrichment that comes from the autonomous activity of creatures, the use of irresistible power will prevent rather than enhance the fulfilment of that purpose. As Whitehead (1978: 346) suggests, the notion of divine agency as the exercise of crushing compulsion is too crude to be appropriate for the divine. The divine agency is more satisfactorily conceived as acting by means of patient persuasion through the vision of ideals and harmonization presented to each individual. By this vision God seeks to lure people into willing co-operation with the divine purposes.

Unfortunately, while the concept of lure or persuasiveness is a considerable advance on that of coercive might, it is not without problems as a way of understanding divine activity. In the first place the notion that God deliberately chooses to respect our personal freedom by having limited influence over what happens is attractive when people are being creative and tolerable when life is tedious — as it is for most people most of the time. But it seems more like careless irresponsibility when they are being demonically destructive. Some psychopaths seem blind to lures and deaf to persuasion. A defence of the freedom to hurt and to harm is not an easy one to sustain. Second, the change from coercive might to lure may not be that important: a sufficiently attractive lure can be as overwhelming as brute force. People are not bullied by force into being martyrs but persuaded by the vision of their cause. Consequently where there is a failure to evoke creative co-operation, it may be held that God is to be blamed for failing to present an effective lure. The rewards for good behaviour should have been made more desirable!

This latter criticism, however, may properly evoke the reply that to render the divine vision overwhelmingly attractive would be contrary to the divine will for the creativity of autonomous creatures. If there are to be some events which are not simply self-expressions of the divine, God must be thought of as obscuring both the divine reality and the material goods whose immediate actualization will give the greatest satisfaction. Furthermore, the notion that God acts by covert influence on individuals fits human experience generally: whatever a few people may claim about a few unusual cases, most people are not aware of pressures or lures that are manifestly divine. It is also a notion that is defensible on the grounds that only the exceptionally perverse would deliberately reject an indisputable awareness of the divine will.

This reply, though, gives rise to a third problem. The notion of covert divine agency presents a morally and theistically suspect understanding of the divine. If, for instance, God influences people in ways of which they are unaware, can divine activity be distinguished from that of a cosmic Svengali? Hegel (1956: 33) describes 'the cunning of reason' as managing to secure its ends in history through the unwitting efforts of others. If this is how the divine agency works, it would be fair to call it 'cunning' and it might gain our admiration for its ability to get others to produce what it wanted without their being aware that they were being manipulated. It is not evident, though, that it would be worshipful. The effectiveness of unconscious luring might be considered inversely proportional to its true divinity. On the other hand, it could be argued that God is eminently to be trusted and therefore covert activities by the divine must be above suspicion. The problem is that the obscurity of this way of acting makes it impossible to get evidence by which to decide between these judgements.

Another reason for doubting the credibility of the notion of divine agency as a detailed guidance of the course of history becomes apparent when the obscurity of divine activity is considered in conjunction with the claim that God seeks to influence each subject each moment by presenting it with a specific aim. Hartshorne, for example, compares God to 'a sensitive parent or ruler', reacting delicately to our individual situations:

> he enjoys observing our feeling and thoughts and responds
> to these with a perfection of appreciation to which no parent
> or ruler can attain. Because only God can appreciate us, or
> our neighbour, in our or their full worth, we unconsciously
> respond to this appreciation as we do to no other . . .

> (Hartshorne 1970: 12)

The divine agency is thus conceived to take the form of an influence upon our self-creative decisions which occurs as we prehend God's perfect evaluation of our state and its optimum possibilities for enriching experiences. As was noted in the last chapter, this way of understanding God's relationship to natural evolution founders on its requirement of a psychical structure in the entities involved. At the human level, though, this way of understanding seems more promising. Human beings are both conscious and self-conscious.

A problem arises, however, over the situation which Hartshorne points to when he describes our response to the divine vision of us as being 'unconscious'. This description accords with how people generally apprehend their experience. While the notion that God presents a distinct material goal to each subject each moment may be attractive to believers, in practice most people most of the time are not aware of such specific divine lures. Furthermore, when some individuals do claim to have had a sense of a divine calling to do particular things, there seems to be no way of showing from the quality of their experience that they have received specific calls from God rather than projected on God their own desires.

The basic problem, then, is that if human experience gives no clearly warranted examples of such divine influence on people, it is questionable whether it is justifiable to claim that God does so act but in such a covert fashion that it is not immediately apprehensible. It seems simpler to use Occam's razor to shave off what may be a desirable illusion that has attached itself to theistic faith. While, of course, reference to conscious experience to object to the notion of particularized divine activity does not prove that God does not provide a specific goal for each occasion, it does add to the suspicion that the notion may be mistaken. What is not directly experienced may not be there to be experienced, even indirectly and obscurely.

Disquiet with the notion of particular but covert divine agency is heightened when it is appreciated that it may not be theistically appropriate to consider that God makes a specific response to each event. While each of us may desire the assurance that our individual contributions to the divine experience are so important that God is intimately concerned that each of our decisions should lead to the optimum result for the whole, is it credible to view God as so fantastically busy? For some the notion that God deliberately forms a specific lure for each person each moment expresses the awesome involvement of God in all events, however trivial: even the hairs on our head are recorded! For others, such a notion seems to reflect not a vision of the holy but a sense of a fussiness and pettiness that is to be pitied rather than worshipped. It is neither worthy of God nor takes sufficiently seriously the significance of the autonomy that creation gives to the creatures. In discussing God's love Whitehead suggests that it is 'a little oblivious as to morals' (1978: 343). Perhaps something similar needs to be affirmed about divine activity and history: it is to be conceived as 'a little oblivious' to individual situations. With this, we come to a final question about the meaningfulness of history: does it require a notion of

God as an agent with particular purposes for each constituent of the historical order?

To suggest that God does not make specific responses to particular events in human lives will seem to many believers to constitute a heartless faith. Entertaining traditional stories, they look to a God whose providence is a source of individual care and security for all. They sing in Luther's words of God as 'a safe stronghold' who will 'help us clear from all the ill that hath us now o'ertaken'. Others who do not share such expectations still place their hope in God's overall superintendency of history as ensuring that whatever individual decisions may be made, the eventual result will be God's reign 'on earth as it is in heaven'. To hold that God does not act in history in particular ways is to confirm that God has forsaken us (cf. Mark 15: 34). Their cry, though, may express the agony of birth into the real world. As Bonhoeffer came to appreciate, God as 'the centre of life' does not come 'to answer our unsolved problems' but wants us to 'know that we must live as men who manage our lives without him' (1971: 312, 360).

To consider, however, that God does not make particular responses to each individual event does not mean that God is utterly inactive and the historical process purposeless. It may not be justified to hold that God tries to lure each individual along an optimum route, adjusting the particular aim for each individual each moment to compensate for how that individual and all other individuals have chosen in the previous moment. At the same time, it may be that individuals find that they are always faced by possibilities for enriching their experience through novel syntheses and disturbed by pressure to take them up. To the extent that the possibilities and pressure are held to be grounded in the reality of God,[1] they may be held to be evidence of divine activity in history. Furthermore, in that they arouse in people discontent with previous achievements and desire for novel experiences of aesthetic value, whatever they may be and however they may be actualized, they may be regarded as providing the process of history with a formal directivity which justifies the assertion that it is significantly meaningful.

To hold, therefore, that God does not seek to influence people moment by moment with context-specific material goals does

---

[1] Note, though, that Whitehead points out that while the concept of God is essential so far as religious awareness of the world is concerned, conversely religious awareness of God is not a condition of God's function in the universe (Whitehead 1978: 207; cf. also Alexander 1933: 298).

God and the processes of reality

not imply that history must be considered to be an ultimately
aimless process, lacking any intentional goal — with all that
follows from this about the insignificance of human being. Such
a conclusion does not follow because particular divine activities
are not the only basis for establishing the directivity of history.
Just as the proper goal of divine activity has to be conceived in
terms of a formal rather than a material end, so the nature of
divine influence on historical events is to be considered to be
general rather than specific. In other words, instead of expecting
God to present each person with a particular lure appropriate
to her or his immediate situation, divine activity in, on, and
through the process of history is to be understood in terms of
an overall influence which stirs people with a general dissatisfaction at what already has been achieved and, as its obverse, a
perpetual desire for what is enrichingly novel.

Such a notion of God's activity may claim to accord with
human experience. Whereas individuals are not aware of anything that may be apprehended as a continual series of lures to
specific decisions and are properly suspicious of claims that
they encounter such lures unconsciously, they may nevertheless
recognize in their experience something that corresponds to talk
about a restlessness that agitates authentic being. It is manifested
in a desire for greater flourishing which, once allowed to come
to consciousness, is hard to suppress and impossible to do so
without reducing living to merely existing. While not thereby
accepting the puzzling ontological status which Alexander gives
to deity (cf. Alexander 1966: II, 394, 398), this understanding
of divine activity resembles his notion of the 'nisus towards
deity' with which all the world is pregnant (ibid.: II, 353), of
which humanity is most aware in the voice of 'conscience' and
the 'passion for truth and beauty' (ibid.: II, 385), and which
involves all in the emergence of 'a higher level of existence'
(ibid.: II, 429). This 'tendency to deity' is found to give 'strength
and sustainment' (ibid.: II, 381) to the minds of those who are
in harmony with it, presumably because they are in accord with
the basic drives of the process of the whole. As a general urge
towards the actualization of ever higher experiences of value,
however, it is also 'blind'. It 'does not forecast exactly' (Alexander
1939: 277) what will emerge from the creative process of reality,
whether natural or historical.

It is in this general and universal drive towards the formal
end of the increase of value and not in the presentation, let alone
the coercive achievement, of specific material goals that the
divine guidance of history — and accordingly the purposiveness

172

or meaningfulness of history — is found. As Lloyd Morgan (1927: 34) puts it, the view of God which results is that of 'the nisus of the universe pressing onwards to levels as yet unattained; or, as I should prefer to say, is the Nisus directive of the course of events.' Such an understanding of divine activity means that history is not a guided journey along a predetermined route to a particular material state of affairs. It does mean, however, that the process of history has purpose and directivity in a form that is both appropriate to the worshipful ultimacy of God and accords with human experience.

In considering earlier in this chapter what might constitute the nature of a divine basis for the meaningfulness of history, four factors were mentioned. History might be held to be meaningful because human beings are drawn towards the divine as an ideal, or because events contribute to the full realization of the divine, or because the experience of what has happened is always present to God, or because events are directed by God. Taken individually and in the form in which they have frequently been interpreted, reflection indicates that none of these factors provides a fully adequate ground for affirming that meaningfulness. If, however, each of them is understood in the light of the concept of God developed in process thought, they may be coherently combined to produce a strong doctrine of the meaningfulness of history.

According to such a position, the divine is to be conceived as that proper object of unreserved adoration which not only affects all events but also incorporates them in the divine being and preserves the memory of them in their individuality. The receptivity of the divine, furthermore, is balanced by an activity which is experienced by people as a ferment for flourishing that persistently disturbs those who are alive. It is an urge, however, towards the enjoyment of values, not a summons to realize any particular material goal. The point of the process of history is thus to produce, enjoy, and preserve the memory of enriching experiences. Each achievement has value as what it is and for what it contributes to the experience of others. It is, however, also to be treated as a resource to be used in the attainment of further values. History is not significant as a movement towards the implementation of a divine plan but in the aesthetic satisfaction provided by its individual events. Its meaningfulness is grounded in God as all-embracing and universally evocative of novel forms of joy-bearing value.

If, then, the purpose of history is to be understood in terms of God's general promotion and individual appreciation of the values realized in human actions, the proper human response is not one of conformity to patterns and obedience to rules laid down by others of supposedly higher authority, whether secular or religious. Nor is the ideal expressed by the continuation of practices whose living riches have been exhausted. We are to be neither contented cows nor regimented robots. The ideal life is one which never ceases to be creative, in which people both experience aesthetic joy and contribute those experiences to the fullness of the divine being. It is a disturbing goal. The life of the artist is uncomfortable. Others may be hostile because their bovine complacency is threatened; the artist's own experience is unsettled because there is no final satisfaction to the pursuit of aesthetic joy. At the same time it is also a profoundly satisfying mode of being when it is appreciated that 'all objects are internal' to God (Alexander 1966: II, 357). Whatever is achieved is thereafter enjoyed cosmically and everlastingly (cf. Whitehead 1978: 244f).

The question rightly asked of believers is whether God makes any difference. Exponents and critics of process ways of under-standing disagree over what may be justifiably maintained about divine activity as a particular luring which seeks to persuade each concrescing subject. Critics have accused process under-standing of theism of being crucially inadequate because it has no place for specific instances of contingent divine activity in the processes of reality. Defenders have replied that on the contrary the process model presents God as influencing every event in a way that is contingent upon its state and situation. The discussion in this and the previous chapter, however, sug-gests that so far as both critics and defenders consider that specific contingent acts of God are required to make it possible to affirm the theistically grounded meaningfulness of the proce-sses of reality, both natural and historical, the debate is unneces-sary. The relation of God's activity to those processes does not require the divine to act in a particularized manner for reality to be theistically meaningful. All that is required is that the divine be aware of all and generally disturbing all with the urge to novel forms of aesthetic joy. Furthermore, while the argument presented is far from demonstrating that God does not attempt to influence each occasion each moment in a selected way, consideration of the nature of God and the intended creativity of the non-divine suggests that such a notion of particularized divine activity may not be an appropriate way of understanding that proper object of worship, 'the lure of the ideal which is the potentiality beyond immediate fact' (Whitehead 1938: 139), to which nature, history, and humanity bear witness.

10   God and human being: the act of God

Consider the cattle, grazing as they pass you by: they do not
know what is meant by yesterday or today, they leap about,
eat, rest, digest, leap about again, and so from morn till
night and from day to day, fettered to the moment and its
pleasure or displeasure, and thus neither melancholy nor
bored. This is a hard sight for man to see; for, though he
thinks himself better than the animals because he is human,
he cannot help envying them their happiness — what they
have, a life neither bored nor painful, is precisely what he
wants, yet he cannot have it because he refuses to be like an
animal.

(Nietzsche 1983: 60)

Whether or not Nietzsche is accurate about the experience of
being a cow, his remarks point to a distinctive characteristic of
human being. An infant who plays 'in blissful blindness between
the hedges of past and future' only grows into a mature adult by
leaving that state of ignorance. If bovine forgetfulness is desirable, it only comes for us with death, according to Nietzsche —
but death 'at the same time extinguishes the present and all
being'. Thus it demonstrates 'that being is only an uninterrupted
has been'. The resulting self-knowledge brings the discovery that
human existence is fundamentally 'an imperfect tense that can
never become a perfect one' (ibid.: 61).

Since, though, fully personal being is essentially in process, it
has a future to anticipate as well as a past from which it cannot
be detached. Persons are conscious of themselves as being at
the point where events are successively determined. Whereas,
therefore, on one side personal being is existence on the growing
edge of the concrete as it is being augmented and thereby
contributes to the constitution of the past, on the other side
personal being is at the receding edge of the abstract as decisions
fix concretely what was previously more or less indeterminate.
And between the two edges is the present where the self is what
it is in each momentary now. Furthermore, it is not just that the
self finds that it has its being between the dimensions of a past
which pays for its concreteness by having perished and a future

which pays for its openness by being indeterminate. To be a self-conscious self is essentially to be characterized by having both these dimensions. Such persons are aware of themselves as emerging from the determinate which continually perishes into pastness and yet scars their present, and as being projected towards a future which is indeterminate and yet inescapable.

Arising from this awareness comes the question of the significance of human life. If this is what it is to be a person, is it possible to affirm the meaningfulness and worth of human being in a credible manner? And since human being is an abstraction from the actual lives of particular persons, this question finds its concrete and pressing form in the question which reflective self-awareness may evoke in any individual: 'What is the point and value, if any, of that unique mode of being which is my own life?'

As the previous chapters have indicated, there seems to be no divinely ordained necessity about the particular states in which human beings find themselves. So far as the natural order is concerned, humankind appears to be a species which a cosmic tendency towards localized complexifications has recently (according to cosmic time-spans) happened to produce, through forces interacting according to a mixture of chance and necessity, in the evolutionary process on this planet. As for its historical character, mention has already been made of H. A. L. Fisher's comment that the study of history indicated to him that the overall story of the events of the past is as purposeless as that of the successive waves which fall upon a seashore (Fisher 1936: v). Furthermore, if the understanding of the relationship of God to creation and to history advanced in the previous three chapters is justified, in neither case does reference to the intentional activity of God seem to be able to provide a credible way of denying the accidental form of the situation in which people find themselves today. Granted, though, that this is the context in which individuals come to raise questions about the significance of human being, is it possible to affirm the intrinsic worth of each individual? In particular, so far as theistic understanding is concerned, is it possible to justify the claim made by various theologians that the ultimate significance of human beings is grounded in their individual and corporate relationship to the divine?

Augustine, for example, classically makes this claim in the opening paragraph of his *Confessions:* 'for Thou hast formed us for Thyself, and our hearts are restless till they find rest in Thee' (Augustine 1876: 1). It is a point which finds many modern echoes. Karl Rahner, for instance, suggests that human existence is correctly perceived only when it is seen to be orientated 'towards the absolute mystery' which is God (Rahner 1978: 44). Bernard Lonergan basically agrees: since 'man is for God ... religion is intrinsic to authentic humanism' (Lonergan 1974: 148). From a different theological standpoint H. Richard Niebuhr maintains that 'without belief in something that makes life worth living men cannot exist', and that the fundamental human conviction of 'the infinite worth of persons' only makes sense in terms of 'some infinite being to whom they are valuable' (Niebuhr 1941: 77, 151). It is also a point which Schubert Ogden strongly endorses. He argues that human beings have a fundamental 'confidence in the final worth' of their existence which cannot be justified without reference to the reality of God as 'the ground' of this 'confidence' — and that this reference to God is intrinsically unsatisfactory unless the attributes of the divine are conceived according to the dipolar panentheistic conception developed in process thought (Ogden 1967: 44, 47; cf. 120ff).

These, however, are very general claims. So far as individual human lives are concerned, the relationship between the significance of that being and the divine breaks down into three issues. First, how can reference to God help persons to cope with their inheritance of the scars and guilt as well as of the achievements and medals of their past as it moulds their present and influences their future? Second, how may God be understood to give a sure ground of hope for whatever future there may be? Third, and embracing the other two questions, how can reference to God be understood to show that human lives have fundamental significance when they exist as cosmically minute sequences of moments of actuality between past events which eventually perish into oblivion so far as this world is aware and future possibilities which disappear into utter vagueness?

The understanding of the relationship between God and the processes of reality developed in the previous three chapters may well be considered to indicate that reference to God provides no convincing way of meeting these three basic questions about the meaning and worth of individual lives. While, that is, these descriptions of God's relationship to creation and to history may be judged to be rationally credible, they may also be judged to be existentially useless so far as our personal being is concerned. Taking up the standpoint of Christian faith, however, critics of the earlier discussions may argue that what has been omitted from them and what in particular is crucial to the present

177

discussion is a recognition of the saving act of God in the life of Jesus who is the Christ.

They may, for instance, assert that attention needs to be given not only to Augustine's outline of the human predicament in the *Confessions* but also to his description of the divine response to that predicament. While he maintains that human beings find their true satisfaction in the divine, he also affirms that such peace is only made possible through the act of God in the Incarnation:

> our very Life descended hither, and bore our death, and slew it, out of the abundance of His own life ... And in this world He was, and into this world He came to save sinners, unto whom my soul doth confess, that He may heal it, for it hath sinned against Him.

> (Augustine 1876: 71)

and

> I sought a way of acquiring strength sufficient to enjoy Thee; but I found it not until I embraced that 'Mediator between God and man, the man Christ Jesus' ... For 'the Word was made flesh,' that Thy wisdom, by which Thou createst all things, might provide milk for our infancy.

> (ibid.: 165)

and

> For Thou art righteous, O Lord, but we have sinned and committed iniquity ... and Thy hand is grown heavy upon us ... What shall 'wretched man' do? 'Who shall deliver him from the body of this death' but Thy grace only, 'through Jesus Christ our Lord,' whom Thou hast begotten co-eternal, and ... in whom the Prince of this world found nothing worthy of death, yet killed he Him, and the handwriting which was contrary to us was blotted out? (ibid.: 171f)

Such claims, of course, are by no means peculiar to Augustine! They pervade Christian faith, belief, and theology as they have been traditionally held. Various models of relationship have been and still are used to express the salvific effect of the life and death of Christ — religious ones such as the notions of sacrifice and ritual cleansing, social ones such as those of ransom, propitiation, and the satisfaction of honour, and personal ones such of those of reconciliation, example, and lure. What is common to them all, however, is the belief that in some way or another the fundamental predicament of human being is met by an act of God in the life of Jesus who is, therefore, the Christ. Salvation — oneness, wholeness, healing, peace (again there are many metaphors used to express the reality) — is achieved through the intervention of God in human affairs.

In view of this understanding, it may well be objected that what has been developed in this study is both a basically flawed appreciation of the nature of God and a critically inadequate appreciation of the relationship between the human and the divine. It is flawed because it fails to take into account the saving act of God — an act which dramatically changes how the relationship between God and the processes of reality, natural and historical, is to be perceived. It is inadequate because it does not recognize how that saving act of God radically changes the human situation and gives a significance to human being which could never be anticipated by reflection on the general course of nature and history. Indeed, so the critics may argue, it is only because of the saving act of God in Jesus as the Christ that it is possible to affirm that human being has any proper, ultimate significance.

So much for the criticisms! What is to be said in reply? In the remainder of this chapter I want to consider the question of the significance of claims about the incarnation of God in the event of Jesus who is the Christ. The next — and concluding — chapter will take up the other issue which has been raised, namely that of the way in which the divine establishes the significance of human being — in other words, how God may be understood as 'Saviour' in a rationally credible manner. Although the discussion will concentrate on the Christian claim that the saving act of God is to be located in the life and fate of Jesus of Nazareth, what is maintained is generally applicable, *mutatis mutandis*, to traditional beliefs of those other faiths which find their identity and focus their understanding of the relationship between God and humanity on some supposed extraordinary act (or acts) by which God has intervened in the processes of reality.

Incarnational references in theology are references to specific events in history, particularly to the series of events that constitute the life of a person, in which it is held that the divine was peculiarly present. God was there, as the term suggests, 'in the flesh'. Why are such events regarded by some believers and theologians as having fundamental significance for religious faith? Why do they not say on hearing about such events,

'How odd' or 'How interesting' but proceed to ignore them in constructing their theological understanding? There seem to be four possible answers to this question: that such an event has fundamental significance for God — either subjectively or objectively — or that such an event has fundamental significance for human beings, again either subjectively or objectively. On examination, however, three of these possible answers appear to be radically unsatisfactory.

An incarnational event may be held, for example, to be basic to faith solely on the grounds that it shows that God knows in the divine experience what it is to be a human being. Hence the divine can be trusted to appreciate our existential predicament. Some interpretations of the doctrine of the ascension,[1] for example, hold that it expresses the incorporation of human experience within the divine reality. But in so far as such a view presupposes that the precise quality of human experience is not available to the divine except through a historical 'incarnation' in which God actually 'becomes' a human being (however this is understood), it implies a theistically unjustifiable limitation of God's awareness of all occasions of actuality. Although we are limited in our awareness of each other's experiences, people in love claim that as their love grows so they become increasingly aware of each other's feelings. If God's knowledge results from unlimitedly sympathetic love and awareness, it follows from the essential character of the divine reality that God shares all human experiences without loss or error. There is no part of human experience that is closed to the divine. If this is so, claims about the significance of a historical incarnation which regard it as making certain experiences available to God are to be rejected. They are based on far too limited an understanding of the divine. In this respect the notion of 'incarnation' is to be held to symbolize what is essentially the case in the divine experience, namely that all actual experiences as such are incorporated in the divine experience.

A second interpretation of the notion of incarnation holds that such an event is needed for God to be able to effect an atonement with humanity. Some believers claim, for instance, that only a divine incarnation could produce the perfect human being required to offer the perfect sacrifice which is the condition of

---

[1] The doctrine of the ascension basically makes the same point as the doctrine of the incarnation but by means of a model whose basic metaphor takes up the notion of movement in the opposite direction — from earth to heaven rather than from heaven to earth.

reconciliation between the divine and the human. This view is also indefensible. If taken seriously, it presumes that the rules of divine purity, justice, and honour prevent God from doing what God wishes to do simply because God wants to do it and it is good. If there is alienation between God and humanity, and if God desires the reconciliation of humanity with the divine, it is incredible to hold that God must undertake an incarnatory event in order to make it possible so far as God is concerned. But if incarnation does not effect anything in God's own being, does its theological significance make sense in terms of what it makes possible for human being?

Third, it is possible to interpret an incarnational event as enabling human beings to appreciate the character of their authentic existence by providing them with an actual example of it. This interpretation is theistically deficient, however, if it turns the 'God' who is allegedly 'incarnated' into 'the ideal human being' and thereby denies that there is any grounding for that ideal which exists outside humanity. What is offered in that case is not anything to do with 'God' in any theistic sense but something which tells us about the 'ideals' which persons must actualize if they are to find authentic being. If this is the function of Jesus as the Christ in the Christian faith, what is given is a human Jesus who is set before humanity as its ideal — as 'the one for others' or as 'the utterly dependent upon God' or as 'the totally open to the future' — but whose nature expresses nothing other than the human. It is not a Jesus of whom the notion of 'incarnation' is properly predicable *unless* (and this is a vital 'unless') such an ideal human life also expresses in some way or another something of the nature of God.

The fourth way of interpreting the notion of incarnation holds that a revelation of the nature of God is given in the events so described. It is not just a perfect human life which is presented. The life of the 'incarnate' one is a human life which discloses the actual nature of the divine and so provides the basis for faith's understanding of and authentic response to reality.

This view of incarnational affirmations as affirmations about points in history at which the nature of ultimate reality is revealed agrees with what Whitehead says in *Religion in the Making*. He states, for example, that 'Religion starts from the generalization of final truths first perceived as exemplified in particular instances' (Whitehead 1927: 110) and, again, that 'religion claims that its concepts, though derived primarily from special experiences, are yet of universal validity ... It arises from that which is special, but it extends to what is general' (ibid.: 21; cf. 32, 37). On these grounds he holds that there is a fundamental difference between the Buddha and Christ: the former provides 'his doctrine to enlighten the world' whereas the latter 'gave his life' — and leaves it to Christians 'to discern the doctrine' (ibid.: 45).

The view that the function of incarnational affirmations is to identify points of insight into the nature of the divine does not seem open to the objection that it depends upon an inadequate understanding of God. It may, however, be objected that on such an understanding any alleged incarnation is redundant. It can only provide a knowledge of God which must already be presupposed in the decision that this event is a revelation of the divine. It may be argued, for example, that the life of Jesus is regarded as a revelatory incarnation of God because it is a life of self-giving love and because it is believed that self-giving love is the character of the divine. Consequently, so it may be maintained, incarnational claims do not provide new insights into the divine character. They only give concrete examples of it. The examples, though, are chosen because they illustrate what is already held to be the divine nature. What may be said in reply to this objection to the significance of incarnational claims as revelatory of the divine?

In response to this objection it needs to be pointed out that claims about an incarnation presuppose first that God exists, second that God's reality is not so utterly transcendent that no carnate form can even be relatively adequate to express something of its character, and third that certain aspects of the divine reality can only be discerned through identifying events where they are given actual expression. It is the third point that is crucial in meeting the objection that incarnational claims are otiose. In order to grasp it, it is necessary to take up the distinction which Hartshorne makes between the 'existence' and the 'actuality' of God which was outlined in Chapter 4.

Whatever metaphysical arguments may be able to establish about the reality of God, their conclusions can only provide information about the abstract existence of the divine. For example, even if Hartshorne were correct in all his claims for the ontological argument (and this is disputable (cf. Pailin 1968, 1969a)), it would only justify such a conclusion as that 'that than which a greater cannot be conceived necessarily exists' or that 'a perfect being exists' or that 'the adequate object of worship exists.' Such information, however, is too abstract to be on its own a sufficient ground for living religious faith: what believers want to know is what the divine greatness, perfection, and

worshipfulness (and other abstract attributes of the divine existence such as creativity, love, and appreciation) are like in actual
practice. They need this information if they are to respond
appropriately to the divine by harmonizing their thoughts and
actions with what is ultimate in being, value, and rationality.

Living religious faith, that is, cannot be satisfied with abstract
knowledge of the existence of God. It requires insight into the
actual character of the divine reality which can only be achieved
by finding occasions in which that reality is held to be manifested
in actual practice. It is at this point that claims about an
incarnation of the divine are significant for these are claims
about a series of events in which it is believed that the *actual*
qualities of the divine are revealed.

In this respect it is useful to make a distinction between what
may be called the 'passive actuality' and the 'active actuality' of
the divine. The former covers the way in which God is 'actually'
affected by what happens in the world through the agency of the
non-divine; the latter refers to the way in which God's nature is
'actualized' in active responses to those events. When Whitehead
and Hartshorne discuss the 'consequent' or actual nature of God,
they are mainly[2] concerned about the passive actuality of the
divine. They argue, for instance, that because God is maximally
influenced by all events, the actual state of the divine depends
in part upon the actual states of those events. What, for example,
God knows now as being the case in this room depends upon
what contingently happens to be the case here. In so far, then,
as God's existence as a perfect being entails that in principle
God is aware at any moment of all that is at that moment to be
known, it follows from this and from my awareness of some
things that are at present the case (e.g. that I am not wearing a
tie, that my watch is on the desk, that I feel slightly thirsty),
that I can know something of the passive actuality of God in
practice — for God's actual knowledge of what is currently the
case must include all my knowledge of what is so (cf. Hartshorne
1970: 39). In more general terms, an understanding of God's
existence and a knowledge of history give us knowledge of some
of the passive actuality of the divine.

The believer, however, wants also to discern the actual character of the concrete values which inform God's creative activity
in and response to events in the world. Such perception is

---

[2] It should be noted, though, that 'mainly' does not mean 'wholly'. Both
Whitehead and Hartshorne do make important affirmations about the active
actuality of God, for instance in giving a basic conceptual aim to each
concrescing entity.

necessary if the believer is consciously and deliberately to try to live according to the will and nature of God. The active actuality of God — as of any entity — can be discovered, however, only by identifying events in which it is concretely displayed. For example, as Hartshorne recognizes, the peculiar character of 'the relations of God to man' referred to in ideas of sin, grace, and forgiveness cannot be determined metaphysically. When we seek knowledge of God 'beyond the bare outline of the dimensions of his being' determinable a priori we have to turn to 'empirical science and theology (revealed theology is in this sense empirical)' for the sources of insight. Consequently, for all his confidence in metaphysical thinking, Hartshorne affirms that

> the final, the highest knowledge is not metaphysical, but empirical in that total sense in which both the generic or merely identical or universal features and also the inexhaustibly growing particularities of experience are included. Only philosophy, science, and religious theology drawing upon special experiences of gifted individuals and groups can together furnish man with his greatest measure of such total knowledge.

> (Hartshorne 1964: 345f; cf. 1965: 300; 1967: 77)

Accordingly, when believers and theologians make claims about an incarnation, they are to be understood to be directing attention to events in which they judge that God's nature and will are to be perceived to be actively actualized in a normative form (cf. Gibson 1970: 246). As Whitehead puts it, 'what further can be known about God' beyond being in general the principle of concretion

> must be sought in the region of particular experiences, and therefore rests on an empirical basis. In respect to the interpretation of these experiences, mankind has differed profoundly. He has been named respectively, Jehovah, Allah, Brahma, Father in Heaven, Order of Heaven, First Cause, Supreme Being, Chance. Each name corresponds to a system of thought derived from the experiences of those who have used it.

> (Whitehead 1927a: 222)

In the case of the system of understanding which is Christianity, the decisive clue to the character of ultimate reality is held to be given by either the reality or the record or the symbol of one personal history, namely that of Jesus of Nazareth.

According to the traditional self-understanding of Christianity, then, the rather small number of reports about the life of Jesus (together with, it should probably be added, a tradition of faith which traces its formation to the effects of his ministry and fate) provide both insight into God's active actuality and the norm by which the correctness of other claims to a knowledge of God's active actuality are to be judged. In Whitehead's view the failure to apply this norm thoroughly in practice has led to major distortions in Christian theology. Although that thought is supposedly based 'upon an intensive study of the significance of certain historical occasions', what has emerged has generally been dominated by alien 'barbaric elements' and 'defects in intellectual comprehension' (Whitehead 1933: 211f). In particular Christian theology has been ruined by refusing to discard its inheritance of pictures of God fashioned on the images of 'the ruling Caesar', 'the ruthless moralist', and 'the unmoved mover' (Whitehead 1978: 343; cf. 1933: 216f). Instead it has tried to fit the revelation of God perceived in the events of Jesus as the Christ on a basis formed by these despotic conceptions. If Christian theology is to be true to itself, however, it should, in Whitehead's view, return to its 'Galilean origin'. According to his interpretation of the significance of that normative origin, this will result in theology finding its dominant motifs in 'the tender elements in the world, which slowly and in quietness operate by love', and the goal for living in 'the present immediacy of a kingdom not of this world' (Whitehead 1978: 343).

In providing normative disclosures of God's active actuality, incarnational claims give insight into the purposive character of the divine ground of the processes of reality. What, therefore, is manifested in an incarnational event is not to be compared to a miracle on the old-fashioned view of miracle as a surd which acts counter to the general order of things. Indeed, to attempt to regard an incarnation as an irrational irruption into this world of a 'totally other' mode of being is probably self-defeating: if such were the case an incarnation would neither make sense to us (as taking a blind person on a visit to a picture gallery would not make sense) nor would it throw any light on the reality in which we find ourselves — except, perhaps, to show that it is 'invadable'. What is correctly grasped as an incarnational event is, rather, to be seen as an event in the processes of reality which makes known the fundamental character and end of all those processes. Such an event is not an exception to those processes. It is, rather, an event which evokes insight into the nature of the divine relationship to all events. Contingent, temporal events of

185

a life in this world, described in ordinary falsifiable propositions (for in principle it is conceivable that later historical investigations might show that Jesus of Nazareth never existed in the way suggested by the Christian tradition), are thus held to reveal what is necessarily and everlastingly true of all events (and so is not empirically falsifiable).

Objections may be raised to this interpretation of the notion of incarnation. On the one hand some may object to the definitive status ascribed to Jesus as being unwarrantable while, from an opposite standpoint, others may object that it fails to recognize adequately the unique status and nature of Jesus as the Christ.

According to the first of these objections, if God is continually active in the processes of reality, no one event or series of events ought to be singled out as giving a normative manifestation of the divine actuality. To this it may be replied that while God is to be held to be involved in all concrescing occasions, other agents also influence what emerges and in particular the concrescing subject. In some occasions the resulting synthesis is closer to the divine will than in others. There is, therefore, good reason for believers to concentrate their attention on those occasions which are justifiably held to come closest to being pure expressions of the divine will for their situation. As Whitehead suggests with his concept of 'importance', certain events are more valuable than others in providing insight into the nature of things. There is, therefore, in principle no reason why a relatively minute number of events (for Christian theology, those of the recorded life of Jesus) should not be held to provide a normative, indeed an unsurpassable and so final, revelation of the divine actuality in relation to the processes of reality.

The second objection argues, in contrast, that what has been said about incarnation does not do justice to the credal claims that Jesus is to be believed to be 'truly God', 'truly man', and 'one person'. It may be, of course, that such a combination of notions is irredeemably incoherent. If so, it ought to be abandoned rather than presented as if authentic Christian faith demanded a sacrifice of the intellect. On the other hand, it is possible that the substance of the credal affirmations may be a justifiable way of expressing the significance of Jesus as the Christ and hence as the incarnation of the divine. How might it be held to be thus justifiable?

If it is correct to maintain that incarnational affirmations are about points at which the divine active actuality is manifested, then to claim that God was incarnate in Jesus is not to claim that Jesus of Nazareth incorporated in his existence the metaphysical qualities of the divine (which may be described in such terms as infinity, necessity, absoluteness, and everlastingness). It is, rather, to claim that in the life of Jesus the qualities of the active actuality of God are manifested — personal qualities like love and mercy and respect for others. Furthermore, since according to panentheistic understanding of the divine there is no unbridgeable gulf between the actuality of God and the world, it is not incoherent to hold that the values of God's active actuality may be expressed in a human life within the limits appropriate to human being.

Is it possible to say anything more about the incarnation in Jesus as the normative revelation of the divine, in particular in relation to the activity of God in the events of his life? Paul, for example, suggests that God took the initiative in what occurred: 'From first to last this has been the work of God. He has reconciled us men to himself through Christ. ... God was in Christ reconciling the world to himself' (2 Corinthians 5: 18f). Although the results are very speculative, some theologians have tried to use the concepts of process thought to show how such an idea may be understood.

John Cobb, for example, holds that to recognize that Jesus was 'fully human' does not rule out the possibility that 'God's presence in Jesus' had a 'structural role' in his personal life which it has not had in other persons (1971: 390). He thus suggests that

> God's aim for Jesus was that he prehend God in terms of that which constitutes him as God — his lordship, his love, and his incomparable superiority of being and value. This prehension was not experienced by Jesus as information about God but as the presence of God to and in him. Furthermore, and most uniquely, it was not experienced by him as one prehension alongside others to be integrated into a synthesis with them. Rather this prehension of God constituted in Jesus the center from which everything else in his psychic life was integrated. This means that at least in *some* decisive moments of his life he perceived the world, his own past and future, his emotions and reason, in terms of the presence of God in him.
>
> (ibid.: 393)

Thus 'the "I" of Jesus' is held to have been 'constituted by his prehension of God' (ibid.). In a later study of Christology Cobb puts it that while Jesus fully 'shares our common humanity',

God gave him 'distinctive possibilities of actualizing himself around the immanent Logos' and Jesus responded by 'freely' choosing 'at least at important times in his life . . . to constitute his own selfhood as one with this presence of God within him' (Cobb 1975: 171, 173). Accordingly his 'certainty and authority' and normative status are explicable because his selfhood expressed the presence in him of 'the fullest incarnation' of the divine 'Logos' of creative transformation (ibid.: 138; cf. 256). Since his 'I' 'was coconstituted by the presence of the Logos in him', it is justifiable to claim that in his activity 'God was indeed immediately active' (ibid.: 141; cf. 171).

Similar views are presented by other theologians influenced by process thought. Since Jesus completely — and freely — conformed to the divine will, Schubert Ogden (1967: 186) puts it that he 'actually *is* God's decisive act'. In his life 'the ultimate truth about our existence before God is normatively re-presented or revealed' (ibid.: 184). J. E. Barnhart expresses the unity of the divine and the human in Jesus in terms of the realization of such 'empathy' that 'indeed God was in Jesus, and Jesus was in God — not literally but effectively' (Barnhart 1967: 230). Norman Pittenger writes of 'the *coincidence* of the divine and human acts' in Jesus (Pittenger 1959: 181), Peter Hamilton of Jesus's aim in life being so 'aligned with God's aim' that in his actions God was 'objectively present' (Hamilton 1967: 206), and Daniel Day Williams of Jesus as living in such unbroken communion with and so totally open to God that in him the nature of God as love is actualized (Williams 1968: 158–72).

As a way of understanding the possible nature of a divine incarnation in history, these notions have much to commend them. They can be seen as developing to its limit the notion of divine vocation. Since the character of my active actuality is revealed in what I do, others may discover what I am like by observing my actions. In some cases, though, I may be unable to be personally present to them and so may arrange for a substitute to act for me. If I give this substitute very precise instructions about my wishes and if she or he carries them out extremely faithfully, it is arguable that people watching the substitute might justifiably claim that they now understand me. Before the modern development of communications, this was ideally the role of an ambassador to a foreign court: so to represent (or, rather, to 'present') the ruler from whom he or she came that that ruler's wishes and responses were displayed in and through those of the ambassador. The above interpretations of the person of Christ may be considered to suggest an analogous model for appreciating the relationship between Jesus and God: God called Jesus to represent the divine will in every situation in Jesus's life; and Jesus, according to Christian faith, completely grasped the character of that will and accurately presented it in his words and deeds. While fully human, with all the limitations and freedom of a human being, Jesus thus 'incarnated' God's active actuality by being completely responsive to God's call to him to represent the divine in the situations of his life.

It may be objected, though, that all people are called to fulfil the will of God; consequently this understanding of the incarnation of the divine in Jesus does not satisfactorily safeguard the uniqueness of Jesus as the Christ. Two replies may be offered to this criticism. On the one hand, it may be claimed that since Jesus fulfilled that vocation perfectly, he may properly be regarded as unique. In no other has the will of God been perfectly expressed. On the other hand, it may be argued that there is no reason why, on this interpretation, Jesus's vocation should not be regarded as a unique one — that he has been called to express God's actuality in ways in which others have not been called. At this point, however, Christological affirmations about Jesus have entered far into the realm of speculations where there is no evidence to determine the issues. Whatever 'metaphysical compliments' Christian believers may wish to pay to Jesus, the reservations of Cobb and Ogden indicate what is rationally warrantable. The former suggests that we do not know if others were called as Jesus was called but failed to fulfil their vocation (cf. Cobb 1971: 394) while the latter emphasizes that we cannot know that there were, are, or will be no other Christs than Jesus (cf. Ogden 1962: 168ff, 183ff). Furthermore, it is possible that others than Jesus were called to represent God fully in their lives and did so completely but that the significance of their lives was not recognized by others and so their revelation of the divine was abortive.

These suggestions about the possible nature of divine incarnation in Jesus are very speculative. The question arises of whether they are necessary. One way to answer this question is to investigate how claims about an incarnation — where an incarnation is understood to have revelatory significance — may be shown to be rationally justified. Such an investigation will indicate what is at stake in these claims and what is essentially involved in justifying them.

Some theologians regard questions about the rational justification of theological understanding as fundamentally misguided. In their judgement claims about a revelatory incarnation are matters of faith. As such they are not open to truth-testing. Rudolf Bultmann, for example, extends the doctrine of justification by faith alone to the epistemology of faith: 'The man who wishes to believe in God as his God must realise that he has nothing in his hand on which to base his faith.' It is contrary to the logic of faith for a person to 'demand a proof of the Word which addresses him' (Bultmann 1964: 211). Such a view of faith, however, makes it impossible, so far as human thought is concerned, to distinguish between what is probably true and what is probably false, and renders believers liable to entertain all kinds of errors and absurdities. As Whitehead recognizes, 'reason is the safeguard of the objectivity of religion: it secures for it the general coherence denied to hysteria' (Whitehead 1927: 53; cf. 53f, 71f, 74; 1933: 138). What, then, may be appropriate tests for showing the rational credibility of claims about an incarnational revelation of the active actuality of the divine?

Some kinds of testing can be immediately ruled out as inappropriate. First, scientific methods of verification which require the repetition of experiments under carefully controlled conditions are not appropriate. So far as an incarnational revelation is derived from past events, its source cannot be produced at will for inspection. Furthermore, if God is held to be agentially involved in the production or in the apprehension of the revelatory significance of the events, human testers ought not to pretend to be able to get God to repeat the divine activity for their observation in the same way that they might hope to get cells to react to specific stimuli under a microscope.

Second, claims to an incarnational revelation cannot be verified in ways appropriate to historical judgements. While historical elements are apparently involved in such claims, the crucial element is not the past event but what is held to be 'revealed' in and through that event. For example, if historians could show to the satisfaction of the canons of history that Jesus had said words of pardon to the woman taken in adultery or had died from crucifixion, they would not have verified in any way the religious claim that in this or that action we have an insight into God's relationship to humankind. Historical support for the accuracy of the Gospel records may be interesting but it does not positively verify the faith derived from them. At most it only shows that the events which evoked the disclosure of the divine did occur as reported. This, though, is not very significant since *something* must have evoked the disclosure and presumably such events would not be completely out of character with what was allegedly disclosed thereby.

Third, incarnationally revealed insights into the divine concern what is necessarily universal in its scope. God's essential nature is compatible with all possible times and all genuinely possible situations. Hence the method of testing by conceivable empirical falsification is ruled out in the case of the divine. This way of testing a claim about what is the case depends on conceiving possible situations whose occurrence would falsify it as being true there and then (although not necessarily elsewhere), and observing whether such situations occur. Take, for example, the claim that all the babies born in Manchester on 4 May 1987 were females. We can easily conceive situations which would falsify that claim, for example, by finding in one Manchester hospital a record of a male who was born that day or by hearing a mother tell about her son being born in Manchester on the May Bank Holiday in that year or by being shown the birth certificate of a boy whose date and place of birth are stated to be that day in a registration district of Manchester. If we never in practice came across any such record, this would not positively prove that all the births there on that day were of females. It would, however, provide what might be called a negative test for the claim. In the case of the divine reality, however, no such possible falsifying circumstances are coherently conceivable. Correct claims about divine existence are in principle universal (and so empirically non-falsifiable) claims about what is fundamentally the case. Furthermore, the perfection of the divine means that claims about God's active actuality have a similar character. God's actions are necessarily what is best in the circumstances and no possible circumstance is beyond their bounds.

Fourth, it might be argued that claims about God being incarnationally revealed in event E as having qualities x and y might be loosely verified by checking whether the qualities x and y are part of some already accepted understanding of the divine. Such an argument, though, would only provide some form of confirmation for the revelatory claim at the cost of making the revelatory insight unnecessary. At best it would show that the alleged incarnational insight agreed with information about God which was already believed to be true. This form of testing would thus render incarnational claims redundant since it would only recognize them as 'true' when they provided information which was already known. Questions might arise about how we came by this information and about how we might test it but the supposed revelation would be of no help.

God and the processes of reality

What kind of testing, then, is appropriate in such cases? Since what is given in an incarnational revelation is knowledge about God and since the epistemological status of God is akin to that of metaphysical principles in that knowledge of the divine provides information about the ultimate character of reality, the tests for claims about God derived from incarnational revelation are tests appropriate for metaphysical statements. To be accepted as being at least possibly true, propositions about the nature of God's active actuality need to satisfy the following six criteria. They must be: internally coherent — contradictions signify nothing; consistent with any ultimate rational and evaluative principles that are independently known — a revelatory insight may change our beliefs about the nature of the ultimate but God is presumably consistent with Godself as the ground of all rationality and value; universally applicable as providing a coherent understanding of all reality — while certain truths about God may be 'derived primarily from special experiences', they must be 'of universal validity, to be applied by faith to the ordering of all experience' (Whitehead 1927: 21; cf. 55f; cf. 1933: 217); adequate — in the sense of being appropriate to the character of the ultimate ground of all reality, both actual and possible; intuitively satisfying[3] — although this criterion may be challenged on the grounds that it is liable to lead to the endorsement of only what fits existing understanding, it may be pointed out in reply that if God is the ground and goal of human being, correct insights into the divine actuality might be expected to have intuitive appeal; and, finally, relevant in that they provide a convincing and significant insight into the fundamental nature of reality as it is currently perceived to be — in the end propositions expressing insights apprehended through past events held to give an incarnational revelation are to be tested by their present existential significance.

It must be appreciated, though, that even if all these tests can be implemented and produce a positive result, they will not show that there is a complete correspondence between the reality of God and what is considered to be the divine actuality revealed in a series of events such as the life of Jesus. Furthermore, these tests cannot show that there will never be an understanding of the divine which surpasses that perceived through consideration

[3] Cf. 'Rational religion appeals to the direct intuition of special occasions, and to the elucidatory power of its concepts for all occasions.... The doctrines of rational religion aim at being that metaphysics which can be derived from the supernormal experience of mankind in its moments of finest insight' (Whitehead 1927: 21).

192

of such a series of events in the past. If Christian believers consider that their faith compels them to affirm that God is unsurpassably revealed in the event of Jesus (or Muslims in the teaching of Muhammad, or Buddhists in the life and teaching of the Buddha, or Jews in the case of the Torah), it is a mark of their commitment to the revelation grasped through that series of events (a 'metaphysical compliment') rather than a rationally warranted claim or a well-founded limitation of the capacity for revelatory insights into the divine. On the other hand, so far as Christian insight into the divine is concerned, what these tests may indicate is that the picture of God as a tenderly operating love, apprehended through 'the brief Galilean vision of humility', is more likely to be true than the pictures of God as 'the ruling Caesar, or the ruthless moralist, or the unmoved mover' (Whitehead 1978: 343) which have dominated — and distorted — so much theistic faith. The existential significance of this view of the divine for human being will be the subject of the next — and final — chapter of this study of God and the processes of reality. Before we turn to it, however, one further question about incarnational claims needs to be discussed.

In view of the primarily metaphysical tests used to justify claims about an incarnational revelation of the divine, the question arises of whether historical factuality is a necessary condition of such claims. This may seem to be a pointless question to ask since, it may be argued, if a revelation is 'incarnational', it must necessarily be given 'in the flesh' and through events in history. Thus it may be asserted: no history, no incarnation and no incarnational revelation. The issue, however, is by no means as simple as this response implies.

Before we tackle the heart of the question, two preliminary points need to be made. The first is the widely recognized point that all records of historical events are biased by the cognitive assumptions, perspective, and selectivity of those who observed and recorded them. We have no unprejudiced records of any event. In the case of such material as the Gospel records of Jesus, the interpretative element is notoriously great. Here we are offered, as John confesses, reports which are intended to lead us to believe that 'Jesus is the Christ, the Son of God' in order that we might 'possess life by his name' (John 20: 31). While, then, the material about Jesus presented in the Gospels (and, biased as it may be, this is practically all the reliable material available to us) is doubtless connected with some historical events, it is not possible to get behind the records to examine the events which evoked the faith. Accordingly Christian apologists who try to justify faith's response to Jesus by reference to Jesus's life and teaching enter into an unconvincingly circular argument. The evidence which they can turn to about his life and teaching is only available as filtered through faith's response to them. What is important for theistic faith today, though, is the insight into God's relationship to the processes of reality and in particular to human life which is believed to be provoked by those records and by reflection upon them in the continuing community of faith centred around them.

The second point is that the writings of both Whitehead and Hartshorne present a story of God as a loving tenderness and an all-embracing care which is apparently based on wholly non-revelatory considerations. Indeed, Whitehead claims that the *Sophist* and the *Timaeus* show that the later Plato had reached an understanding of 'the divine element in the world ... as a persuasive agency and not as a coercive agency' (Whitehead 1933: 213; cf. 205f). If such a reason-derived picture of God in many ways resembles that given in the incarnational events of Jesus, and if, as was suggested earlier, the only credible understanding of an incarnational event is as revelatory, the question arises whether an incarnational event is necessary — except, perhaps, to provide illustrations (divinely acted parables) of the nature of God already apprehensible by rational reflection. It may be, of course, that Whitehead and Hartshorne are considerably influenced by a Christian background (the fathers of both were clergymen) but this does not apply to Plato. Perhaps, however, it should not be too surprising in view of the universal providence of God to find that important insights into the divine are not restricted to those who share a particular tradition centred on certain events believed to be incarnationally revelatory.

Furthermore, as Newman points out in *The Grammar of Assent*, real apprehensions are more effective than notional ones. For all the perceptiveness and precision of abstract thought, concrete exemplifications of the divine nature are both more determinate and more effective in influencing thought and behaviour. In this respect it should thus be noted that according to Whitehead what Plato discerned in theory, Christ displayed in reality and thereby 'evoked a response from all that is best in human nature'.

The Mother, the Child, and the bare manger: the lowly man, homeless and self-forgetful, with his message of peace, love, and sympathy: the suffering, the agony, the tender words as

life ebbed, the final despair: and the whole with the authority
of supreme victory.

(Whitehead 1933: 214)

This one-sentence sketch of the compelling story of Jesus is
tinged with the hues of an epoch that has passed away but it
draws attention to characteristics which have traditionally been
considered to give insight into the divine actuality. Thus Whitehead goes on to ask, 'Can there be any doubt that the power of
Christianity lies in its revelation in act, of that which Plato
divined in theory?'

This, though, brings us to the main issue, namely, is the
happenedness of an incarnational revelatory event essential or
even important for its theological employment? Indeed, bearing
in mind Lessing's point that there is a logical difference between
a matter of history and a matter of faith, it may even be
asked whether a historical element is possible in a theological
understanding of an incarnational revelation of the divine. The
standard Christian answer is in the affirmative. Donald Mac-
Kinnon (1968: 74, 76f, 82-9), for example, maintains that the
Christian faith essentially includes the assertion of propositions
about the occurrence of a number of contingent historical events.
Thomas Torrance is typically more forceful:

> By the Incarnation Christian theology means that at a
> definite point in space and time the Son of God became
> man. . . . Thus it is the faith and understanding of the
> Christian Church that in Jesus Christ God Himself in His
> own Being has come into our world and is actively present
> as personal Agent within our physical and historical
> existence.

(Torrance 1969: 52)

Similarly, though not so vehemently, Daniel Day Williams (1968:
157) suggests that we cannot 'separate all the original empirical
facts from [the] later interpretation' of faith. It should not
be forgotten that the credal confessions of the Christian faith
apparently include historical references — 'born', 'suffered',
'crucified, dead and buried', and 'the third day'.

If, however, the religious and theological function of an incarnational claim is revelatory, the purpose of references to an
allegedly incarnational occurrence is to point to particular events
(or to records of them) which are held to give insight into the
character of God and of the relationship of the divine to the

195

processes of reality. In that case, it is not the happenedness of the events nor the accuracy of the records of them but the correctness of the insight into the divine which they arouse that is the crucial issue. The supposedly 'historical' stories which arouse insight may not correspond to what actually happened. But this is not important if, like parables, they evoke a correct perception of the actual relationship of God to the processes of reality. It is this actuality which is vital: not the factuality of the story which provides the insight.

To affirm this, however, is not to deny that some historical occurrences led to the insight. As a matter of historical probability, furthermore, it is plausible to consider that the overt character of the life of Jesus was not widely unlike the character of the divine held to be revealed thereby. It would be surprising, for example, if disciples, however overwhelmed by their master's charisma, would come to perceive the loving concern of God as exemplified in and through the career of one whom they knew to be an egocentric, rabble-rousing, boozy, and selfish fanatic! What must be recognized, however, is that the contingent facts of the historical life of Jesus do not in the end constitute the actuality that is vital to belief. The actuality that is indispensable to belief belongs to a quite different mode of reality — the reality of the actuality of the divine. This is the actuality in which theistic faith puts its trust and by which it is orientated. The investigations of historians and biblical critics may lead to interesting results but they do not provide the 'facts' on which faith is grounded. They only help to identify what seem to have been the events which evoked in the first Christians incarnational insights into the character of the divine actuality. The truth of those insights is not verified by the tests for historical accuracy but by the tests for metaphysical actuality.

It may be objected that the historical factuality of the incarnation as an actual act of God should not be evaluated in this way since it guarantees the truth about God revealed therein. In other words, it may be held that it is because God was operative in those events that the divine nature is known thereby. There is, however, no such guarantee for faith. What happened in history and what is historically recorded are the events of the life of a particular human being. Even if it could be shown beyond a shadow of doubt that Jesus healed the sick, fed the hungry, enlightened the ignorant, and reproved the life-denying, it would not be unreasonable to respond 'So what? He was a good man and he came to a nasty end. I don't deny it. But there have been other good people in the past and some are alive today.' Past

196

events, that is, guarantee nothing beyond the fact that the records of them are correct — for instance, that a particular person lived in a specific manner. They do not show that in that person's activity God is revealed. The truth of this latter claim has to be justified in a different way.

To sum up, then, what is the significance of incarnational claims? A coherent and theologically adequate understanding of 'incarnation' is to be found in terms of the notion of 'revelation'. Particular stories about events may give rise to particular revelatory insights but they do not, in themselves, demonstrate the truth of those insights. According to the Christian faith, the events of the life of Jesus, as recorded, give the clearest insight into the concrete character of the active actuality of God in relation to the processes of reality. The truth which is revealed by those events (or, rather, by the records of them) was not only true in the apostolic age: it is truth about the fundamental character of God that today and ever in the future is the ground and goal of all being. In this sense the 'incarnation' is to be thought of as a continuing reality.[4]

What does all this mean about the significance of human being? With this question we come to the final chapter of this study of God and the processes of reality.

---

[4] Cf. 'It is better to say that incarnation is perpetual, and what is unique about the Incarnation of God in Christ is its definitive form and direction: it perfects a long-standing process, and provides for its perpetuation in the perfected form' (Gibson 1970: 246).

11   God and human being: the significance of the human

Does it matter what the truth is about God and processes of reality? Much of the discussion in the preceding chapters may seem to imply that the only credible way of understanding God renders the divine too remote from human affairs to be important for human being. If this is so, theological understanding may reasonably be judged to be an intellectual exercise which has nothing positive to contribute to the conduct and appreciation of human life. At the same time it is hardly to be ignored as a harmless pastime for those who can find nothing better to do. While it affirms a kind of theism, its implications for the significance of human being may appear to be no less disturbing than the atheistic image presented by Nietzsche's madman: on this planet humankind plunges directionless 'as through an infinite nothing' (Nietzsche 1954: 95). Ultimately no one cares. Those, then, who find guidance and comfort in the stories of religion may seem well advised to avoid theology if they do not want their illusions to be shattered. Ignorance is bliss!

To make such a response to what seems to be the truth is practical atheism. It prefers to worship idols responding to human desires than to recognize the holiness of what is ultimate in being, value, and rationality. Authentic theism demands openness to and acknowledgement of the truth about the divine, whatever its implications. And, as Anselm perceived, there is an intrinsic demand in faith to seek understanding. A religious belief which tries to protect itself by shutting out the light of truth fosters an internal contradiction which will grow within it like a malignant cancer until it perishes in its self-imposed darkness.

But is a credible apprehension of the reality of God as hostile to the value of human life as the above comments have assumed? It is arguable that instead of devaluing human being, a proper appreciation of the divine is the only basis for affirming its real and ultimate significance. The final chapter of this study, therefore, considers how such a case may be made and what it indicates about the relationship between the divine and the human.

198

In the treatment of the nature and significance of incarnational claims in the previous chapter, one issue was not discussed. This is the issue posed for Christian belief by the question, 'Why Jesus?' Why was it that the incarnational revelation of the divine was initially considered to be given in Jesus? Why did the first Christians come to regard Jesus as the focus of their faith?

For most of the history of Christian understanding, this question has received two answers. First, it has been argued that Jesus established his divine status by the 'miracles' which he wrought. These were his credentials. Second, it has been argued that since he claimed such a status for himself and since the character of his life shows that he was neither bad nor mad, his claim must be accepted as a correct self-understanding. Such arguments no longer convince. The first answer raises more problems than it solves. In the first century of this era such claims were not distinctive to Jesus and comparative claims that one person's miracles were 'bigger and better' than another's cast doubt on the significance of them all. Today the identification of events as 'miraculous' is a product rather than a source of a form of faith — and a form of faith which is questionably credible. The second argument collapses once it is recognized, as it must be, that sincere and good-living people can be deluded in their basic self-understanding. Was it, then, on the basis of such unsatisfactory arguments that the first followers of Jesus came to centre their faith in him?

Although the paucity of the evidence means that any answer must be somewhat conjectural, the most likely reason why some people came to affirm that the divine had been incarnationally manifested in Jesus lay in what they considered to be the effect of encounter with Jesus. In brief, Jesus was held to be the Christ *because* he was experienced as 'saving'; he was not held to be 'Saviour' *because* he was independently perceived to be the 'Christ'. Frances Young, for example, states that

> Galilean fishermen and learned rabbis, Zealots and 'Gnostics', Pharisees and sinners, Jews and Gentiles — somehow he was all things to all men. ... All manner of men found their salvation in him and were driven to search for categories to explain him. ... Different christological positions were intimately related to different ways of understanding salvation.

> (Young 1973: 22f)

Accordingly she holds that 'historical study' shows 'the primacy of soteriology' (ibid.: 14). Similarly, Maurice Wiles (1986: 86) holds that 'christological doctrine is the reflective judgement of the church as to what must be true about the person of Jesus' if its conviction that 'in Christ God had been reconciling the world to himself' is valid. Again, in terms of contemporary thought, Gordon Kaufman suggests that Christian theology is justified in regarding Jesus as 'the normative paradigm or model for understanding who or what God is and what true humanity is' because and in so far as that 'image/concept' is powerfully effective in fulfilling the role of the divine in humanizing and relativizing us (Kaufman 1981: 135, 154).

What, in that case, was and is the salvific significance of Jesus as the Christ? As Whitehead remarked, 'Christ gave his life. It is for Christians to discern the doctrine' (1927: 45). What, then, is the significance of human being that is affirmed by the divine nature as incarnationally revealed in Jesus — or as discernible through some other mode of theological reflection?

Many of the classical attempts to express the nature of salvation that are found in the Christian tradition now speak only to a declining cognitive minority. Self-conscious members of the post-Enlightenment world are bemused when they hear that on the cross Christ led 'the cosmic powers and authorities ... as captives in his triumphal procession' and that as they 'die with Christ', they 'pass beyond reach of the elemental spirits of the universe' (Colossians 2: 15, 20). They do not understand their fundamental predicament as human beings and its solution in such terms. Similarly Methodists today may well wonder how John Wesley aroused great emotional responses in their predecessors by preaching to them as people who felt themselves to be condemned sinners abiding under 'the wrath of God' and calling on them to 'cast' themselves with all their sins 'on the Lamb of God' (Wesley 1820: 89, 102). Such utterances are not readily (if at all) recognizable now as identifying the malady of human being and its remedy. Nor, although the music might stir them, do contemporary Methodists find their self-understanding illuminated by the words of Charles Wesley:

> And can it be that I should gain
> An interest in the Saviour's blood? ...
> Alive in Him, my living Head,
> And clothed in righteousness divine,
> Bold I approach the eternal throne,
> And claim the crown, through Christ, my own.

What they would probably find easiest to affirm is the opening phrase of another verse: 'Tis mystery all!' While such notions clearly made an impact in the past, providing people with a way of understanding their experience of salvation, for many contemporary people they belong to the language and thought-forms of a dead culture. At best they provide slogans and rallying cries for a faithful remnant. They do not give clear insights into the saving relationship between the human and the divine.

What is needed is an understanding of that relationship which makes sense now to real people living in the real world. In this respect Schubert Ogden's (1973: 3f) criteria for theological understanding, namely credibility and appropriateness, should be replaced by those of credibility and significance. It is crucially important to satisfy the first of these criteria, credibility, in order to make it clear that theological affirmations are not the expression of dreams about a desirable never-never land but are rationally justifiable claims about the character of reality. Accordingly claims about salvation need to show that they meet 'the relevant conditions of meaning and truth universally established with human existence' (ibid.) and hence are 'credible to human existence as judged by common experience and reason' (Ogden 1982: 4).

The satisfaction of the criterion of appropriateness, however, is only important to the extent that it is considered important to show that a theological affirmation is in harmony with a particular tradition of faith. Ogden, for example, holds that a statement of Christian theology should be in accordance with what he considers to be the foundational and normative expression of the Christian faith given in the 'the primary symbols' of 'the "datum discourse"' of the apostolic witness (Ogden 1973: 3; cf. 1982: 4). This demand, though, is at odds with the rationale which led both to the apostolic apprehension of the faith and to later revisions of its formulations. That rationale is that formulations of faith should express, admittedly in the thought-forms of the time and so in a culturally conditioned manner, the truth about the relationship between God and human being. It is this concern to be faithful to the truth as they perceived it, and not fearfully hiding behind the authority of established traditions, that led people in the past to make and remake Christian doctrine. It is this same concern which governs authentic developments in theological understanding today.

If theistic understanding is to be able to claim that its insights are not only true but also crucial for the completion of human self-understanding and the flourishing of human being, then it also needs to show that they are significant. By satisfying this criterion it will indicate that it is not to be dismissed as a matter of irrelevant intellectual speculation for whiling away idle hours. It is, instead, affirming matters that are manifestly decisive for the fulfilment of human life. I have sometimes called this criterion 'the Bright Hour Test' since in effect it asks of a theological claim 'Can the mature women of the Bright Hour (or some other church fellowship) who have long experience of what life is like be reasonably expected to see that what is being proposed is important for actual living?' This criterion expresses what Paul Tillich lays down in a more sophisticated manner when he states that only those propositions are genuinely theological whose object 'can become a matter of ultimate concern for us' in that it 'determines our being or non-being' (Tillich 1953: 14, 16). It is crucial, therefore, that the Gospel message of the 'New Being in Jesus as the Christ' is correlated to contemporary human existence as symbolically disclosed in its cultural expressions (Tillich 1957: 194; cf. Tillich 1956: 85; cf. Ogden 1973: 2).

As was indicated by the illustrations from Colossians and the Wesleys, many traditional attempts to make sense of the experience of salvation fail to satisy one or both of the criteria of credibility and significance. Some expressions of the nature of salvation employ models of relationships whose fundamental character is alien to an acceptable appreciation of the relationship between the divine and the human. It is not theistically credible to suggest, for example, that the relationship of God to human beings is to be understood in terms of the need to satisfy the impugned honour of an over-sensitive despot, or to pay a ransom to a bandit, or to meet the bureaucratic regulations of a sacrificial system, or to appease an offended lord.

It may be replied, however, that such criticisms are based upon a failure to take proper account of the point of referring to such relationships. Notions such as those of the satisfaction of honour, ransom, vicarious sacrifice, and propitiation are not used to describe either the existential situation from which humanity needs to be saved or the means by which salvation is secured. Their role, rather, is to express indirectly — by analogy — the character of the state of salvation: being 'saved', that is, feels somewhat like having been reconciled to another, released from captivity, having had one's obligations met by someone else, and restored to a right relationship. While this reply is not without justification, it must also be recognized that many of the doctrinal expositions of these expressions of the nature of salvation do not manage to avoid implying views of

God which are incompatible with a proper understanding of the holiness, ultimacy, and perfection of the divine.

Another objection to many traditional treatments of salvation is that they refer to situations which are no longer regarded as matters of fundamental concern requiring divine intervention. In some cases this is because what they present as the state of salvation is in fact contrary to what are considered to be God's creative purposes for human being. To interpret the attainment of salvation, for example, as a heteronomous state in which the 'saved' rejoice that God has taken total control of their lives contradicts the recognition that the creative will of God is for the development of persons, not the manipulation of puppets. It treats the aim of salvation — the 'making whole' of the self — as a matter of the effective destruction of those who are supposedly 'saved'. Although some people may be so unhappy with themselves that they look forward to what amounts to personal suicide, this is no reason to hold that God similarly despairs about the possibilities for their lives.

Other notions of salvation are untenable because they look to the divine for matters which are no longer credibly considered to be provided by divine agency. Just as the underlying ontology renders it implausible today to suggest humanity has been captured by cosmic forces from whose thrall God compels release, so awareness of human history makes it implausible to consider divine salvation as a protection against threats to communal well-being. While, for example, the Jews may have seen their deliverance from slavery as due to divine intervention, today it seems more plausible to hold that liberation from unjust regimes comes through political activity. The likely result of telling the exploited to pray and to wait for God to rescue them is to condemn them to remain oppressed.

Other views of salvation suggest that God may be expected to overcome various physical threats to the welfare of individuals. Such expectations are not only what Freud calls illusions (the product of wishes); experience suggests that they are to a large extent delusions. Whatever may be meant by divine power and by such intercessions as 'Give us today our daily bread', neither faith in the reality of the former nor praying the latter protect people from violence and starvation. It is blasphemy against the divine goodness, furthermore, to try to explain the fates of those who suffer and of those who do not as due to divine choice. Such an 'explanation' transforms the object of unqualified adoration into a monster. So far as handicap, want, disease, and warfare are concerned, theistic believers have to realize that it is their responsibility to find and effectively implement the remedies. Enormous as the practical problems of the human condition may be, their solution will not be found by people expecting God 'to do something' but by human actualization of the divine will. Physical needs will be met, diseases eradicated, the threat of war diminished, and moral guilt answered, if at all, as people take measures to control population, establish a fair distribution of the world's resources, develop medical research, make political systems more mature and responsible, and provide counselling for offenders — and for the offended.

When attention moves from the cosmic, the natural, and the historical to the internal state of personal existence, many traditional notions of salvation are still found to be problematic. One view of salvation sees it as the receipt of God's forgiveness for harm done to other human beings: David, for example, may have wronged John but, feeling repentant, he may seek and receive forgiveness from God. Such a view of salvation is not open to the criticism that it allows David to avoid the embarrassment of seeking John's forgiveness, for genuine repentance will generally require this. What is questionable about it is that the reference to God may obscure the fact that since it is John and the human community who have been disrupted, it must be John in particular and the community in general who must pardon if social harmony is to be restored and guilt released. Where this is no longer possible (as when those who have been wronged have died), the important human response to those feeling guilt must be to assure them of their acceptance in the community. At its best, therefore, reference to divine forgiveness is a way of reinforcing the unlimited character of what ought to be the community's forgiveness; at worst it suggests a failure to appreciate the significance of sin for human lives.

Even less satisfactory is the view of the human predicament and divine response which sees salvation as the paying of penalties incurred through breaking God's commandments — as if the divine were a regulatory body which demanded compensation from those who broke sacred rules. Such a view not only fails to appreciate the nature of moral goodness — and of sin as the failure to actualize it. It also demeans God by treating the divine as a combination of a petty magistrate and a compensation-grasping litigant. While moral evil is to be taken seriously, co-operation with the creative urgency of the divine makes it important to avoid the inhibiting scrupulosity which arises from conceiving God as a 'ruthless moralist' who notes every tiny speck of evil and makes an issue of it. In this respect Whitehead shows clearer insight into the divine than moralizing (and bullying) pernickety preachers when he remarks that God, operating 'in quietness ... by love', is 'a little oblivious as to morals' (Whitehead 1978: 343). The positive freedom of love accords with divine creativity much more than the negative fear of offending.

Is, then, the notion of divine salvation a symbol which no longer has significance for human being? Or does it express an illusion which has no substance? To answer 'Yes' to either question might leave the issue of the reality of God intellectually interesting — like that of the discovery of the smallest prime number which has more than a million digits — but it would mean that theism cannot be regarded as significant for human being. The affirmation of God's saving activity may have comforted believers in the past but it is now to be seen as a materially inert placebo. As Nietzsche, Freud, and Monod suggest, beliefs about divine salvation must then be classed with other childish comforts like teddy bears. It is time we grew beyond such things.

Such analyses of the human situation may, however, be judged to reveal the shallowness of some current forms of human self-understanding and to deny the possibility of discerning any ultimate significance in human being. Instead, so theists may argue, the notion of divine salvation is the only way of affirming that significance in the face of fundamental threats to which human activity can provide no answer.

When properly understood, this argument is not susceptible to the criticism that it merely seeks to identify gaps for which 'God' can act as an imaginary plug until human beings find 'real' ways of coping with them. It is not maintaining, that is, that while God is no longer credible as a solution to the problems of social, political, and economic liberation, or to physical ills, or to things that go bump in the night, there are certain identifiable contingent problems of human existence for which it is credible to posit divine salvation as a solution. What this argument does hold is that whatever may currently happen to be the contingent state of human being, its fundamental significance can only be justifiably affirmed, if it is affirmable at all, by reference to what transcends the empirical and contingent mode of being in the world.

What are the grounds for doubting the significance of human being — and hence the significance of the lives of each person constituting human being? Reflection on the nature of human being indicates that there are cosmic, historical, and individual threats to its significance.

On the cosmic scale, human being seems to be a brief incident in the story of a planet with finite duration. Even if the exhaustion of the resources needed to sustain life, nuclear warfare, or a chance genetic change in a virus do not destroy human being sooner, the earth will eventually be cremated by its expanding sun. All the physical remains of humanity will utterly perish. In terms of the cosmos at large, the existence of this planet, let alone the human life that very temporarily inhabits it, is but one of a vast number of localizations of forces that will eventually disperse, leaving practically no trace of ever having existed. As Whitehead puts it, in its slow decay the physical universe is transmuted into a new order in which the world 'as we at present know it, will be represented by a ripple barely to be distinguished from non-entity' (Whitehead 1927: 144).

Consideration of its historical dimension provides no better grounds for a confident affirmation of the significance of human being. Although each person inherits a genetic structure determined by the interactions of a myriad ancestors, who those ancestors were and what they achieved is for the most part wholly forgotten. Gravestones weathered smooth, shelves of long unread books in the depositories of great libraries, and the worn artefacts in museum cases are memorials to some people long dead. The survival of these memorials only reminds us that in the case of most people death brings practically total obliteration in a very few generations. There is no memorial whatsoever of all but a tiny fraction of those who have lived. We may know who our grandparents were and even who our great great grandparents were but, unless we belong to an exceptional family, the addition of a few more 'greats' leads to impenetrable ignorance. While historians preserve the memory of a few people and events, there is no means of recollecting the vast majority of those who have lived. Even where scraps indicate that individuals existed — a mason's mark on a cathedral stone, a nameless drawing by a child from an extermination camp, a skull dug up in an Iron Age settlement — we do not know who they were. As persons they have utterly disappeared from human ken. Even major human achievements like empires and cultures have their day and cease to be as the records of them fade away.

If reflection turns from the historical aspect of human being to the current being of individual persons, it becomes apparent that their significance is threatened by the accidental nature of their existing at all, the continual perishing of their past, and the finitude of their future. There is no necessity about the actuality of a particular individual. Her or his existence is the product of a fantastic number of accidents in the meeting and mating of forbears. Furthermore, the reality of the self that she or he was some years ago has now gone. The actual self at one moment is constituted by massively inheriting the characteristics of the self the previous moment together with, since to be a self is to be a living (i.e. a responding) being, room for slight modifications to that datum. The present self, however, with its living modifications of its inheritance only comes to be through the perishing of its predecessor. To be an actual *I* is thus to be a point of actuality whose identity as a persisting *me* is an abstraction referring to a series of massively overlapping inheritances as well as to modifications to them in a route of occasions of actual being. What, though, is true of the previous states of a self is also true of its successive present states while that self continues to live: each present moment continuously slips into the non-being of pastness. For example, just as the actual self I was thirty years ago is now no more, so if I continue to live the self I am now will perish to be succeeded in the route of occasions that is me by other, more or less different actualities. What those actualities will be is unclear for the near future and quite unpredictable for the more distant. I may continue to develop as a person and die suddenly while still enjoying a creative existence. Or in time I may wander into senility, neither contributing to the enrichment of the lives of others nor able to enjoy life for myself. What is certain, though, is that the process of my being a physical self will eventually stop. A time will come when my momentary actuality as a physically living self perishes and has no successor.

In view of these threats, is it possible to affirm the significance of human being in general and of the lives of individuals in particular? No credible way is to be found by asserting the importance of each individual's contribution to fashioning the human future. There seems to be no reason to expect that future states will not share the perishing and forgetting that characterize what is now the human past. Nor is any solution to be found by reference to ideas of subjective immortality. The self I was thirty years ago has gone and my present self finds no affirmation of its significance in being told that some future self which I will have become — perhaps senile and exhausted — will continue after the death of its body.

Neither is there any way of affirming the significance of human being by reference to God if the divine, as perfect, is held to be a timeless *actus purus*, unchanging and impassible in every respect, aware only of the eternal and simple essence of deity.

207

Such a conception of God, when meant seriously, totally devalues human being. It entails that human actions either make no impression whatsoever on the divine (and so cannot be held to have any ultimate significance) or are all simultaneously present to the divine (and so their supposed worth as expressions of contingent freedom is a delusion).

If, however, the basic concept of God is modified to present God as active, but the divine is conceived to be an all-controlling agent whose creative power determines all that occurs, human being must still be considered to have no significance. To interpret the faith that 'He's got the whole world in his hands' as meaning that God finally fixes everything is to imply that human beings — and the rest of creation — are puppets who dance according to the ways in which their strings are pulled. In that case any value in their behaviour is to be ascribed to their manipulator. If, though, the notion of divine power is qualified to allow some creative freedom to human beings but salvation is regarded as a result of contingent acts of divine intervention which change the state or the status of particular individuals, the ultimate importance of each individual remains the product of a specific divine decision. Individuals still have no significance of their own.

Is there, then, any way of avoiding the conclusion that reality as a whole and human life in particular are pointless processes, vain and wearisome attempts to avoid nothingness? Does talk about people's 'ineradicable confidence in the final worth' and meaningfulness of their existence (Ogden 1967: 37; cf. 35) describe illusions by which they try to keep up their courage? Or can this confidence be justified? A sentence by Whitehead in the final chapter of *Process and Reality* suggests a way of understanding the divine and the human that establishes the significance of the latter through its relationship with the former — though, as will be indicated at the end of this discussion, something more needs to be said than is directly implied in this sentence. Whitehead states that God 'does not create the world, he saves it: or, more accurately, he is the poet of the world, with tender patience leading it by his vision of truth, beauty and goodness' (Whitehead 1978: 346).

In saying that God 'does not create the world' Whitehead is recognizing that creatures contribute to the determination of the successive actual states of the world. What, however, is important for the present discussion is that the sentence contains two basic insights into the relationship between God and the human aspects of the processes of reality. Both are necessary for a credible understanding of the ultimate significance of human being and both indicate that that significance is only conceivable in terms of God as the one to whom all being is finally referred. We shall consider each idea in turn.

The first idea finds an answer to the problem of the continual perishing of the past in the preservation of the quality of each actual occasion in the divine. According to Whitehead's notion of God's consequent nature and Hartshorne's view of the passive aspects of the divine actuality, every moment of experience which occurs, without exception, is part of the divine experience and as such is never forgotten. The genuine contingency of future events (which means that their actuality cannot be known prior to the decisions which determine them) and the absolute aspect of the divine awareness (which means that in principle God is neither ignorant nor forgetful of whatever is knowable) thus combine to entail the final denial of the ultimacy of the perishing which threatens the significance of the reality of human being. Whitehead sums up this point when he states that God 'saves the world as it passes into the immediacy of his own life' (Whitehead 1978: 346). All the events which constitute a personal life have significance because they are incorporated into God's everlasting reality.

In this respect the divine may be said to 'save' human being in a way somewhat analogous to that in which we 'save' souvenirs and works of art. In the human case, however, attempts to preserve creative achievements of the past and to re-present past experiences are never more than temporary and partial. Artefacts decay and our recollection of past experiences quickly blurs and dims. It is difficult to be clear about how one felt at a particular moment a week ago; it is impossible to recollect even vaguely and approximately almost all of the moments of one's being twenty years ago even if there are diaries and letters to bring some of them to mind in a general way (cf. Hartshorne 1962: 252). God, in contrast, loses none of the past. In the clarity of the divine mind, each actual occasion of experience — and so the individuality of each person constituted by every moment of her or his being — is preserved with all the sharpness of its immediate occurrence.

While, then, Whitehead properly warns against trying to perceive too much about how the world appears in God's experience of it, he states that 'what does haunt our imagination is that the immediate facts of present action pass into permanent significance for the Universe.' It is wrong, therefore, to class every activity as 'merely a passing whiff of insignificance' (Whitehead

1941: 698). Similarly Hartshorne maintains that 'our adequate immortality' lies in God's knowledge of us since this knowledge is 'coextensive with reality'. The divine omniscience, furthermore, is indestructible: 'what we once were to Him' we will never cease to be (Hartshorne 1962: 252f). Accordingly Hartshorne holds that 'the permanence of life's values' extends beyond their contribution to 'human posterity'. Their 'abiding value' lies in their being incorporated into the life of 'the Holy One' who 'survives all deaths and for whose life all life is precious' (ibid.: 242). While this understanding of objective immortality (i.e. everlastingness as an object in God's awareness) neither entails nor excludes subjective immortality (i.e. everlastingness as an experiencing and responding subject), it does entail that nothing that each self achieves is ever lost. As the momentary actuality of being a self perishes, the subjective immediacy of that experience is lost but its objective quality becomes a distinctive part of the divine.

In this incorporation of the human into the divine, we see one facet of the significance of human being. Although all occasions of experience have value and are to be treasured as such, and although each self and each group of selves have to balance present satisfaction against richer experiences that may be enjoyed in the future at the price of sacrificing comfort now, the ultimate significance of human being is not merely a matter of the human enjoyment of present and future moments of value. It is found in what is thereby contributed to the richness of the divine actuality. The goods which enrich our experience are also experienced by God in and through us — and in a way which fully appreciates and preserves their qualities.

The divine incorporation of human experiences, furthermore, is not an unconcerned absorption of further data by an unconscious cosmic data bank. It is a warm, personal appreciation of them. From this it follows, as Hartshorne points out, that the first commandment — that 'we are to love God unreservedly' — sums up all the rest (ibid.: 256). Those who properly seek to realize the fullest joy in the divine experience will do it by seeking the highest aesthetic satisfactions that are attainable for all persons, including themselves. It is a point that Teilhard de Chardin makes in *Le Milieu Divin*: 'God ... pushes to its further possible limit the differentiation among the creatures He concentrates within Himself' so that 'at the peak of their adherence to Him, the elect also discover in Him the consummation of their individual fulfilment' (Teilhard de Chardin 1960: 104).

The claim that the proper end of human being is to enrich the divine may be criticized on the grounds that it is absurd. What any individual can contribute to the divine reality is so minuscule that it cannot have perceptible worth for God. This, though, is the absurdity at the heart of theistic faith — that each individual 'exists *before* God ... on the most intimate terms' (Kierkegaard 1955: 216). Furthermore, while it may seem unbelievable that God shares our joys and our sorrows, the stories of the widow's mite and the lost coin are reminders that magnitude and worth are not commensurable. What makes the idea that the divine appreciates every occasion of actuality seem incredible to us may be our failure to grasp the greatness of the divine.

What this view of human fulfilment presents is a radical alternative to the self-centred view of 'heaven' which dominates much religious thought. Rather than envisaging 'heaven' selfishly as a state where each person finds endless pleasure for herself or himself, it applies to the whole of human being the understanding that people only find completely satisfying joy by giving to and sharing experiences with others in genuine love — and so without self-seeking thoughts of any return. In the divine–human relationship, though, what a person gives to God is what that person enjoys. At this point, then, selfish and unselfish forms of love are transcended in a giving of joy to the other which is nothing other than the joy which the giver experiences. God, therefore, is not to be judged as selfish because the divine reality shares in and preserves — and so to some extent benefits from — what we feel and lose. We are not deprived of anything appropriate to our finite nature because the divine retains what perishes for us. Nor, unless we are so immaturely selfish that to share an experience spoils it for us, does the divine incorporation of our actual occasions diminish our enjoyment of them. On the contrary, the sense that the divine shares and preserves our experiences enhances our appreciation of them. Hence, as Whitehead suggests, God not only extends our purposes 'beyond values for ourselves to values for others' but also provides that 'the attainment of such a value for others transforms itself into value for ourselves' (Whitehead 1927: 142f). In this way the quality of our 'reasonable, holy, and living sacrifice' to God depends on the depth of our 'devotion to all good things' in 'generous openness to others' and 'to the beauty of the world' (Hartshorne 1962: 257).

To regard the significance of human being in terms of the preservation of all its constituent experiences in the divine is, however, only one of the ideas that Whitehead puts forward in

211

the sentence quoted earlier (see p. 208, quoting Whitehead 1978: 346). God not only gives human beings the peace of knowing that all their actual occasions are incorporated in the divine reality: God also judges them with 'a tenderness which loses nothing that can be saved' and 'a wisdom which uses what in the temporal world is mere wreckage' (Whitehead 1978: 346). Divine 'judgement', that is, is not to be regarded as a destructive rejection of what is bad but rather as a perception of how what has been, good or bad, may be used in the further creation of aesthetic riches. God fosters the future actualization of what is good as well as preserving what has been achieved.

The realization of this aspect of the divine activity is partly brought about through the creative freedom which characterizes human being. People do not have to conform completely to their immediate past (cf. Whitehead 1941: 695). Being able, within limits, to respond to what they remember about the past and anticipate about the future, they can use their situation, whatever it may be, creatively in order to give material expression to the formal 'ideals of perfection, moral and aesthetic' embodied in the divine nature (ibid.: 697). The basic structure of reality, that is, gives to each person the significance of being able to use what may seem at first sight to be a wretched situation — 'mere wreckage' — as material for creatively envisaging and producing what is good.

In Whitehead's view God's activity in this respect is not simply that of ensuring in an utterly general way that the processes of reality are such that human beings have the freedom to respond creatively to their situation. Having, in the concluding section of *Religion in the Making*, described God as 'that element in life in virtue of which judgment stretches beyond facts of existence to values of existence', he goes on to speak of God both as the source of 'all forms of order' and as confronting 'what is actual . . . with what is possible for it' (Whitehead 1927: 142ff; cf. 1941: 694). The latter phrases indicate that he understands God's role in this respect to be a form of activity.

As has been suggested in earlier chapters, though, the divine cannot be credibly regarded as presenting a specific optimum goal to each person (let alone to each concrescing occasion) each moment of the process of reality. On the other hand, contrary to the assumptions of Nietzsche and Cupitt, it must also be recognized that the freedom of people to choose does not require of God a distancing — whether benevolent or unfeeling — or a refusal to be actively involved in influencing what occurs. Furthermore, it may be considered by some to be theistically

unsatisfactory to conceive of God as a remote source and pre-
server of the process of reality whose relationship to its particular
events is merely one of knowing — and perhaps also of
enjoying — whatever happens to occur in it. Whitehead suggests,
for instance, that while God does not wholly determine whatever
occurs, God has a real influence on the processes of reality as a
lure or a persuasion. In *Process and Reality* he speaks of God as
affecting events through 'the patient operation of the overpowering rationality of his conceptual harmonization' (Whitehead
1978: 346). The use of the adjective 'overpowering' should not
be taken to mean that God coerces people so that they have no
option but to conform to the divine will. Such an interpretation
would contradict Whitehead's denial that God acts in such a
way, as well as contradicting human experience and God's
creative intentions. What the adjective describes, not wholly
felicitously, is the quality of the divine perception of the most
rewarding possibilities, not its irresistible effect on people's
actions.

The activity of the divine as both attracting and enabling grace
is more happily expressed by Whitehead when he writes of God
as 'the poet of the world, with tender patience leading it by his
vision of truth, beauty, and goodness'. This image suggests that
just as the poet takes the commonplace words of everyday
conversation to evoke fresh insights into truth, beauty, and
goodness, so the divine uses the present constituents of reality
in the creation of future riches. It is noteworthy, though, that on
reconsidering this phrase Whitehead deleted 'leading' in his copy
of the work and wrote both 'persuading' and 'swaying' in the
margin (ibid.: 413). His image, that is, is not of a poet who takes
the data of the 'language' provided by the actual occasions of
human reality and manipulates them according to the poet's
creative insights. Nor is it of a poet as having in mind a
particular state of affairs which characterizes the final end of the
processes — and hence of all reality. Instead Whitehead is
suggesting that God is quietly, patiently, and persistently stirring
people to be discontented with their present state, whatever it
may be and however fulfilling it may have been when it was first
reached. This happens as they are influenced by the divine vision
of truth, beauty, and goodness as formal goals for the processes
of reality. These ideals can never be completely satisfied by any
material state of affairs and so inspire the divine with a restless
creativity. They are communicated to people and similarly
disturb their living as, whether consciously or not, whether
willingly or not, people become aware of the divine. God,

God and the processes of reality

therefore, is considered both to enjoy the value of what is actualized in the process of reality and, as the spirit of creative transformation (cf. Cobb 1975), to be a ceaseless pressure on the constituents of that process for the production of further expressions of value. This aesthetic understanding of the divine reality indicates another aspect of how God establishes the significance of human being. God 'saves' not only by preserving all that has been but also by evoking in its constituents the production of novel expressions of aesthetic worth.

Whitehead's image of the poet, however, may usefully be augmented by other models of divine activity. Whereas poets struggle to control words and structures to express their perceptions, novelists sometimes report finding that as a story progresses its characters develop their own personalities. The way in which a novelist fosters and appreciates such a growth in the characters as they respond to their situations may then be seen as providing another model for the nature of the divine activity as creator and saviour — two notions which refer to what is essentially the one divine activity that establishes the significance of human being.

The characters in a novel, though, are wholly products of the novelist's imaginative projections, however surprising they may seem to the novelist. The divine–human relationship is hence more appropriately modelled in terms of personal interactions where all those involved have some — if limited — autonomy. God's saving activity may, for instance, be compared to the role of imaginative and courageous play-group leaders. Such people seek to stimulate children to explore their potential. They do not try to determine the children's activity but, granted the environment and the resources available, they try to excite the children into creative activity. Appreciating what is then produced, they provoke the children to discover how they can turn to further good use what has been produced and to try out other activities when they appear, for the time being, to have exhausted the potential for novel enrichment in what they have been doing. Another possible model for divine activity is that of the producer of an improvised play. In such a situation the producer does not seek to control the actors' every word and gesture but, having outlined the plot and its characters, encourages them to discover dramatic riches by exploring the possibilities in what is so given.

The models of poet, novelist, play-group leader, and producer are only models for understanding the character of divine activity. They are not to be pressed too far. But they bring out,

214

in a way that models of sacrifice, satisfaction, cosmic victory, ransom, and expiation seem now unable to do (even if they ever were so able), how the ultimate significance of human being may be understood to be established by the way in which human achievements are fostered and preserved by the divine. According to the insights of Whitehead and Hartshorne, God is to be held to 'save' people by everlastingly incorporating in the divine reality, without any loss of their individuality, the value of all the actual occasions of each person's life and by ceaselessly seeking to evoke in each person further creative responses to his or her situation.

As was mentioned earlier, though, this way of understanding how the divine establishes the ultimate significance of human being needs to be modified — or perhaps developed — in a fundamental way. What has been presented so far is in danger of being interpreted as offering a very elitist view of the significance of human being. Those who are able by circumstance and natural capacity to create novel expressions of value may be seen as authentically responding to the divine and as ensured of being for ever remembered by the divine. This suggests that objective immortality gives the highest degree of ultimate significance to the *Übermenschen* to whom Nietzsche looked forward but leaves very much in question the significance of those — the overwhelming majority of human beings — who largely lack such abilities or possibilities. Does, then, a credible understanding of the divine imply that there is little or no significance in the life of a severely mentally handicapped child or in the life of an adult whose struggle to exist precludes any opportunity for aesthetic creativity? Such a view may seem to be a radical but justifiable extension of Hartshorne's view that 'we are more important *for God*' and so have more value than 'the other animals' (Hartshorne 1967a: 23; cf. 1987: 85). It is, however, an elitist view which is compatible neither with a recognition of the universal providence of God nor with the assertion of the worth of each person.

As has already been mentioned, Hartshorne describes God as existing everlastingly as 'the Holy One' for whom 'all life is precious'. The worry with the view that the significance of human being lies in what of aesthetic worth it can contribute to the divine reality is that it is liable to suggest a scale of value in which those who contribute more are to be judged to be ultimately more significant than those who contribute less. From this it may be considered to follow that those who contribute less are less precious to God — precious to some extent perhaps but, if their contribution is minimal, not a great deal. As for those who are unable to contribute anything of value, they must be deemed to have no significance.

One response to this conclusion is to hold that all human beings are capable of some realizations of value. A mother struggling to survive and to help her family to survive in the midst of famine and disease may not have opportunities to create works of art but she can know the pangs and the glory of self-sacrificing love. Because of his severe handicaps a baby boy may not be able to do much but he may be able to smile and to try to communicate by blowing bubbles. Even if someone is not capable of the least response to others, she or he may be capable at least of enjoying a feeling of warmth or a sense of security. In such ways, it may be argued, all people have some experiences to contribute to the divine reality and are for ever treasured in the divine memory. Furthermore, the scales of richness and of novelty by which the intellectually elite (in their own eyes) judge between human efforts may seem important to them but be trivial and unwarranted in God's eyes.

Such a response, though, accepts the principle that human significance depends upon the worth of human efforts. It is an assumption which reflects the anthropocentric pride prevalent in human being and against which Paul and Luther protested when they affirmed that salvation is by grace and not by works. As they perceived it, the 'right relationship' ('righteousness') between the human and the divine is established by the latter and bestowed freely upon the former. What does this mean in terms of contemporary human self-understanding?

It basically means that worth is to be recognized to be something that is given by the interest of others. Although the reasons for the ascription of worth are complex matters which we cannot go into here, in the end an object does not possess, earn, merit, or attain worth because of its intrinsic qualities. A piece of gold has worth, whereas a handful of earth does not, only among people who have chosen to regard gold as valuable. A painting does not have worth because of the effort that the artist has put into it; a photograph is not treasured because of the value of its constituent materials; a person does not have worth because he or she is an intricate organism. Each of them has worth because and so far as they are valued by others. The significance, worth, value of human beings — call it what you will — is something that is given to them by others and which they give to others by their concern for them. The fundamental worth of a handicapped baby boy, then, whatever his problems and possibilities, is that he is loved. His significance is not a matter of what he manages or does not manage to do. It is not achieved by his efforts but is received from those who are concerned about him.

What, though, is the significance of those who feel that they are unwanted and unloved? If some of these unfortunate people are correct in thinking that no other human being cares about them, does this mean that they have no significance? Similarly, does it mean that when no one at all remembers us, our being has lost all value? In one sense the answer must be 'Yes'. The correlate of the principle that to have worth is to be valued by another is that to be that for which no one is concerned, that to which no one responds, that about which no one bothers is to be worthless. If, though, the theistic understanding which has been expounded in the previous chapters is correct in its perception of the ultimate character of things, such an answer is in a fundamental respect utterly wrong in practice. And so too is the self-understanding of those who consider that they establish their final worth by their own efforts. Both the utterly despairing and the self-confidently proud need to appreciate that in the end each person has worth because the divine cherishes each individual. The love and the concern that parents and friends have for a handicapped child (and the joy he may give to one somewhat cynical old puzzler by blowing bubbles at him in his attempts to communicate) are but hints of the ceaseless and total concern that God has for him. Not one of his experiences will ever be alone or ever forgotten. This is not because God looks to gain from his experiences but just because he exists. Simply as such he is incorporated in the universal love of all-embracing deity. That is where his (and everyone else's) significance lies — in the divine as totally aware and completely loving.

This may seem a surprising and perhaps even an unexpectedly warm place to end a rather arid study of the relationship between God and the processes of reality. But although there is much more that could be said about it, it is here that the argument leads. The human has worth because of the divine.

This study of God and the processes of reality has thus come full circle. It began with 'the problem of God today'. It ends with the problem of the significance of human being. Only if the former problem can be solved can a satisfying solution to the latter problem be envisaged. In the intervening chapters an attempt has been made to indicate how, by taking up and modifying insights suggested by the works of Whitehead and Hartshorne, it is possible to develop an understanding of the God of theistic faith. Is that understanding credible? The answer to this fundamental question for the significance of human being depends on whether the resulting understanding of God is to be judged to present a coherent and comprehensive grasp of the ultimate and universal character of reality. In seeking to make such a judgement the limits of human thought should not be forgotten. Those who want neat and incontrovertible solutions to fundamental questions should take account of Whitehead's warning that 'the final outlook of Philosophic thought cannot be based upon the exact statements which form the basis of special sciences. The exactness is a fake' (Whitehead 1941: 700). Rather they — and we — must consider the significance of 'the reaction of our own nature to the general aspect of life in the Universe' (ibid.: 698). It is a rational assessment which we must make for ourselves. In the end faith — and the understanding which it embodies — is the responsibility of each person.

References

Adolfs, Robert (1967) 'Is God dead?', in Bernard Murchland, (ed.) *The Meaning of the Death of God*, New York: Vintage Books.

Alexander, Samuel (1933) *Beauty and Other Forms of Value*, London: Macmillan.

—— (1939) *Philosophical and Literary Pieces*, London: Macmillan.

—— (1966) *Space, Time and Deity*, with a new Foreword by Dorothy Emmet, London: Macmillan.

Anselm (1962) *Basic Writings*, trans. S. N. Deane, Introduction by Charles Hartshorne, La Salle, Ill.: Open Court.

Aquinas, Thomas (1964) *Summa Theologiae*, vols 1-60, Blackfriars in connection with London: Eyre & Spottiswoode.

—— (1975) *Summa Contra Gentiles*, trans. A. C. Pegis, Notre Dame and London: University of Notre Dame Press.

Aristotle (1955) *The Nicomachean Ethics*, trans. J. A. K. Thomson, Harmondsworth: Penguin Books.

—— (1960) *Metaphysics*, trans. R. Hope, Ann Arbor: University of Michigan Press.

Augustine, Aurelius (1876) *The Confessions*, in M. Dods (ed.) *The Works of Augustine*, Edinburgh: T. & T. Clark.

Barbour, Ian G. (1966) *Issues in Science and Religion*, London: SCM Press.

Barnhart, J. E. (1967) 'Incarnation and process philosophy', *Religious Studies* 2 (2), April 1967.

Barth, Karl (1933) *The Epistle to the Romans*, trans. E. C. Hoskyns, London: Oxford University Press.

—— (1960) *Church Dogmatics III*, 3, trans. G. W. Bromiley and R. J. Ehrlich, Edinburgh: T. & T. Clark.

—— (1967) *The Humanity of God*, London and Glasgow: Collins.

Bartholomew, D. J. (1984) *God of Chance*, London: SCM Press.

Beckett, Samuel (1965) *Waiting for Godot*, London: Faber & Faber.

—— (1972) *The Lost Ones*, London: Calder & Boyars.

Berdyaev, Nicolas (1953) *Truth and Revelation*, trans. R. M. French, London: Geoffrey Bles.

Bergson, Henri (1911) *Creative Evolution*, trans. A. Mitchell, London: Macmillan.

—— (1935) *The Two Sources of Morality and Religion*, trans. R. A. Audra and C. Brereton, New York: Henry Holt.

Beveridge, William (1846) *Ecclesia Anglicana Ecclesia Catholica: or, The Doctrine of the Church of England consonant to Scripture, Reason, and Fathers*, Oxford: Oxford University Press.

Birch, Charles and Cobb, John B. Jr (1981) *The Liberation of Life*, Cambridge: Cambridge University Press.

God and the processes of reality

Birch, L. Charles (1968) 'Creation and creator', in Ian G. Barbour (ed.) *Science and Religion: New Perspectives on the Dialogue*, London: SCM Press.

Bonhoeffer, Dietrich (1971) *Letters and Papers from Prison*, enlarged edn, ed. Eberhard Bethge, London: SCM Press.

Braithwaite, Richard B. (1966) 'An empiricist's view of the nature of religious belief', in Ian T. Ramsey (ed.) *Christian Ethics and Contemporary Philosophy*, London: SCM Press.

Bultmann, Rudolf (1964) 'Bultmann replies to his critics', in Hans Werner Bartsch (ed.) *Kerygma and Myth: a Theological Debate*, trans. R. H. Fuller, London: SPCK.

Buren, Paul M. van (1963) *The Secular Meaning of the Gospel*, London: SCM Press.

Burnet, Gilbert (1705) *An Exposition of the Thirty-Nine Articles of the Church of England*, London: Ri. Chiswell.

Calvin, John (1953) *Institutes of the Christian Religion*, trans. H. Beveridge, London: James Clarke.

Camus, Albert (1987) *The Plague*, trans. S. Gilbert, London: Folio Society.

Cobb, John B. Jr (1969) *God and the World*, Philadelphia: Westminster Press.

—— (1971) 'A Whiteheadian Christology', in Delwin Brown, Ralph E. James, and Gene Reeves (eds) *Process Philosophy and Christian Thought*, Indianapolis and New York: Bobbs-Merrill.

—— (1975) *Christ in a Pluralistic Age*, Philadelphia: Westminster Press.

Cupitt, Don (1980) *Taking Leave of God*, London: SCM Press.

—— (1985) *Only Human*, London: SCM Press.

Davies, Paul (1984) *God and the New Physics*, Harmondsworth: Penguin Books.

Dean, William D. (1972) *Coming To: A Theology of Beauty*, Philadelphia: Westminster Press.

Derham, William (1723) *Physico-Theology: or, A Demonstration of the Being and Attributes of God from His Works of Creation*, London: W. & J. Innys.

—— (1738) *Astro-Theology: or, A Demonstration of the Being and Attributes of God from a Survey of the Heavens*, London: W. Innys & R. Manby.

Eliot, T. S. (1961) *Selected Poems*, London: Faber & Faber.

Feuerbach, Ludwig (1957) *The Essence of Christianity*, trans. G. Eliot, New York: Harper & Brothers.

Findlay, J. N. (1955) 'Can God's existence be disproved?', in Antony Flew and Alasdair MacIntyre (eds) *New Essays in Philosophical Theology*, London: SCM Press.

—— (1964) 'Reflections on necessary existence', in William L. Reese and Eugene Freeman (eds) *Process and Divinity*, La Salle, Ill.: Open Court.

Fisher, H. A. L. (1936) *A History of Europe*, London: Edward Arnold.

Flew, Antony (1966) *God and Philosophy*, London: Hutchinson.
Ford, Lewis S. (1978) *The Lure of God: a Biblical Background for Process Theism*, Philadelphia: Fortress Press.
—— (1978a) 'Some proposals concerning the composition of *Process and Reality*', *Process Studies* 8 (3), Fall 1978.
—— (1984) *The Emergence of Whitehead's Metaphysics, 1925-1929*, Albany: State University of New York Press.
Freud, Sigmund (1962)*The Future of an Illusion*, trans. W. D. Robson-Scott and James Strachey, London: The Hogarth Press.
Gibson, A. Boyce (1970) *Theism and Empiricism*, London: SCM Press.
Gilkey, Langdon (1973) 'Process theology', *Vox Theologica* 43.
Goldman, Ronald (1965) *Readiness for Religion: A Basis for Developmental Religious Education*, London: Routledge & Kegan Paul.
Gore, Charles (1926) *The Reconstruction of Belief*, London: John Murray.
Griffin, David (1971) 'Schubert Ogden's Christology and the possibilities of process philosophy', in Delwin Brown, Ralph E. James, and Gene Reeves (eds) *Process Philosophy and Christian Thought*, Indianapolis and New York: Bobbs-Merrill.
Gunton, Colin (1973) 'A critique of process theology', *The Expository Times* LXXXIV (10), July 1973.
Gunton, Colin E. (1978) *Becoming and Being: the Doctrine of God in Charles Hartshorne and Karl Barth*, Oxford: Oxford University Press.
Hamilton, Peter (1967) *The Living God and the Modern World*, London: Hodder & Stoughton.
Harnack, Adolf (1901) *What is Christianity?*, trans. T. B. Saunders, London: Williams & Norgate.
Hartshorne, Charles (1948) *The Divine Relativity: a Social Conception of God*, New Haven and London: Yale University Press.
—— (1953) *Reality as Social Process: Studies in Metaphysics and Religion*, Glencoe, Ill.: The Free Press and Boston, Mass.: Beacon Press.
—— (1962) *The Logic of Perfection and Other Essays in Neoclassical Metaphysics*, La Salle, Ill.: Open Court.
—— (1964) *Man's Vision of God and the Logic of Theism*, Hamden, Conn.: Archon Books.
—— (1965) *Anselm's Discovery: a Re-examination of the Ontological Proof for God's Existence*, La Salle, Ill.: Open Court.
—— (1966) 'Is God's existence a state of affairs?', in John Hick (ed.) *Faith and the Philosophers*, London: Macmillan and New York: St Martin's Press.
—— (1967) *A Natural Theology for our Time*, La Salle, Ill.: Open Court.
—— (1967a) 'God and the social structure of reality', in Schubert M. Ogden and Charles Hartshorne, *Theology in Crisis: a Colloquium on the Credibility of 'God'*, New Concord, Ohio: Muskingum College.
—— (1970) *Creative Synthesis and Philosophic Method*, London: SCM Press.

God and the processes of reality

—— (1973) 'Ideas and theses of process philosophers', in Lewis S. Ford (ed.) *Two Process Philosophers: Hartshorne's Encounter with Whitehead*, Tallahassee, Fla: American Academy of Religion.
—— (1976) *Aquinas to Whitehead: Seven Centuries of Metaphysics of Religion*, Milwaukee: Marquette University.
—— (1978) *Whitehead's Philosophy: Selected Essays, 1935-1970*, Lincoln and London: University of Nebraska Press.
—— (1982) 'Grounds for believing in God's existence', in Leroy S. Rouner (ed.) *Meaning, Truth, and God*, Notre Dame and London: University of Notre Dame Press.
—— (1983) *Insights and Oversights of Great Thinkers: an Evaluation of Western Philosophy*, Albany: State University of New York Press.
—— (1984) *Omnipotence and Other Theological Mistakes*, Albany: State University of New York Press.
—— (1985) 'Postscript', in Santiago Sia, *God in Process Thought: a Study in Charles Hartshorne's Concept of God*, Dordrecht, Boston, and Lancaster: Martinus Nijhoff.
—— (1987) *Wisdom as Moderation: a Philosophy of the Middle Way*, Albany: State University of New York Press.
Hartshorne, Charles and Reese, William L. (1953) *Philosophers Speak of God*, Chicago: University of Chicago Press.
Hatch, Edwin (1890) *The Influence of Greek Ideas and Usages upon the Christian Church*, ed. A. M. Fairbairn, London: Williams & Norgate.
Hegel, G. W. F. (1956) *The Philosophy of History*, trans. J. Sibree, New York: Dover Publications.
Hemingway, Ernest (1955) *For Whom the Bell Tolls*, Harmondsworth: Penguin Books.
Hepburn, Ronald W. (1958) *Christianity and Paradox: Critical Studies in Twentieth-Century Theology*, London: Watts.
Hume, David (1935) *Dialogues concerning Natural Religion*, ed N. K. Smith, Oxford: Clarendon Press.
Jantzen, Grace M. (1984) *God's World, God's Body*, London: Darton, Longman & Todd.
Kafka, Franz (1961) *Metamorphosis and Other Stories*, Harmondsworth: Penguin Books.
Kant, Immanuel (1933) *Critique of Pure Reason*, trans. N. K. Smith, London: Macmillan.
Kaufman, Gordon D. (1975) *An Essay on Theological Method*, Missoula, Mont.: Scholars Press.
—— (1981) *Theological Imagination: Constructing the Concept of God*, Philadelphia: Westminster Press.
Kierkegaard, Søren (1955) *Fear and Trembling and the Sickness Unto Death*, trans. W. Lowrie, New York: Doubleday & Co.
—— (1959) *Either/Or*, trans. D. F. and L. F. Swenson, rev. H. A. Johnson, New York: Doubleday & Co.
Krause, K. C. F. (1900) *The Ideal of Humanity and Universal Federation*, ed. W. Hastie, Edinburgh: T.& T. Clark.

222

Küng, Hans (1977) *On Being a Christian*, trans. E. Quinn, London: Collins.

Lloyd Morgan, C. (1923) *Emergent Evolution*, London: Williams & Norgate.

—— (1926) *Life, Mind, and Spirit*, London: Williams & Norgate.

—— (1933) *The Emergence of Novelty*, London: Williams & Norgate.

Lonergan, Bernard (1974) *A Second Collection: Papers by Bernard J. F. Lonergan, SJ*, London: Darton, Longman & Todd.

MacKinnon, Donald (1968) *Borderlands of Theology and Other Essays*, ed. G. W. Roberts and D. E. Smucker, London: Lutterworth Press.

McPherson, Thomas (1955) 'Religion as the inexpressible', in Antony Flew and Alasdair MacIntyre (eds) *New Essays in Philosophical Theology*, London: SCM Press.

Maimonides, Moses (1956) *The Guide for the Perplexed*, New York: Dover Publications.

Mansel, Henry Longueville (1858) *The Limits of Religious Thought*, Oxford: for J. Murray, London, and J. H. and Jas Parker, Oxford.

Mascall, E. L. (1949) *Existence and Analogy: a Sequel to 'He Who Is'*, London: Longmans, Green & Co.

Mays, Wolfe (1977) *Whitehead's Philosophy of Science and Metaphysics*, The Hague: Martinus Nijhoff.

Monod, Jacques (1972) *Chance and Necessity: an Essay on the Natural Philosophy of Modern Biology*, trans. A. Wainhouse, London: Collins.

Neville, Robert C. (1978) *Soldier, Sage, Saint*, New York: Fordham University Press.

—— (1980) *Creativity and God: a Challenge to Process Theology*, New York: Seabury Press.

—— (1981) 'Concerning *Creativity and God:* a response', *Process Studies* 11 (1), Spring 1981.

Newman, John Henry (1870) *An Essay in Aid of a Grammar of Assent*, London: Burns, Oates & Co.

Nicholas of Cusa (1960) *The Vision of God*, trans. E. G. Salter, New York: Frederick Ungar.

Niebuhr, H. Richard (1941) *The Meaning of Revelation*, New York: Macmillan.

Nietzsche, Friedrich (1954) *The Portable Nietzsche*, ed. Walter Kaufmann, New York: Viking Press.

—— (1983) *Untimely Meditations*, trans. R. J. Hollingdale, Cambridge: Cambridge University Press.

O'Donnell, John J. (1983) *Trinity and Temporality: the Christian Doctrine of God in the Light of Process Theology and the Theology of Hope*, Oxford: Oxford University Press.

Ogden, Schubert M. (1962) *Christ without Myth*, London: Collins.

—— (1967) *The Reality of God and Other Essays*, London: SCM Press.

—— (1973) 'What is theology?', *Perkins Journal* XXVI (2), Winter 1973.

—— (1980) 'Christian theology and neoclassical theism', *The Journal of Religion* 60 (2), April 1980.

—— (1982) *The Point of Christology*, London: SCM Press.

Otto, Rudolf (1950) *The Idea of the Holy*, trans. J. W. Harvey, London: Oxford University Press.

Owen, H. P. (1969) *The Christian Knowledge of God*, London: Athlone Press.

—— (1971) *Concepts of Deity*, London: Macmillan.

Page, Ruth (1985) *Ambiguity and the Presence of God*, London: SCM Press.

Pailin, David A. (1967) 'Christian and atheist? An introductory attempt to understand the theology of the "Death of God" ', *The London Quarterly and Holborn Review*, October 1968.

—— (1968) 'Some comments on Hartshorne's presentation of the ontological argument', *Religious Studies*, October 1968.

—— (1969) 'A Christian possibility of proclaiming the "Death of God" ' *The Church Quarterly*, January 1969.

—— (1969a) 'An introductory survey of Charles Hartshorne's work on the ontological argument', *Analecta Anselmiana* I.

—— (1974) 'Neville's critique of Hartshorne', *Process Studies* 4 (3), Summer 1974.

—— (1986) *Groundwork of Philosophy of Religion*, London: Epworth Press.

Paley, William (1837) *Natural Theology* in *The Works of William Paley, DD*, ed. D. S. Wayland, London: George Cowie.

Peacocke, A. R. (1979) *Creation and the World of Science*, Oxford: Clarendon Press.

Peacocke, Arthur (1986) *God and the New Biology*, London and Melbourne: J. M. Dent.

Peirce, Charles Sanders (1931-5, 1958) *The Collected Papers of Charles Sanders Peirce*, vols 1-6 ed. C. Hartshorne and P. Weiss, vols 7–8 ed. A. Burks, Cambridge, Mass.: Harvard University Press.

Phillips, D. Z. (1970) *Death and Immortality*, London: Macmillan.

Pittenger, Norman (1959) *The Word Incarnate*, London: Nisbet.

Plato (1955) *The Republic*, trans. H. D. P. Lee, Harmondsworth: Penguin Books.

Rahner, Karl (1978) *Foundations of Christian Faith: an Introduction to the Idea of Christianity*, New York: Seabury Press.

Ramsey, Ian T. (1957) *Religious Language: an Empirical Placing of Theological Phrases*, London: SCM Press.

—— (1964) *Models and Mystery*, London: Oxford University Press.

—— (1965) *Christian Discourse: Some Logical Explorations*, London, Oxford University Press.

Ray, John (1692) *The Wisdom of God Manifested in the Works of the Creation*, London: Samuel Smith.

Richter, Jean Paul Friedrich (1877) *Flower, Fruit and Thorn Pieces*, trans. A. Ewing, London: George Bell & Sons.

Runzo, Joseph (1986) *Reason, Relativism and God*, London: Macmillan.

Russell, Bertrand (1975) *Why I am not a Christian and Other Essays*, London: George Allen & Unwin.

Scharlemann, Robert P. (1981) *The Being of God: Theology and the Experience of Truth*, New York: Seabury Press.
Schulweis, Harold M. (1984) *Evil and the Morality of God*, Cincinnati: Hebrew Union College Press.
Sherburne, Donald W. (1971) 'Whitehead without God', printed in Delwin Brown, Ralph E. James, and Gene Reeves, (eds) *Process Philosophy and Christian Thought*, Indianapolis and New York: Bobbs-Merrill.
—— (1971a) 'The "Whitehead without God" debate: the rejoinder', *Process Studies* 1 (2), Summer 1971.
—— 'Decentering Whitehead', *Process Studies* 15 (2), Summer 1986.
Shideler, Emerson W. (1966) 'Taking the death of God seriously', in Bernard Murchland (ed.) (1967) *The Meaning of the Death of God*, New York: Vintage Books.
Smuts, J. C. (1926) *Holism and Evolution*, London: Macmillan.
Spinoza, Baruch (1958) *The Book of God*, ed. D. D. Runes, New York: Philosophical Library Inc.
—— (1959) *Ethics and On the Correction of the Understanding*, trans. A. Boyle, London: Dent and New York: Dutton.
Swanson, D. L. and Swanson, E. S. (1978) 'Review of John B. Cobb and D. R. Griffin (eds) *Mind in Nature*', *Process Studies* 8 (1), Spring 1978.
Teilhard de Chardin, Pierre (1959) *The Phenomenon of Man*, London: Collins.
—— (1960) *Le Milieu divin: an Essay on the Interior Life*, London: Collins.
—— (1971) *Christianity and Evolution*, trans. R. Hague, London: Collins.
Tennyson, Alfred (1912) *Poems*, London: Oxford University Press.
Tillich, Paul (1953) *Systematic Theology*, I, London: Nisbet.
—— (1956) *The Religious Situation*, trans. H. R. Niebuhr, New York: Meridan Books.
—— (1957) *Systematic Theology*, II, London: Nisbet.
—— (1958) *Dynamics of Faith*, New York: Harper & Brothers.
Torrance, Thomas F. (1969) *Space, Time and Incarnation*, Oxford: Oxford University Press.
Voltaire (1947) *Candide*, trans. J. Butt, Harmondsworth: Penguin Books.
—— (1962) *Philosophical Dictionary*, trans. P. Gay, New York: Harcourt, Brace & World, Inc.
Wesley, John (1812) 'Serious thoughts occasioned by the late earthquake at Lisbon', *The Works of the Rev. John Wesley*, XI, London: T. Cordeux.
—— (1820) 'Sermons on several occasions', *The Works of the Rev. John Wesley*, VII, London: T. Cordeux.
Whiston, William (1725) *Astronomical Principles of Religion, Natural and Revealed*, London: J. Senet, W. and J. Innys, J. Osborn, & T. Longman.

Whitehead, Alfred North (1927) *Religion in the Making*, Cambridge: Cambridge University Press.

—— (1927a) *Science and the Modern World*, Cambridge: Cambridge University Press.

—— (1933) *Adventures of Ideas*, Cambridge: Cambridge University Press.

—— (1938) *Modes of Thought*, Cambridge: Cambridge University Press.

—— (1941) 'Immortality', in Paul Arthur Schilpp (ed.) *The Philosophy of Alfred North Whitehead*, Evanston and Chicago: Northwestern University.

—— (1968) *Essays in Science and Philosophy*, New York: Greenwood Press.

—— (1978) *Process and Reality: as Essay in Cosmology*, corrected edn, ed. D. R. Griffin and D. W. Sherburne, New York: The Free Press.

Wiles, Maurice F. (1986) *God's Action in the World*, London: SCM Press.

Williams, Daniel Day (1964) 'How does God act?: an essay in Whitehead's metaphysics', in William L. Reese and Eugene Freeman, (eds) *Process and Divinity*, La Salle, Ill.: Open Court.

—— (1968) *The Spirit and the Forms of Love*, London: Nisbet.

Wittgenstein, Ludwig (1961) *Tractatus Logico-Philosophicus*, trans. D. F. Pears and B. F. McGuiness, London: Routledge & Kegan Paul.

Young, Frances (1977) 'A cloud of witnesses', in John Hick (ed.) *The Myth of God Incarnate*, London: SCM Press.

The Cloud of Unknowing, trans. by C. Wolters, Harmondsworth: Penguin Books.

Index

God *cont.*

awareness of, 16, 31, 33, 37, 61f, 70f, 79f, 83f, 87f, 102f, 108f, 116f, 124, 180, 183f, 210; beatitude of, 80, 87f, 109; as being itself, 14; as calling, 158f; as cause, 34, 78, 120; as changing (unchanging), 16f, 28, 31ff, 36, 58, 68f, 78f, 88f, 101f, 109f, 161f, 207f; as choosing, 129; cognitive content of talk about, 38f, 40, 181; as compassionate, 16f, 29f, 31, 59, 88, 109f; completeness of, 104f (*see also actus purus*, perfection); concept of, coherence, viii, 16f, 18, 27ff, 34; concept of, requirements, viii, 21, 24, 26f, 31f, 65, 75, 123; consequent nature of, 60, 62f, 64, 139, 164, 209f; contingency of, 32, 69f; as controlling events, 165f, 169, 208; as covertly influencing, 168, 170f; as creator, creative, 15f, 18, 29, 39, 69, 92, 109f, 112, 114, 118–32, 133–53 *passim*, 208, 213; credibility of belief in, 4, 24, 93; 'death' of, 10f; as deliverer, 90; dipolar view of, 32, 37, 64f, 70f, 74, 81, 84f, 90f, 101; as directing all reality, 56, 62f, 64, 133–53, 154–74 *passim*; divinity of, 15; dual transcendence of, 108f (*see also* perfection); as embracing all events, 22, 56, 62f, 84, 89f, 91f, 94f; as *ens realissimum*, 28f, 74, 78, 101, 110f; as eternal, 28, 32, 68f, 83, 85, 113, 117; as eternal urge of desire, 64, 172; as evoking aesthetic value, 173f; as exemplifying metaphysical principles, 55, 60; existence of, viii, 22, 47; experience of, 62, 115, 121; as explanation, 8, 11, 15, 24, 40, 123, 130; as finite and infinite, 28, 34, 61, 68f,

104; foreknowledge of, 12, 84f, 116f (*see also* awareness of); formal and material qualities of, 69f, 73f, 91, 97f; as free, 36; goal of activity of, 114f, 131f, 139f, 143f, 151, 153, 167, 172f; and good, 23, 33, 41, 75, 97f, 109f, 111f; as grace, 69; as grading eternal objects, 64; as ground of all, 13f; as holy, 21, 24; to be imitated, 57, 164; immanence of, 125; as immutable: *see* changing; as impassible, 16, 28f, 31f, 36, 58, 62f, 78f, 88f; as ineffable, 13f, 20, 25; as influencing all, 91f, 94, 124f; as integrating all, 63f, 164; as intentional, 33, 83, 85, 91f, 94, 97, 124f, 135, 146f, 160f, 176, 185f; as having internal relations, 87f, 108, 161f; judgement of, 212f; as knowing: *see* awareness of; as known by revelation, 34, 111, 180f, 185f 193; limitlessness of, 13, 17f, 116; as living, 31, 105f; as loving, 22, 29, 31f, 36, 59, 64, 71f, 88f, 101f, 126, 145, 154, 205, 208, 217; as luring, 59, 64, 93f, 110, 125, 140f, 144f, 148f, 150, 156f, 159, 165f, 167f, 171f, 213; as necessarily creative, 126f, 130, 132; necessary aspects of, 28, 32, 70; necessary existence of, 17, 22f, 47, 68, 90, 131f; necessity of belief in, 7; negative content of descriptions of, 26f; neo-classical view of, 28; notions of in religion, 57; 'omni-', 27, 94f; omnipotence: *see* power of; omniscience: *see* awareness of; as omnitolerant, 22f, 68; as ontologically independent, 41, 127; as paradoxical, 36; passivity of: *see* as affected by all; perception of will of, 156f, 168, 170; perfection of, 16, 23,